The Campus History Series

WRIGHT STATE UNIVERSITY

On the Front Cover: The first commencement to take place on the campus of Wright State University was on Sunday June 23, 1968. Hosted on the Founders' Quadrangle, 356 graduating students represented several colleges. With its message of change and growth, the inspirational keynote address resonated not only to the graduating students, but also to the larger campus community as well. (Courtesy of Wright State University Libraries.)

Cover Background: Pictured is the Founders' Quadrangle where the school held its first on-campus commencement ceremony in the summer of 1968. The hundreds of graduates pictured are representing the Colleges of Business and Administration, Education, Liberal Arts, and Science and Engineering. The keynote address discussed graduates going on to adjust to changes not only in their communities but as productive members of society. (Courtesy of Wright State University Libraries.)

Contents

ACKNOWLEDGMENTS

I am grateful to the following individuals for their invaluable assistance and unwavering support in helping this project come to fruition: Dawne Dewey, director of the Public History program; Chris Wydman, archivist and records manager of the Special Collections and Archives; and Chris Snyder, Communications and Marketing, for helping me to locate images.

I would also like to acknowledge the support of my colleagues, friends, and family who have encouraged me in this venture and have expressed just as much enthusiasm as I have in this project.

Unless otherwise noted, all images appear courtesy of the archives at the Wright State University Libraries.

INTRODUCTION

Plans to establish the first public institution of higher education in the Dayton region were laid in 1961. At the time, Dayton was the second-largest metropolitan city in Ohio, according to information in the Wright State University Archives. The need for a public higher education institution became critical as Dayton emerged as a high technology center that needed an educated workforce. Many key business leaders throughout the community, such as Charles S. Allyn, Robert S. Oelman, and Eugene Kettering, as well as Pres. Novice Fawcett and Pres. John Millett from Ohio State and Miami University respectively, led a communitywide fundraising effort in 1962 to raise the necessary seed money for the branch campus of Ohio State University and Miami University. The goal was to establish a branch campus that would quickly transition into an independent university. The area's large businesses, such as General Motors and National Cash Register, established payroll deduction plans, and more than 2,000 campaign workers recruited 10,000 contributors, which led to raising over $3 million in three months. The land needed for the campus was partially purchased and partially deeded to the state by the US government from an available 190 acres adjacent to Wright-Patterson Air Force Base. Another 428 acres was acquired from private owners, and the construction of the campus's first building, Allyn Hall, began.

In the fall of 1964, with the completion of Allyn Hall, the "campus within a building," the Dayton campus of Ohio State University and Miami University opened its doors to 3,203 enrolled students. Wright State University was characterized by its rapid growth very early on, and within the next 10 years, enrollment increased to over 12,000 students. The second phase of campus development soon began, with greater amenities being provided for students. The university's first president, Dr. Brage Golding (1966–1973), faced mounting pressures from different sources pushing the branch campus to sever ties to Ohio State and Miami University and to become independent. Senate Bill No. 210 stated that the university could become independent when enrollment reached 5,000 but not before July 1, 1967. On October 1, 1967, the university became independent. When the university reached independent status, the next mission was to name it. The goal was to disassociate from the University of Dayton and separate its identity from Ohio State and Miami University. The Sigma Tau Epsilon fraternity set up a contest to name the university. It attracted suggestions such as Wright Brothers University, Martin Luther King University, and Whatsamatta University. The General Assembly decided on Wright State University in order to honor aviation pioneers Orville and Wilbur Wright, who invented the world's first successful airplane in their Dayton bicycle shop. In fact, the Wright brothers conducted most of their early test flights at Huffman Prairie, just a short drive from the Dayton campus.

By 1967, Oelman Hall, Millett Hall, and Fawcett Hall had been completed, forming the campus commons known as the Founders' Quadrangle or "the Quad." Also in 1967, the University Center opened, providing recreational space, food service, a bookstore, and event rooms for student activities, and the School of Graduate Studies was created. As the campus grew, so did the need for on-campus traditional student housing. Hamilton Hall, a dormitory housing over 300 students, was built in 1970 and remained the sole residence hall for the university for years. The second president, Robert J. Kegerreis (1973–1985), oversaw a $14 million building program, helping Wright State University to flourish with the construction of the University Library, Physical Education Building, and the Creative Arts Center, home to outstanding art, theater, dance, and music productions that enrich the area's cultural life.

In 1985, Dr. Paige E. Mulhollan (1985–1994) was named the third president of Wright State University. Under his leadership, the university kept up its reputation for rapid growth. The 1980s saw exponential physical growth as the campus expanded to include buildings for the College of Business, the College of Engineering and Computer Science, and the College of Health Sciences, home to the School of Professional Psychology and Pharmacology and Toxicology Department. The university hired its first African American president and fourth overall president in 1994 with the appointment of Dr. Harley E. Flack (1994–1998). He was also the first African American president of a major metropolitan university in Ohio. The 1990s was also an era of enormous growth, as Wright State University added the Ervin J. Nutter Center, a state-of-the-art sports and entertainment complex. In 1992, the Russ Engineering Center opened, serving as a centerpiece of engineering and computer science education and research for the area. During the fall of 1994, the Student Union opened, providing students, faculty, staff, and the community with conference and meeting facilities. The school's fifth president, Kim Goldenberg, MD, (1998–2007) continued the traditions of increasing enrollment, retaining students, and awarding research endeavors.

Today, under the leadership of its sixth president, David Hopkins (2007–present), Wright State University continues to expand its campus while build lasting relationships with the community. The university is a founding partner of the Dayton Regional STEM School. Since 2009, Wright State has supported the STEM school and its model of offering students a relevant, real-world educational experience. The Wright State University community takes pride in its diversity, from the makeup of the student body to the departments, programs, and organizations that benefit not only the campus but the region as well. Innovation, research, and scholarship have been strong areas for Wright State University. In 2012, the Boonshoft School of Medicine, Wright State Research Institute, and Premier Health Partners formed the Clinical Trials Research Alliance to give physicians more opportunities for medical research and boost clinical trials in the region. Also, Wright State's ArtsGala has turned into the arts event of the year in the Dayton region and has funded student scholarships in theater, dance, art, music, and motion pictures.

Today, Wright State University has nearly 20,000 enrolled students on its main campus situated just 12 miles outside Dayton, Ohio. Across eight colleges within the university and three different campus locations, well over 200 undergraduate, graduate, and professional degrees are offered. The Lake Campus, located in Celina, Ohio, is crucial to the Wright State University community as it offers numerous programs of study for associate's and bachelor's degrees.

One

Humble Beginnings

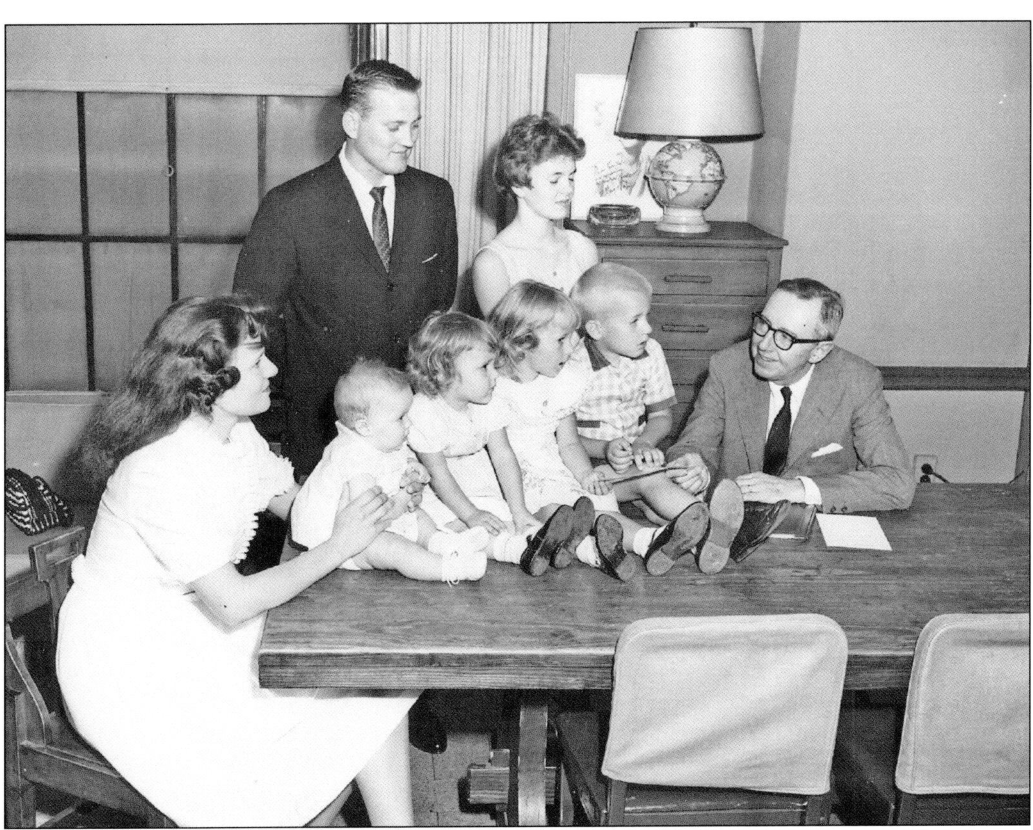

No Public University. The city of Dayton experienced a tremendous population growth between the years of 1940 and 1960, where numbers grew from approximately 295,000 to roughly 400,000, according to information in the WSU Archives. Within the next eight years, the population grew by 36 percent for a total of 540,000 residents. It was during this time that Dayton became known as a technology hub. What was needed was an educated workforce for the employment opportunities the city had to offer.

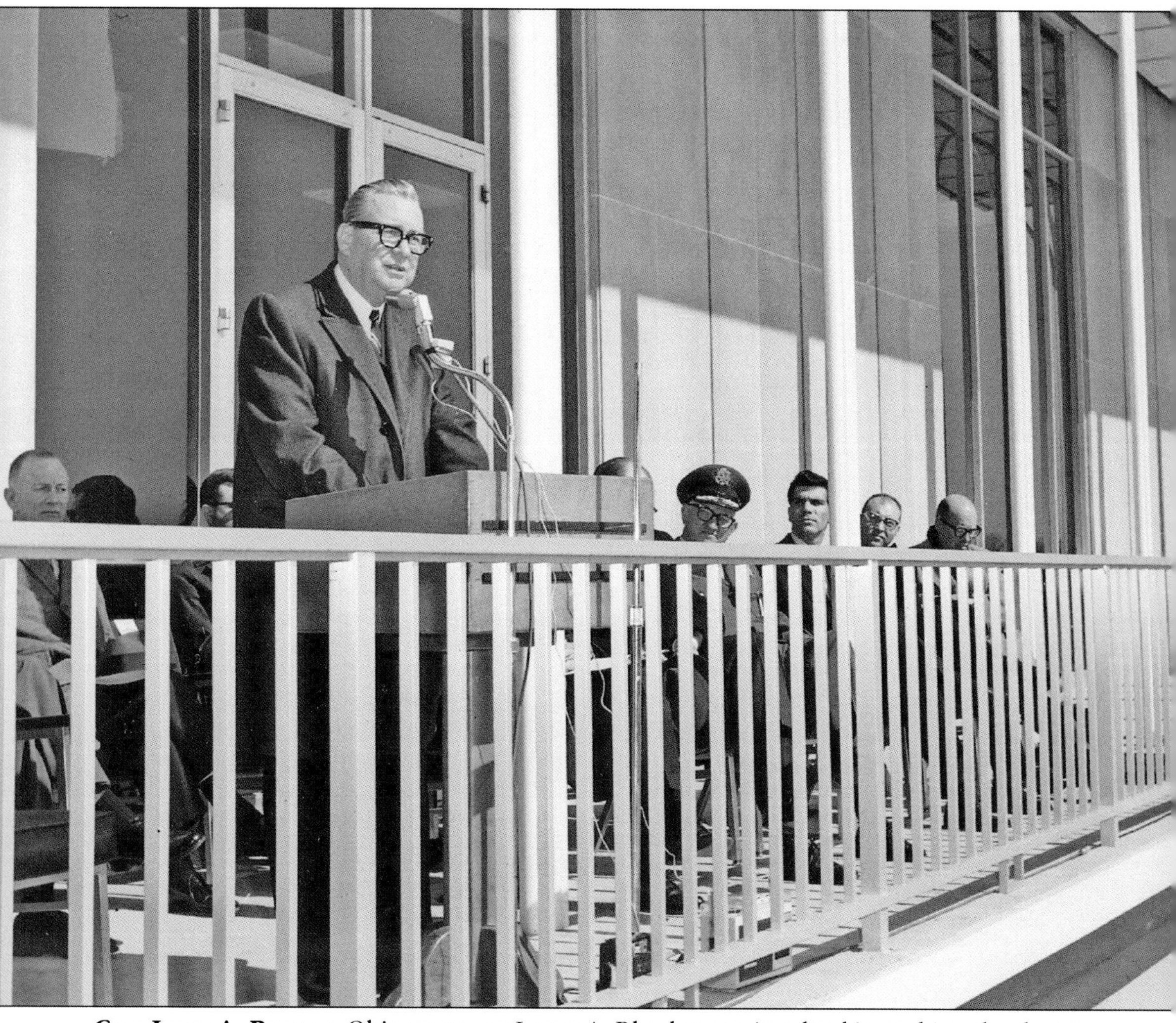

Gov. James A. Rhodes. Ohio governor James A. Rhodes was involved in making the decision to create a new public institution of higher education. During his tenure, he pushed for the development of the state's infrastructure by supporting the building of airports, parks, bridges, roads, universities, and colleges. He pledged to place public higher education within 30 miles of every citizen in Ohio.

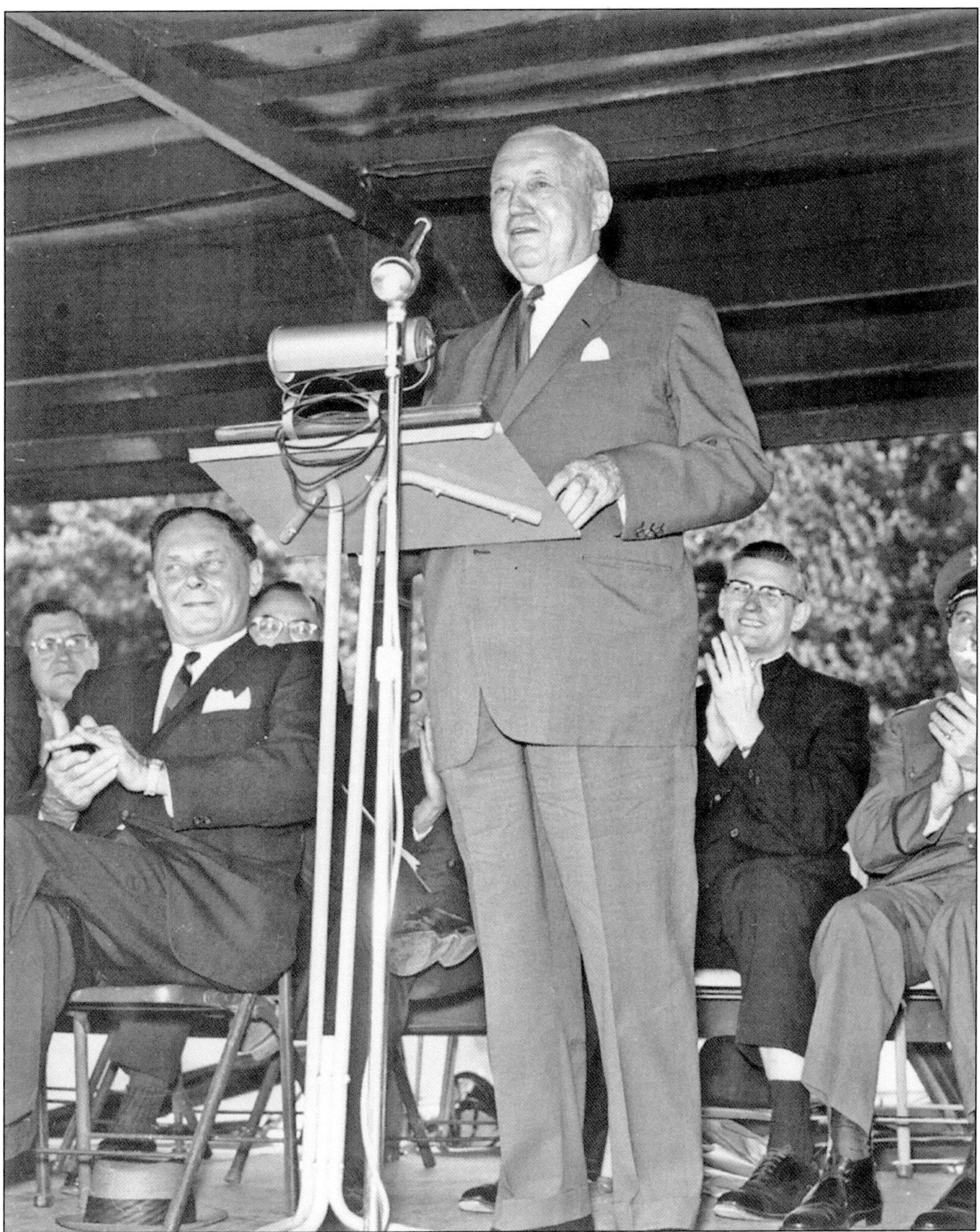

Stanley Charles Allyn. Responding to the need for an educated workforce within the city, Stanley Charles Allyn, chief executive officer of National Cash Register, made it a priority to create a public university in Dayton. He sought out to do this as the founder and first chair of the Area Progress Council.

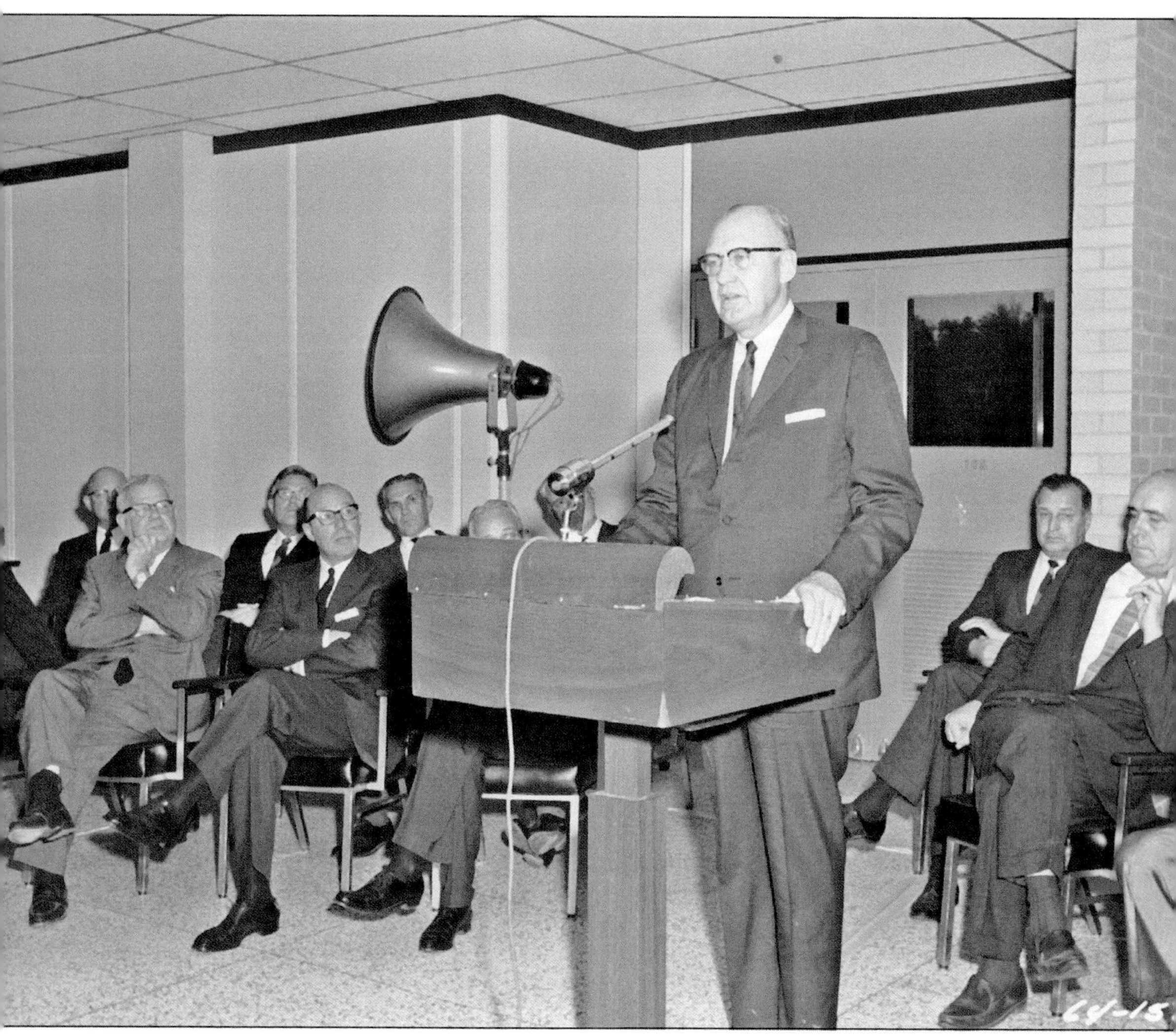

Novice Fawcett. Dr. Novice Fawcett, the president of Ohio State University, ensured that Ohio State fully supported the efforts to build a new public education institution in Dayton. He recognized that such an institution was necessary. Due to his support, the Dayton campus received the state-level support necessary to move forward.

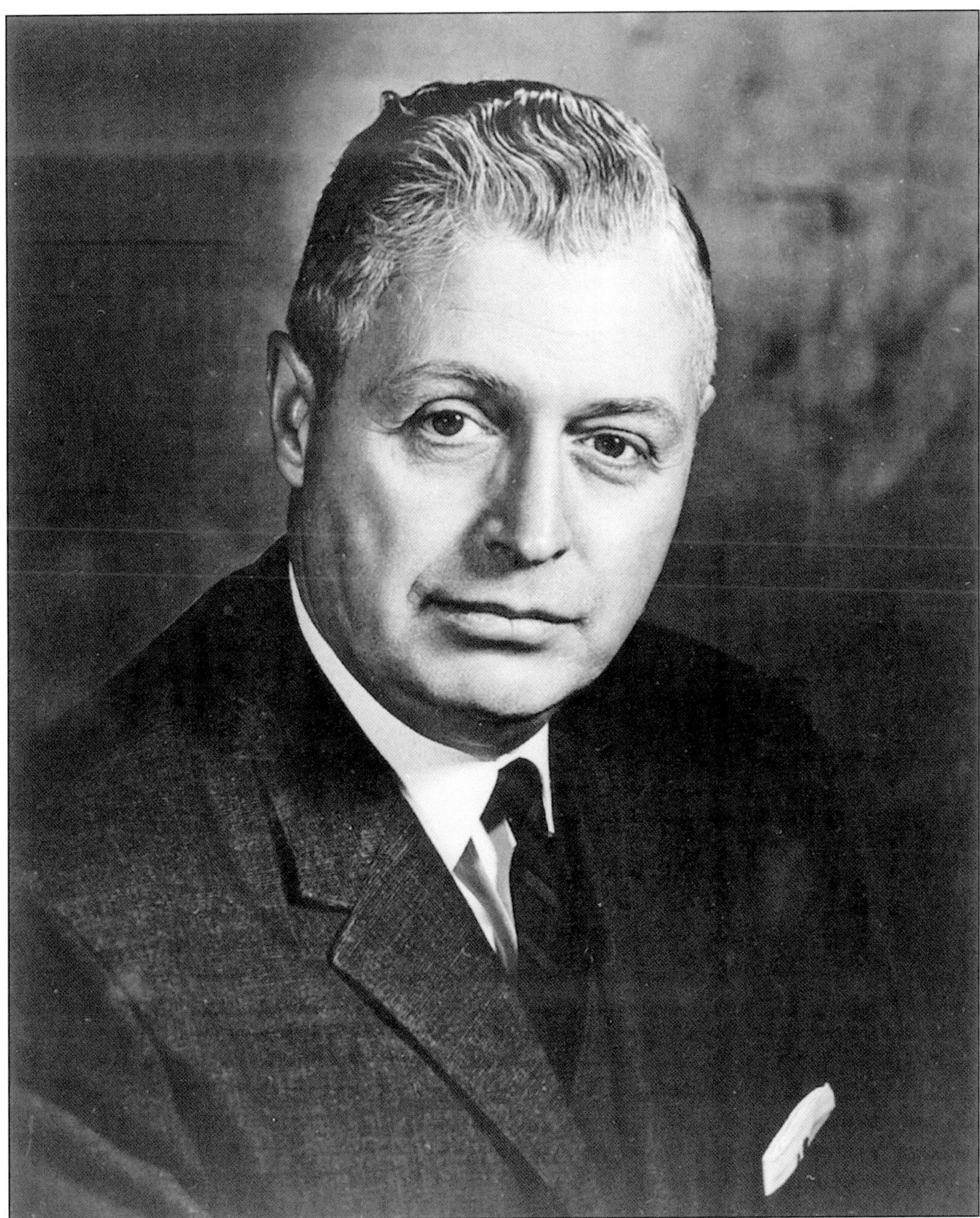

DR. JOHN MILLETT. The 16th president of Miami University in Oxford, Ohio, Dr. John Millett played a critical role in the effort to create an independent university in Dayton. In his capacity as the first chancellor of the Ohio Board of Regents, he supported this project by providing necessary resources such as funding mechanisms.

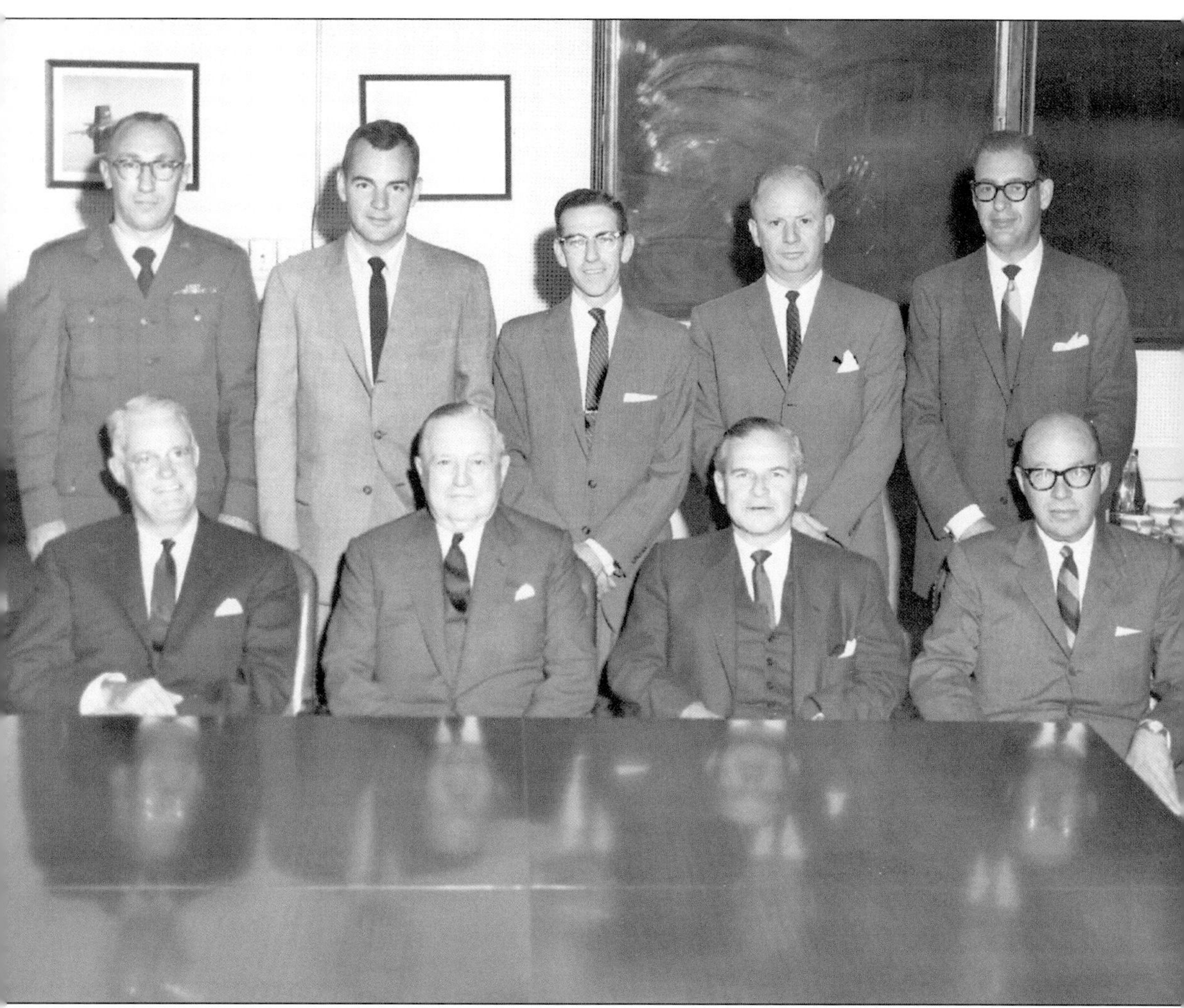

Area Progress Council. The Area Progress Council was comprised of area civic leaders such as Stanley Allyn, Robert Oelman, and David Rike. These men were from major Dayton businesses such as General Motors, National Cash Register, Delco, and Frigidaire, as well as Wright-Patterson Air Force Base. The first initiative of the council was to establish a new public university. The council put up the initial $3 million of the $6 million needed.

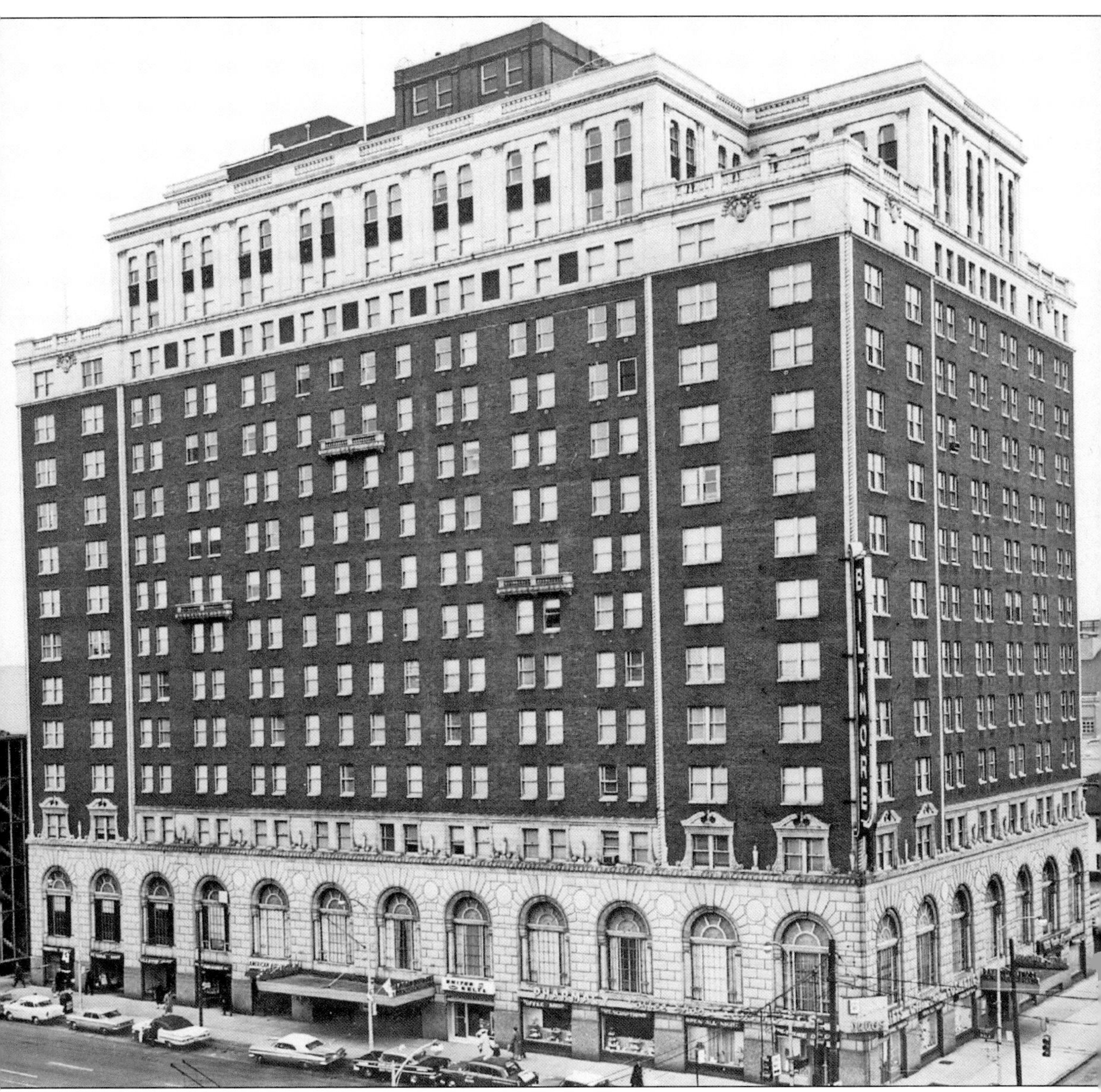

Downtown Dayton, the Dayton Biltmore. Downtown Dayton was the center of toolmaking and electromechanical and automotive manufacturing. The area reconstructed itself to keep up with ever-changing technologies. In 1961, Stanley Allyn made his civic-agenda speech, in which he called for the expansion of higher education. The Dayton Biltmore Hotel, located in downtown Dayton, is where the newly established Area Progress Council made plans to move forward with a new university.

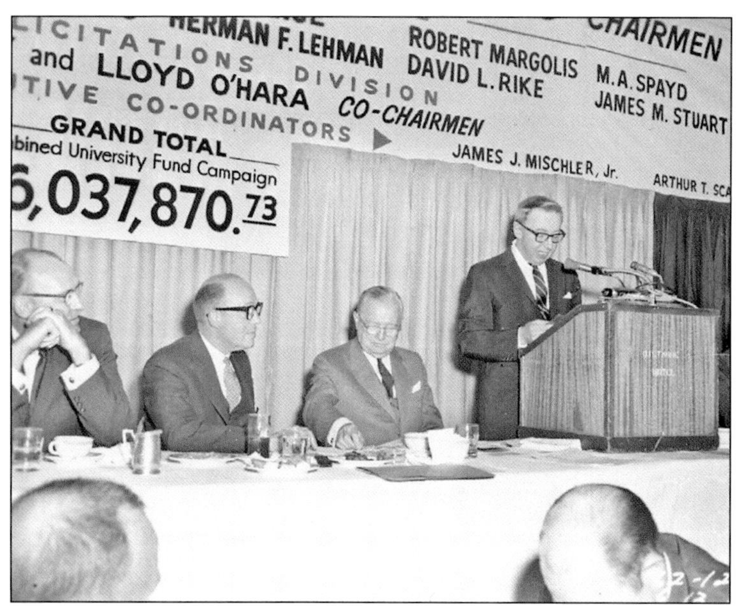

Combined University Building Fund. The Combined University Building Fund was launched in April 1962. A proposal was put forth to accommodate the State of Ohio and the two state universities with respect to acquisition of the site of the Dayton division. Over 2,000 campaign workers reached out to the people, and more than 10,000 contributors helped the campaign reach its goal of $3 million by June.

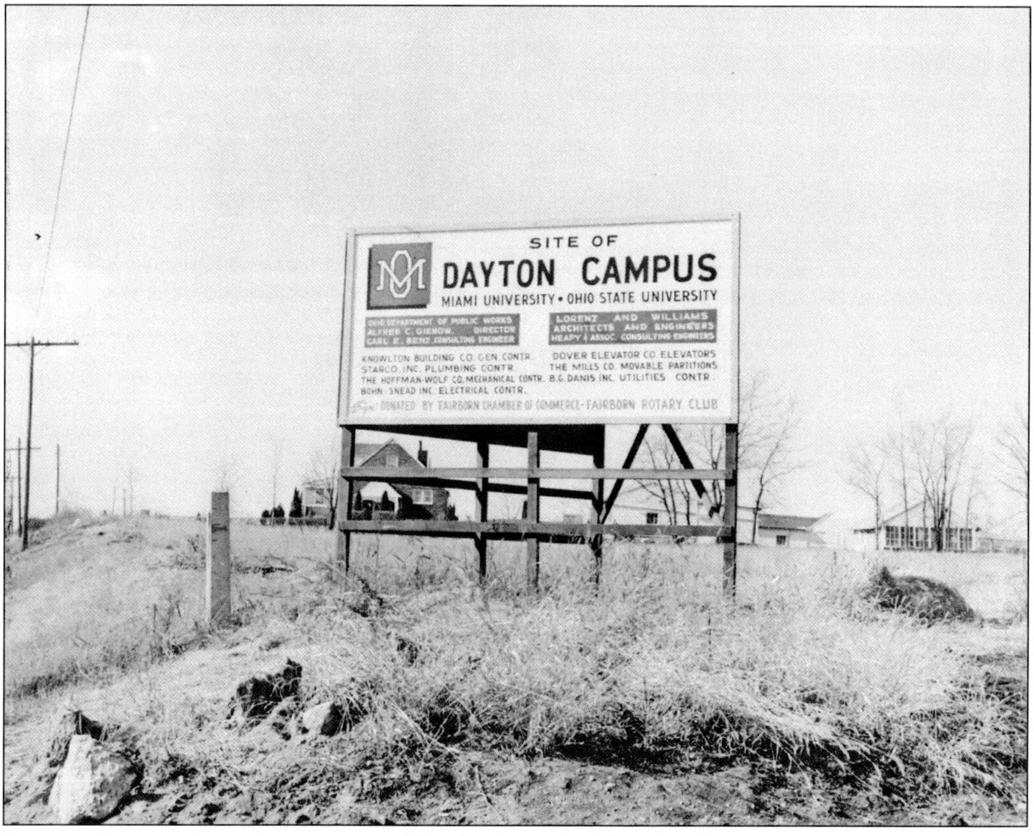

Dayton Campus Land Acquisition. The land needed for the Dayton campus was partially purchased and partially deeded to the state by the US government, including 190 acres adjacent to Wright-Patterson Air Force Base. Another 428 acres was acquired by Henry Bader from private owners such as the Rockafields, Warners, Kooglers, Casads, and the Bateses.

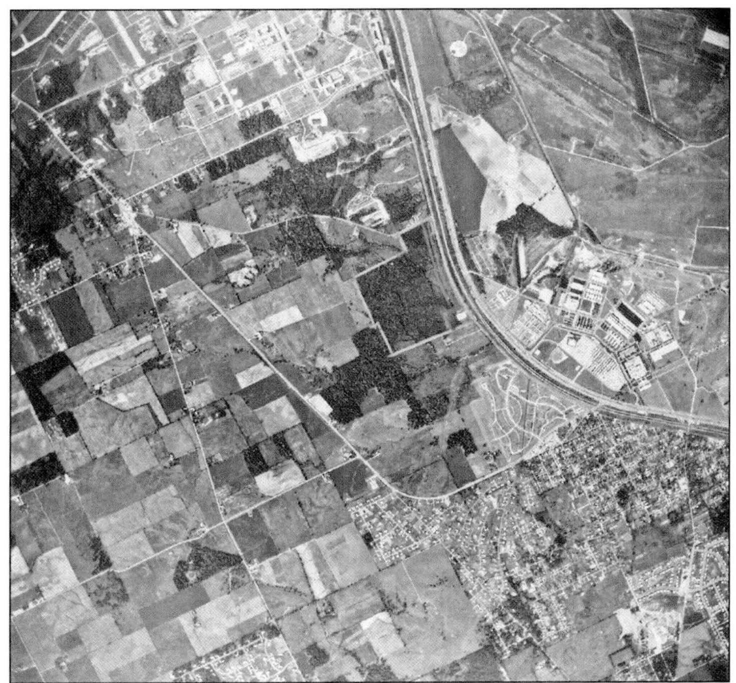

AERIAL VIEW OF THE LAND. Initially, the campus had a total of 618 acres as a result of the land issued from the government and from the efforts of Henry Bader. It was decided that the location of the branch campus of Ohio State University and Miami University would be in Bath Township, Greene County. The site of the campus would be located on Airway Road (later Colonel Glenn Highway), Kauffman Avenue, and Zink Road.

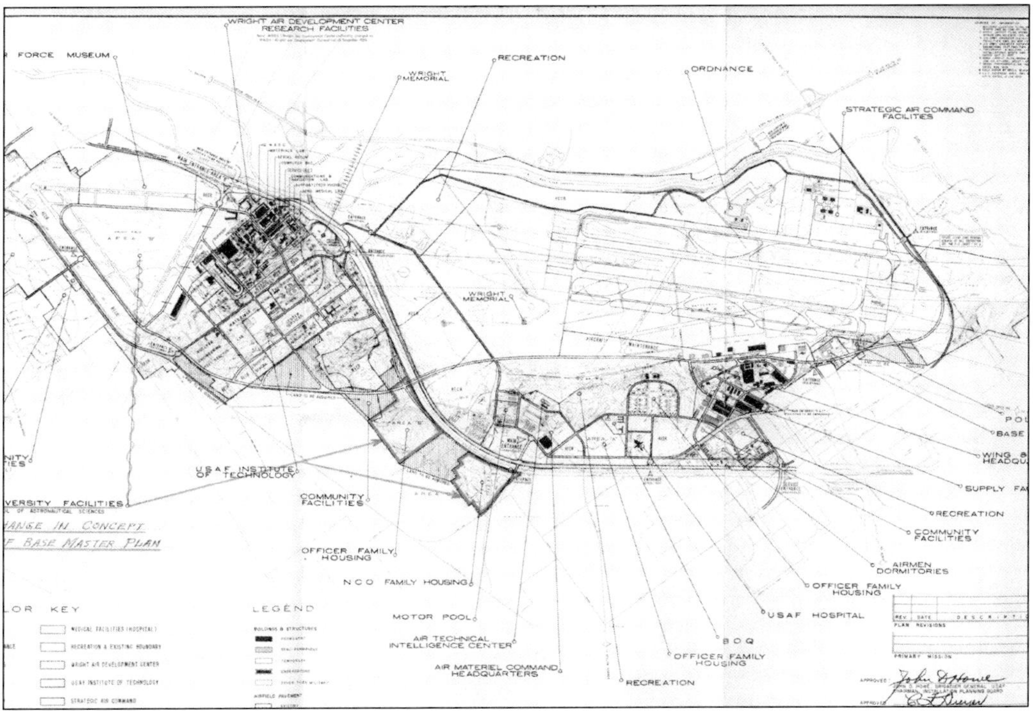

WRIGHT-PATTERSON AIR FORCE BASE. The decision was made to situate the newly formed campus on land in Bath Township. Since the land was unincorporated, the city's government could not provide services like sewer and water systems. Officials from the neighboring Wright-Patterson Air Force Base not only supported the project but also provided temporary water and sewer services.

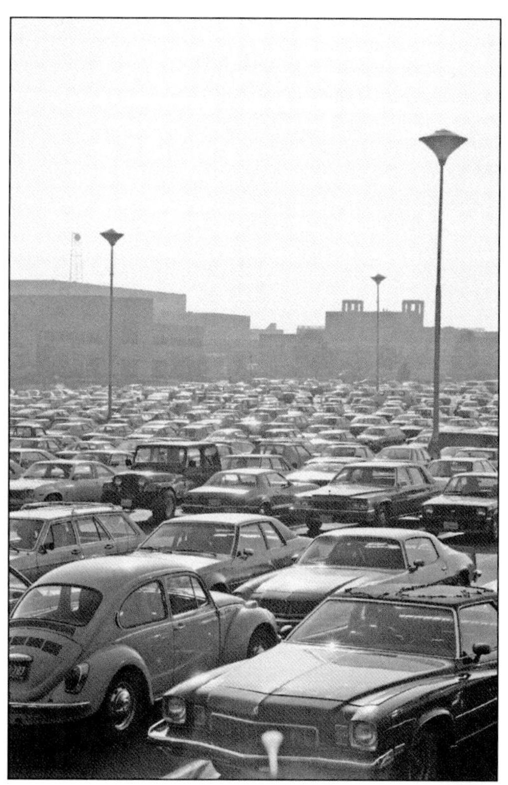

Early Parking Problem. In the original campus plans, there was only enough room for roughly 1,300 parking spaces. This proved to be problematic for the commuter campus. Money was a huge issue, since funding was allocated for parking, landscaping, and sewer and water services after permits for land and building construction were purchased.

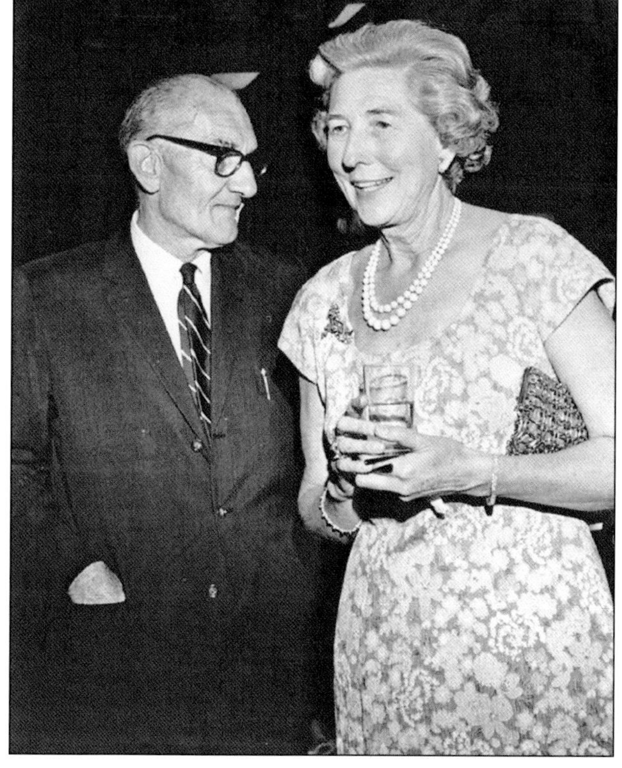

Eugene Kettering. Eugene and Virginia Kettering greatly supported the efforts to establish a public university. They contributed significantly to the city of Dayton—whether it was making financial contributions to the school via endowments or helping to establish a hospital in the city, the Ketterings were known to be generous. Eugene Kettering was also active in the Combined University Building Fund. After he passed, Virginia Kettering continued to support Dayton philanthropically.

Frederick White. In 1962, Frederick White, an administrator with General Motors Corporation and a close follower of the new university project, was appointed as the business manager. Wearing many hats in this position, he finalized land acquisitions; helped to establish zoning controls, power lines, community relations, and bus services; worked with architects; and made long-range plans for campus development. White became known as the "first employee" of the new university.

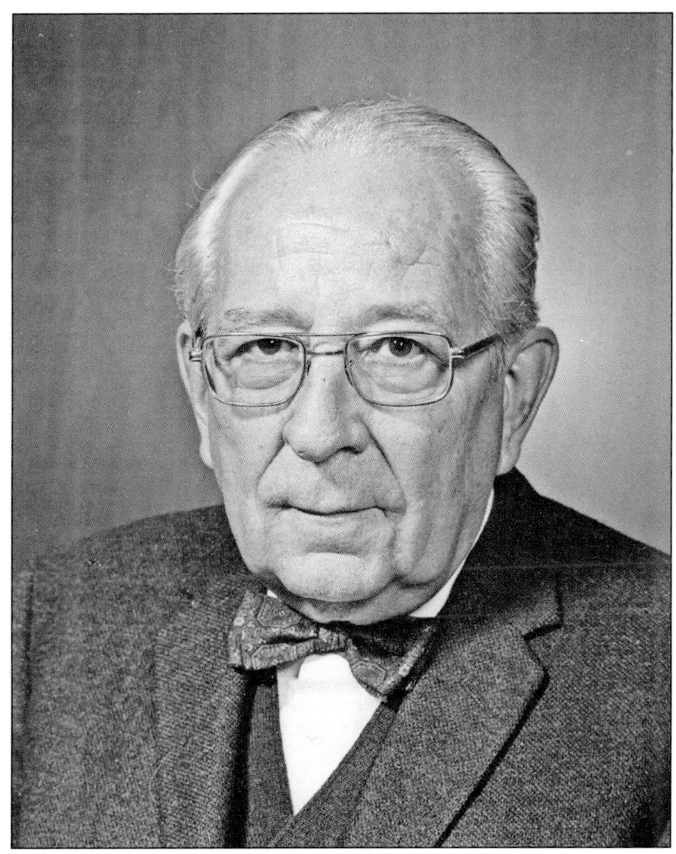

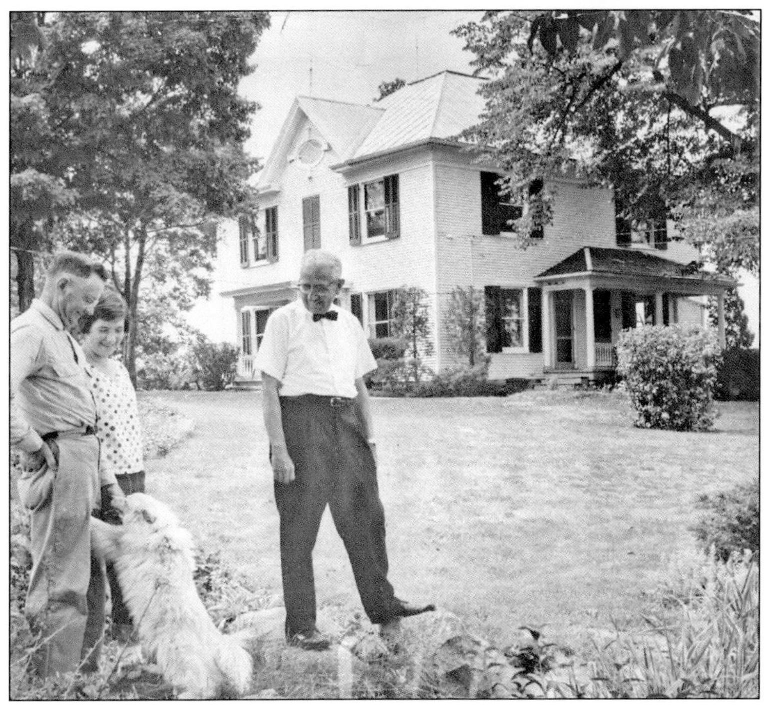

Warner House. The Warner House was owned by the Warner family. The farmhouse was the first administration building for the Dayton campus. It was used by Frederick White as an office, meeting space, and an overall space to get things together for the school. Henry Warner was still living at the house at the time and was in the process of moving.

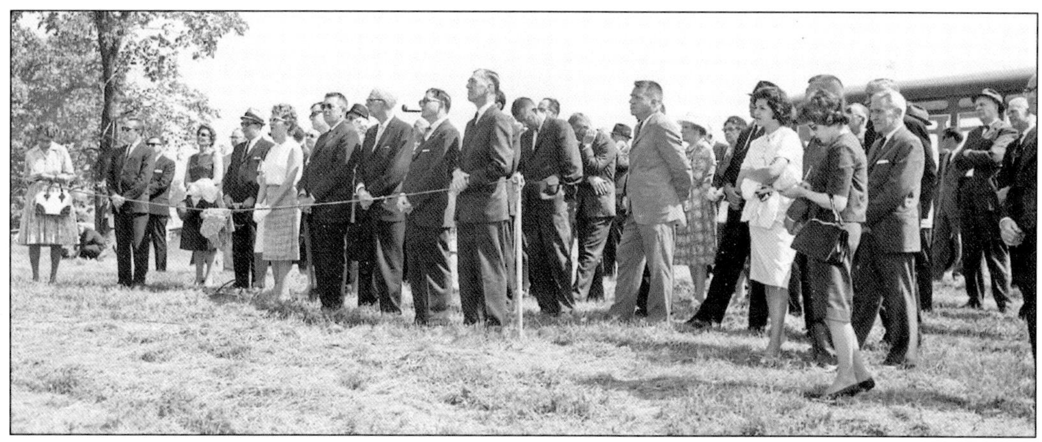

Ground Breaking for Allyn Hall. The ground-breaking ceremony for Allyn Hall, the first building on campus, took place on May 31, 1963, at 3:00 p.m. Known as a "college within a building," it housed all of the academic programs and administrative offices under one roof. Frederick White was the master of ceremonies, and the Reverend Raymond Roesch, SM, president of the University of Dayton, gave the invocation. It was announced that the building would be named Allyn Hall.

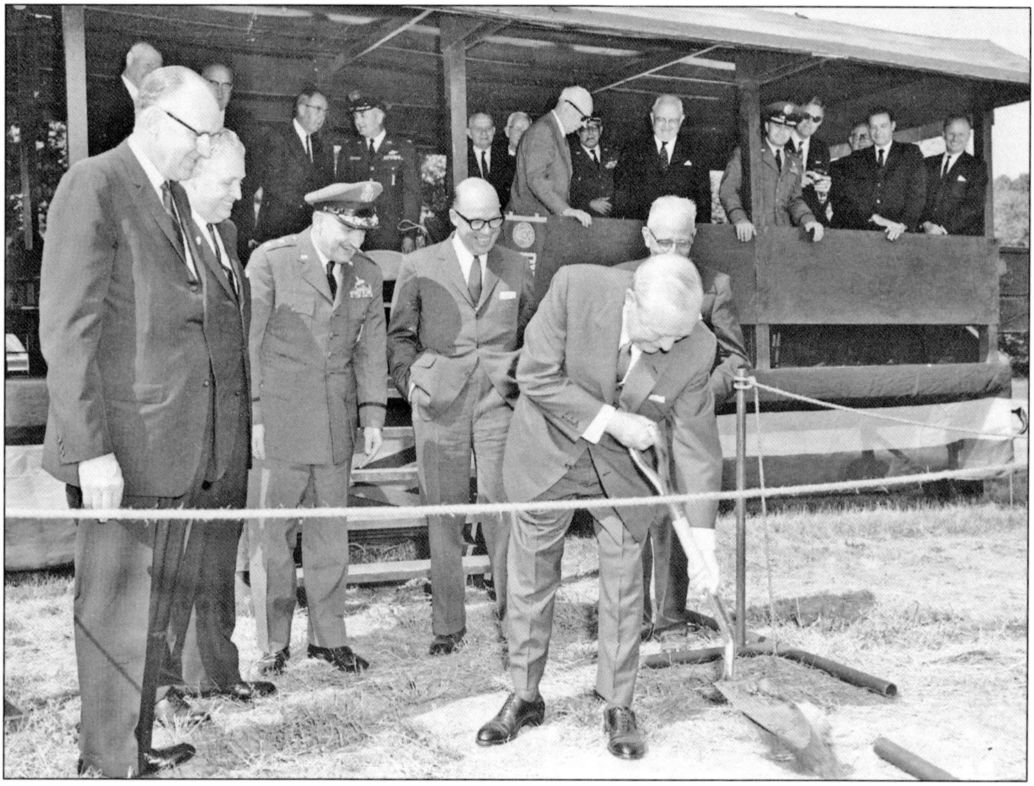

US Air Force. The US Air Force had been a collaborator in the establishment of a new area university since the beginning. At the ground-breaking ceremony for Allyn Hall, the Air Force provided the band, speakers' platform, and bus transportation for the audience. Maj. Gen. T.A. Bennett (with shovel) of the Air Force Logistics Command assisted in breaking ground for the first campus building.

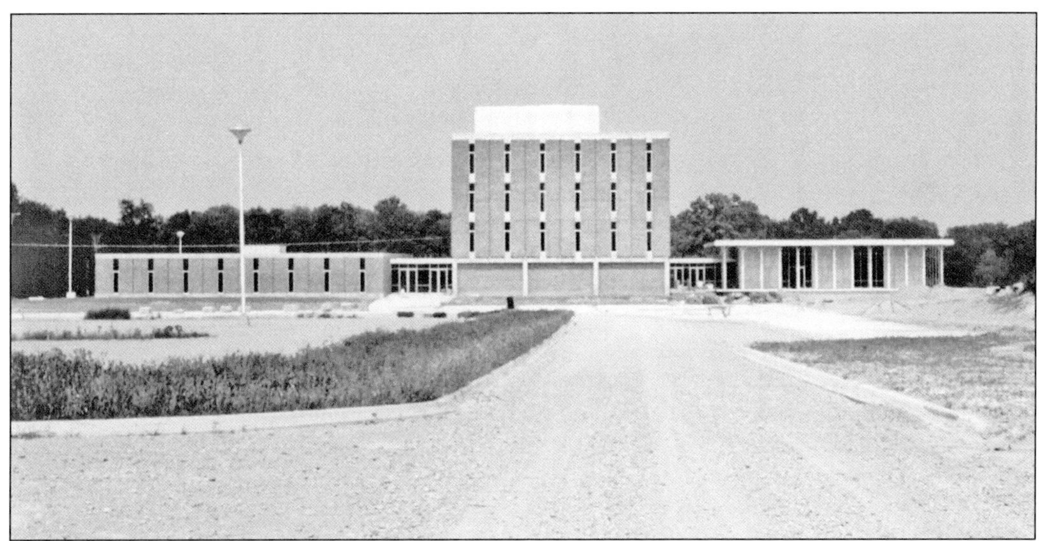

Allyn Hall. On September 8, 1964, the Dayton campus of Miami University and Ohio State University opened. The first building, Allyn Hall, was named in honor of Stanley Charles Allyn. When the building was constructed, it was a self-contained university consisting of the General College, College of Science and Engineering, Dayton Academic Center of Miami University, and Graduate Center of Ohio State University. This small university was home to 3,203 students.

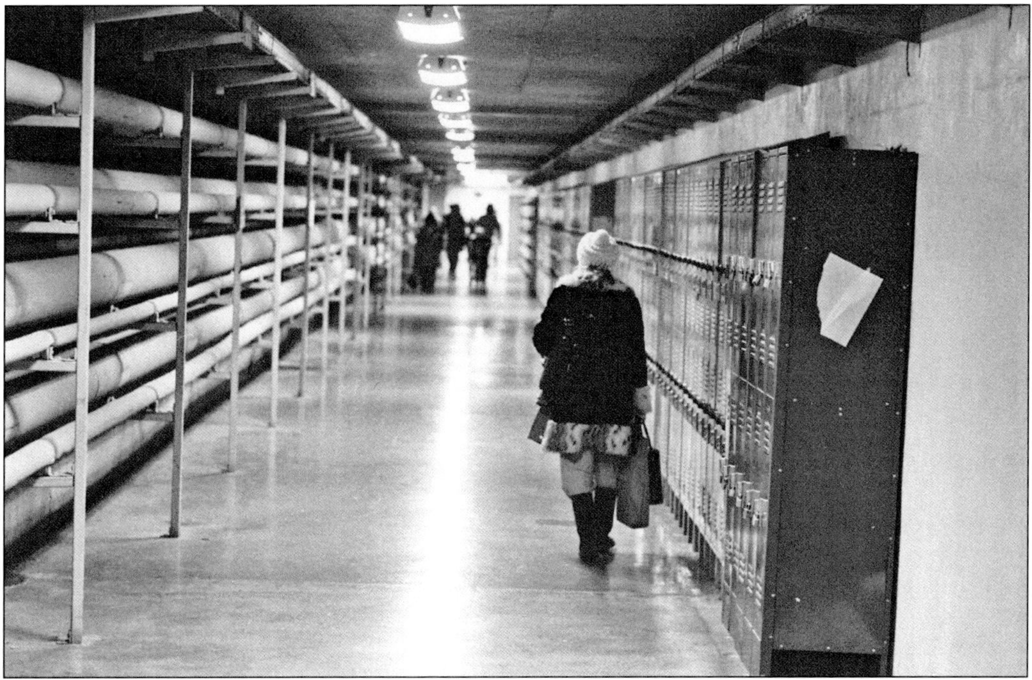

Tunnel System. Belowground is an elaborate tunnel system connecting the campus buildings. This tunnel system was originally constructed for infrastructure/electrical grid connectivity. It was also used for delivery services. During winter months, the tunnels became flooded with pedestrian traffic. Over time, the tunnel system also attracted students with disabilities. There is no evidence that the tunnel was conceived for accessibility.

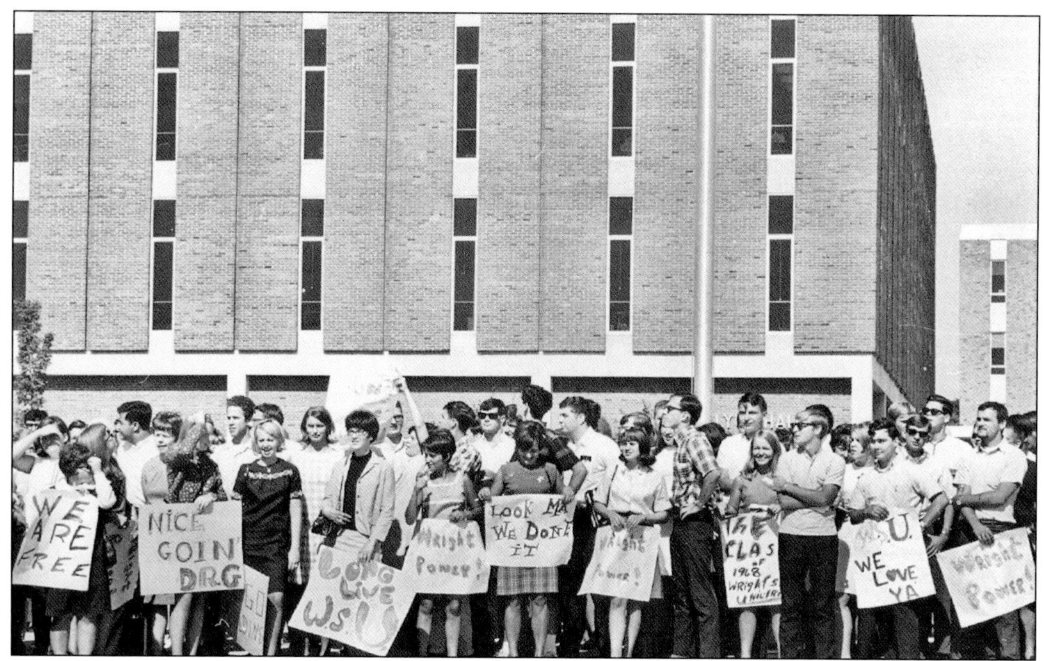

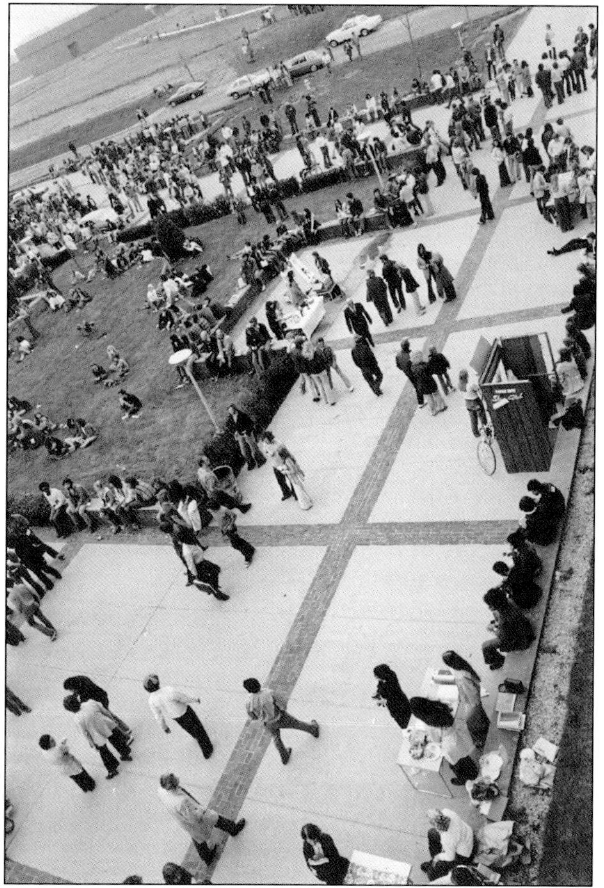

Wright State University Opens. On September 8, 1964, the branch campus of Ohio State University and Miami University opened. There were 3,203 enrolled students, surpassing the Community Research, Inc., estimate of 1,400–1,500. At the time, there were 55 faculty members. During this first year, the campus operated on the trimester system. Although there was construction work going on and the walls were still wet with paint, classes started.

Instruction and Curriculum. During the first year of operation, faculty members from Miami University and Ohio State University instructed students. By the second year, as the school rapidly expanded in size and population, this Dayton campus had well over 100 faculty members and offered 600 courses at the undergraduate and graduate levels.

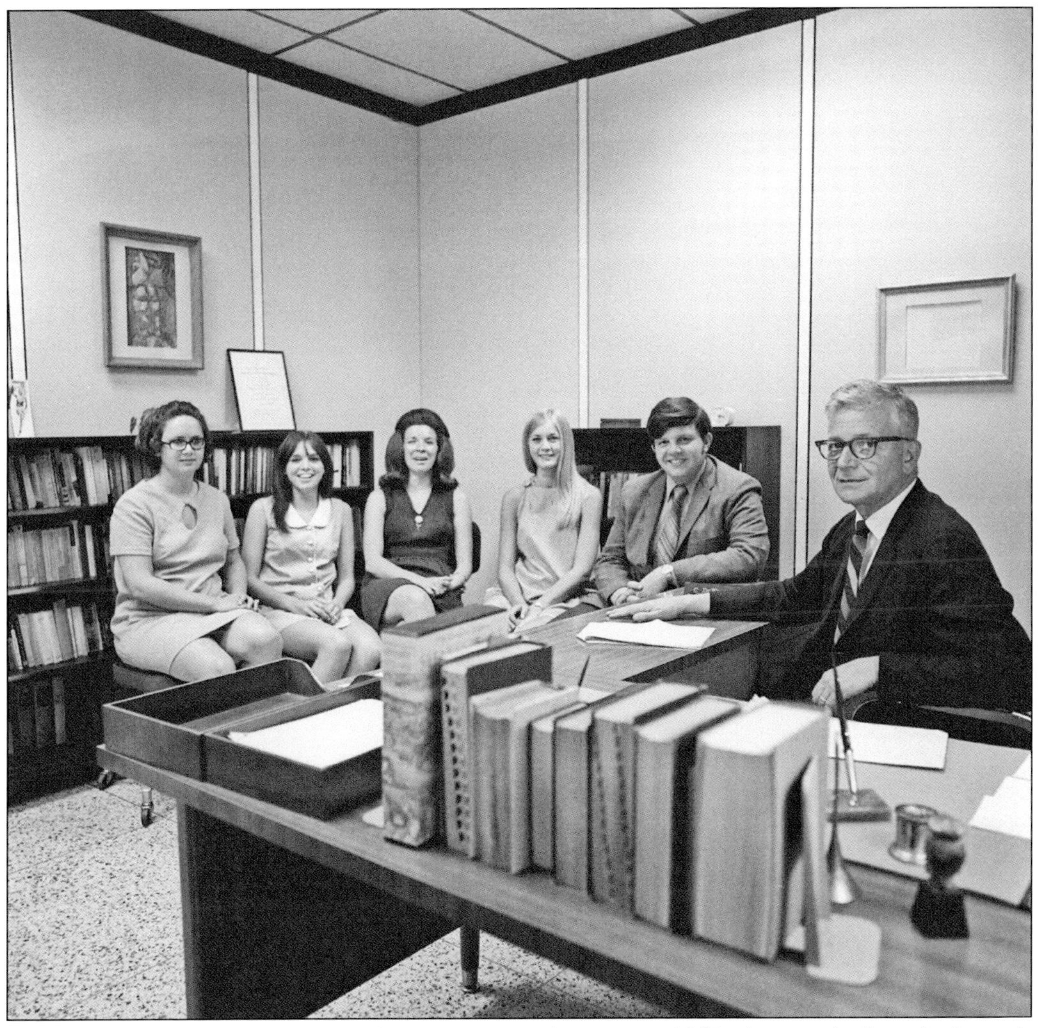

C. DEWITT HARDY. C. Dewitt Hardy came to Wright State in 1963, the year before the branch campus opened. When he arrived, none of the buildings had been built. He is credited as being the first academic instructor. He was the first director of admissions for the campus and found the university's students. In 1970, he moved from administration duties to teaching history. In 1976, Hardy retired from the university.

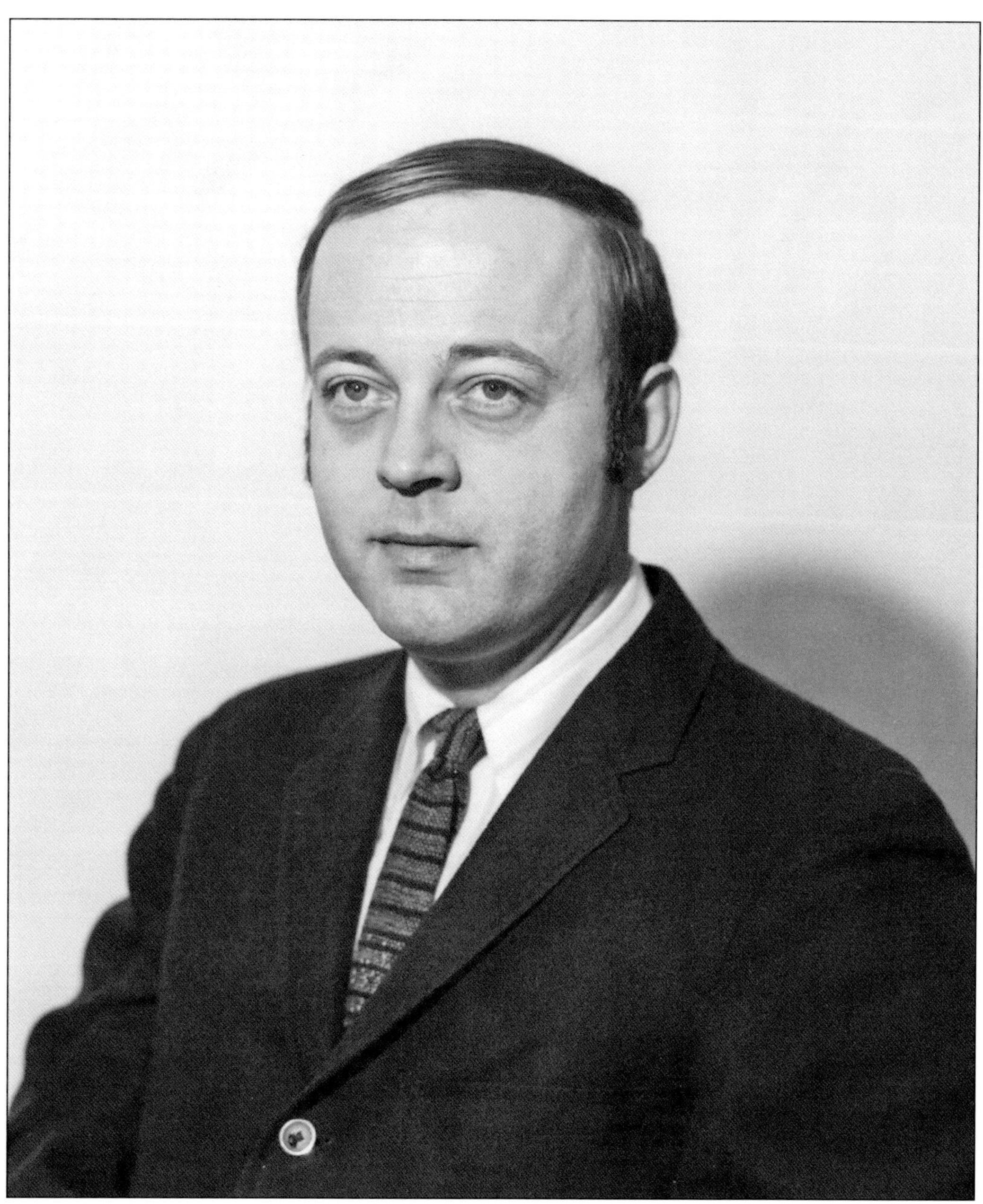

Gary Barlow. Gary Barlow was one of the first faculty members. When he first started working at the campus, it was nothing but grassland and fences with cows in the fields. The first class he taught was in a classroom that was still under construction. He would teach, stop so that construction workers could install ceiling tiles, then start teaching again.

Nontraditional Student. The university consisted of nontraditional students. The average student was 29 years old, and a majority were first-generation college students. This new university provided students with opportunities for a college education that, prior to this branch campus, were not available. On any given day, pedestrian traffic included students dressed in blue jeans and sneakers, those wearing Air Force uniforms, and a mixture of various races.

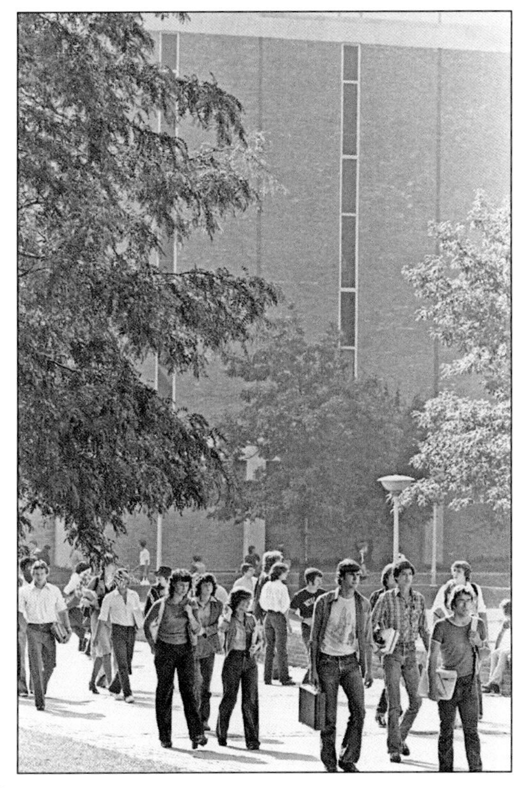

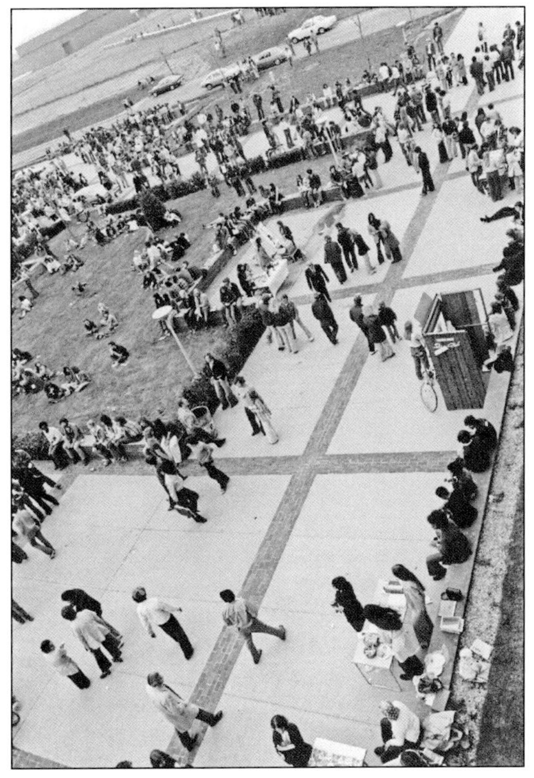

The Overall Student Body. When the branch campus opened in the fall of 1964, the number of enrolled students totaled 3,203. Ninety percent of the students were undergraduates. Thirty-nine percent of them were full-time, and 61 percent were part-time. Graduate students made up the last 10 percent. Only one percent of the graduate students were full-time. Fifty-four percent of the students were men; 46 percent were women.

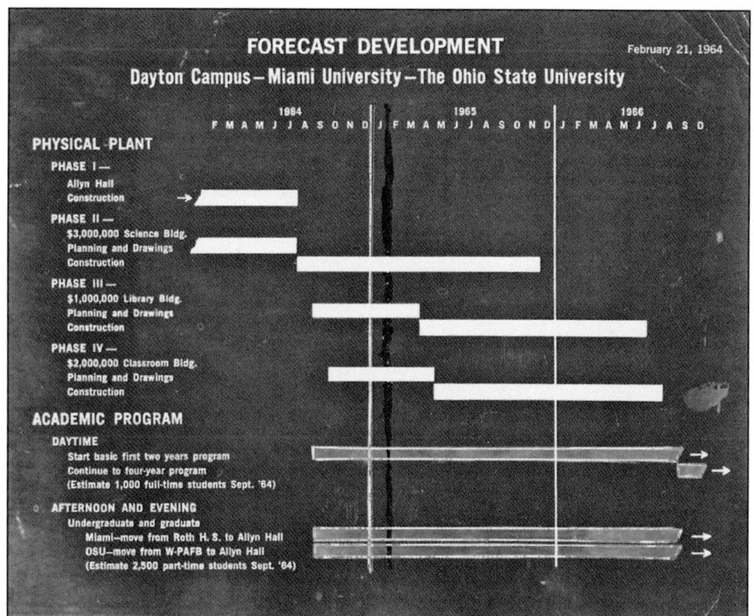

Financial Obligations and Issues. For the first year, the campus operated on a $1 million budget. About three-fourths of the budget was allocated for academic and department support. The remaining quarter of the budget went to maintenance, student support, and administration duties. The tight budget left no room for fundamentals such as a library, research, and various equipment.

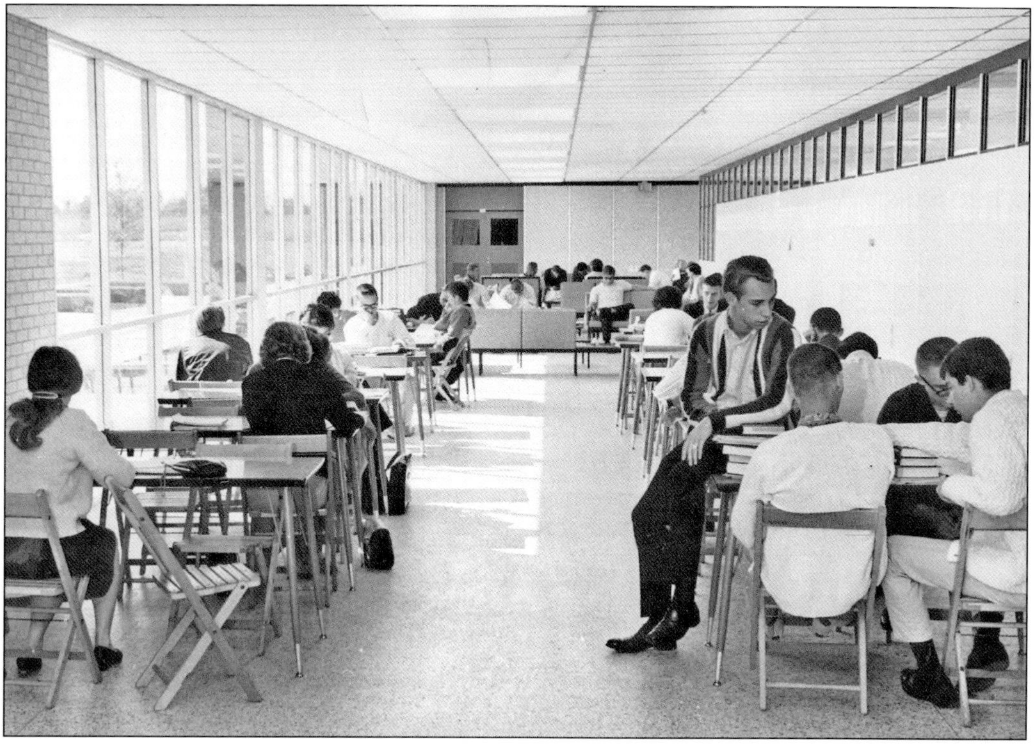

Allyn Hall. The university's first building, Allyn Hall, offered students and faculty the bare minimum, like classroom and a vending machine for drinks, snacks, and sandwiches in the basement. On the ground level were spaces for bursar services, student records, and the registrar. In the building's south wing was a humble library. In the north wing were science laboratories. The building's limited space offered no room for study, lounge, or recreational spaces.

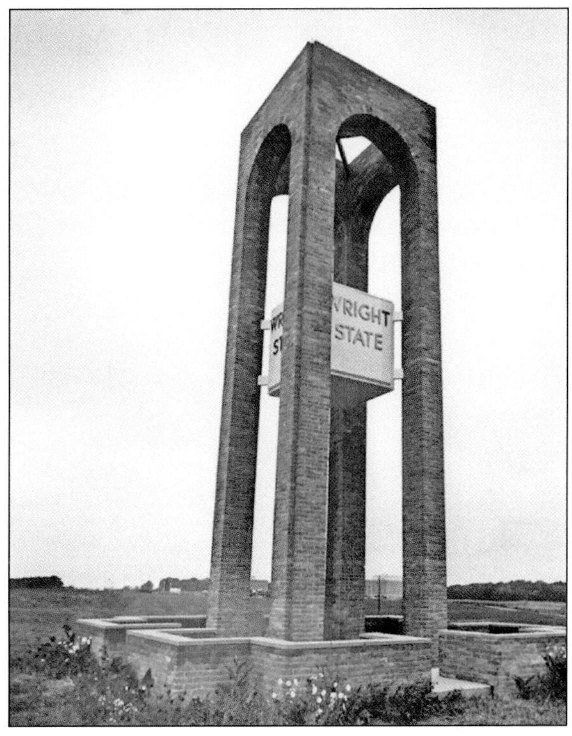

Bell-Less Tower. In 1964, community funds left over from the construction of Allyn Hall were used to build the "Bell-less Tower." It was erected at the school's main entrance on Colonel Glenn Highway. This landmark became the unofficial logo of the campus on advertisements, publications, and stationery.

Ground Breaking for Oelman Hall. The planning committees from Ohio State and Miami University, architects, and Frederick White moved forward with plans for Oelman Hall after funding for more campus buildings was secured. Ground was broken for the second building on March 31, 1965. This new building was designated for the science and engineering department.

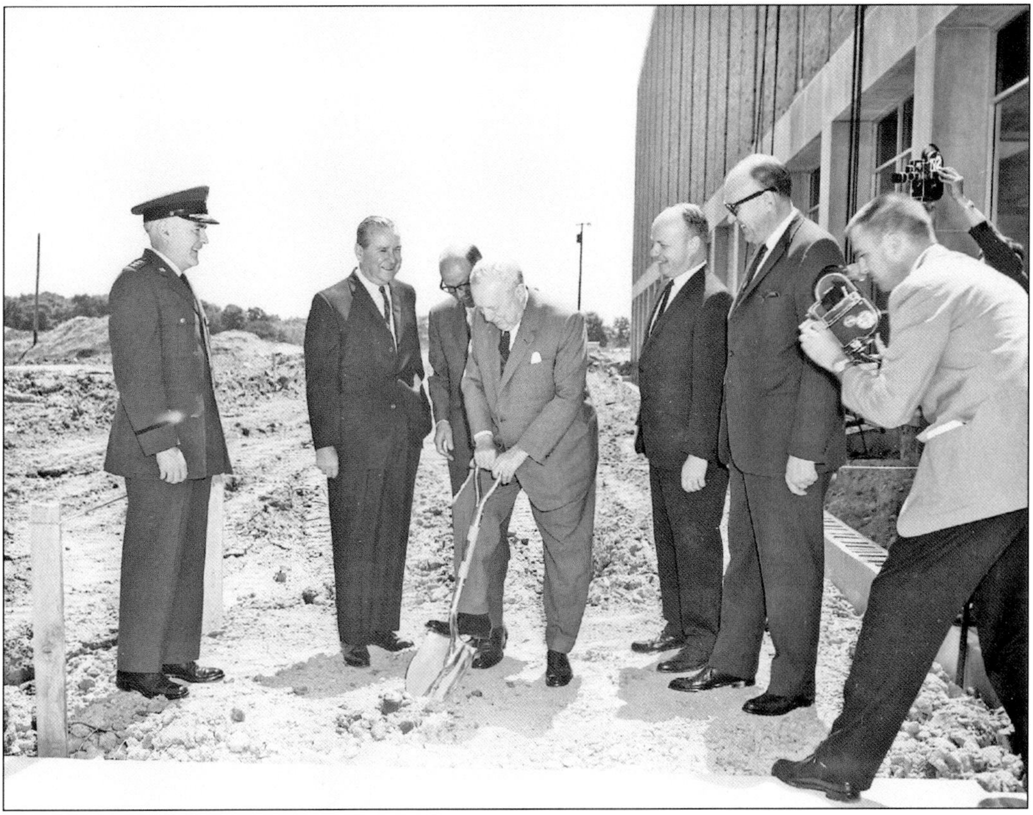

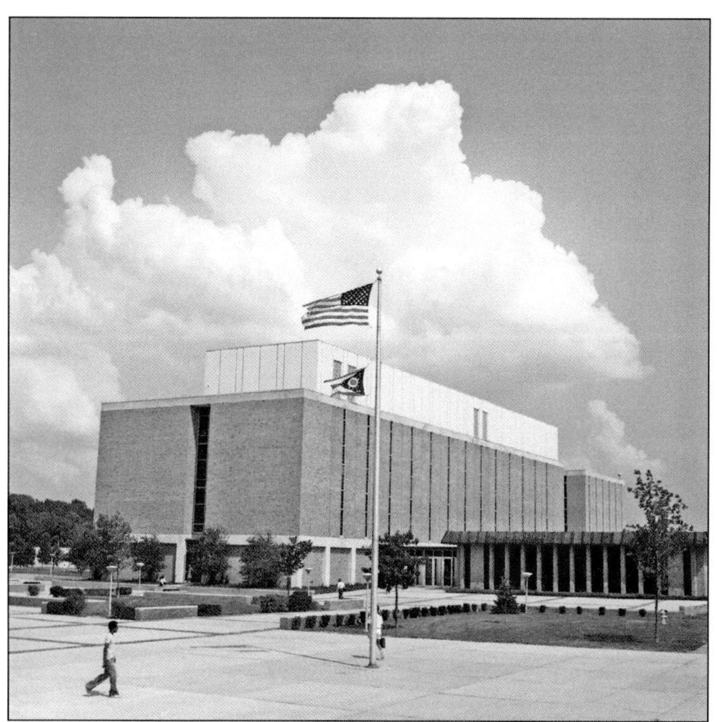

Oelman Hall. The university's second building was completed in 1966. Oelman Hall was named in honor of Robert Oelman. It holds the Oelman Auditorium, which is used for faculty meetings, performances, and guest speakers. Initially, it was also used as an office space for Pres. Brage Golding. It is now home to the Chemistry Department, classrooms, and various departments and offices.

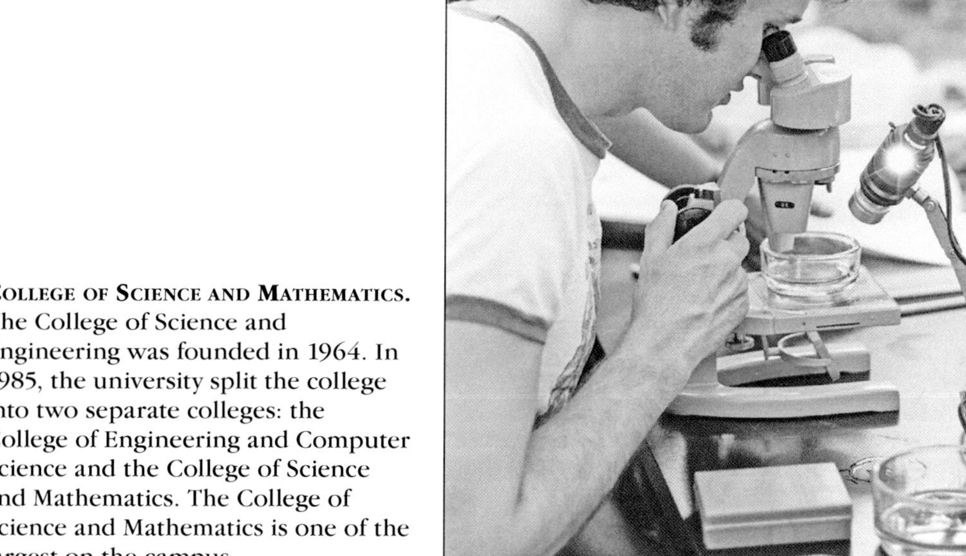

College of Science and Mathematics. The College of Science and Engineering was founded in 1964. In 1985, the university split the college into two separate colleges: the College of Engineering and Computer Science and the College of Science and Mathematics. The College of Science and Mathematics is one of the largest on the campus.

Millett Hall. The third building to be constructed was Millett Hall. The ground breaking for Millett Hall took place on July 2, 1965; it was completed in 1966. The building was designated for additional classrooms as well as the campus library. It was named for John D. Millett, who was the president of Miami University at the time of Wright State's initiation.

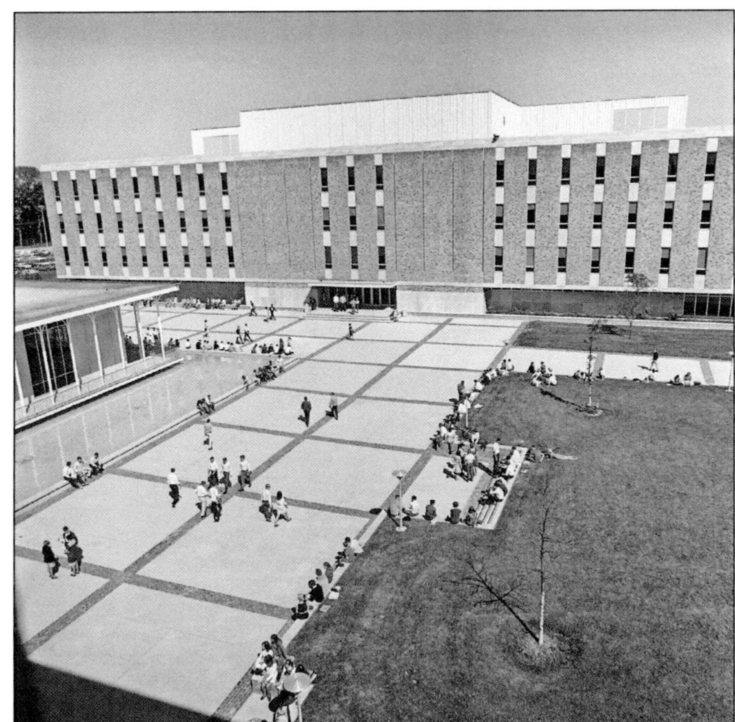

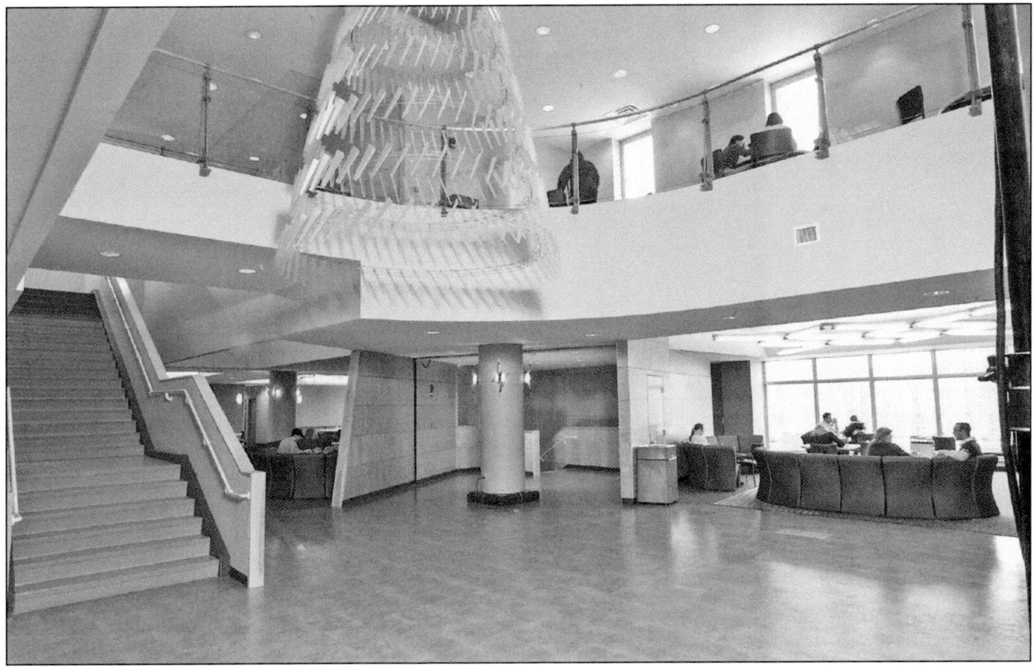

College of Liberal Arts. The College of Liberal Arts is situated in Millett Hall. It is home to departments such as Sociology and Anthropology, Applied Behavioral Science, Classics, Communication, English, History, Modern Languages, Political Science, the University Honors Program, and the Multicultural Center, which houses the Asian/Hispanic/Native American Center, the Bolinga Black Cultural Resources Center, and the Women's Center.

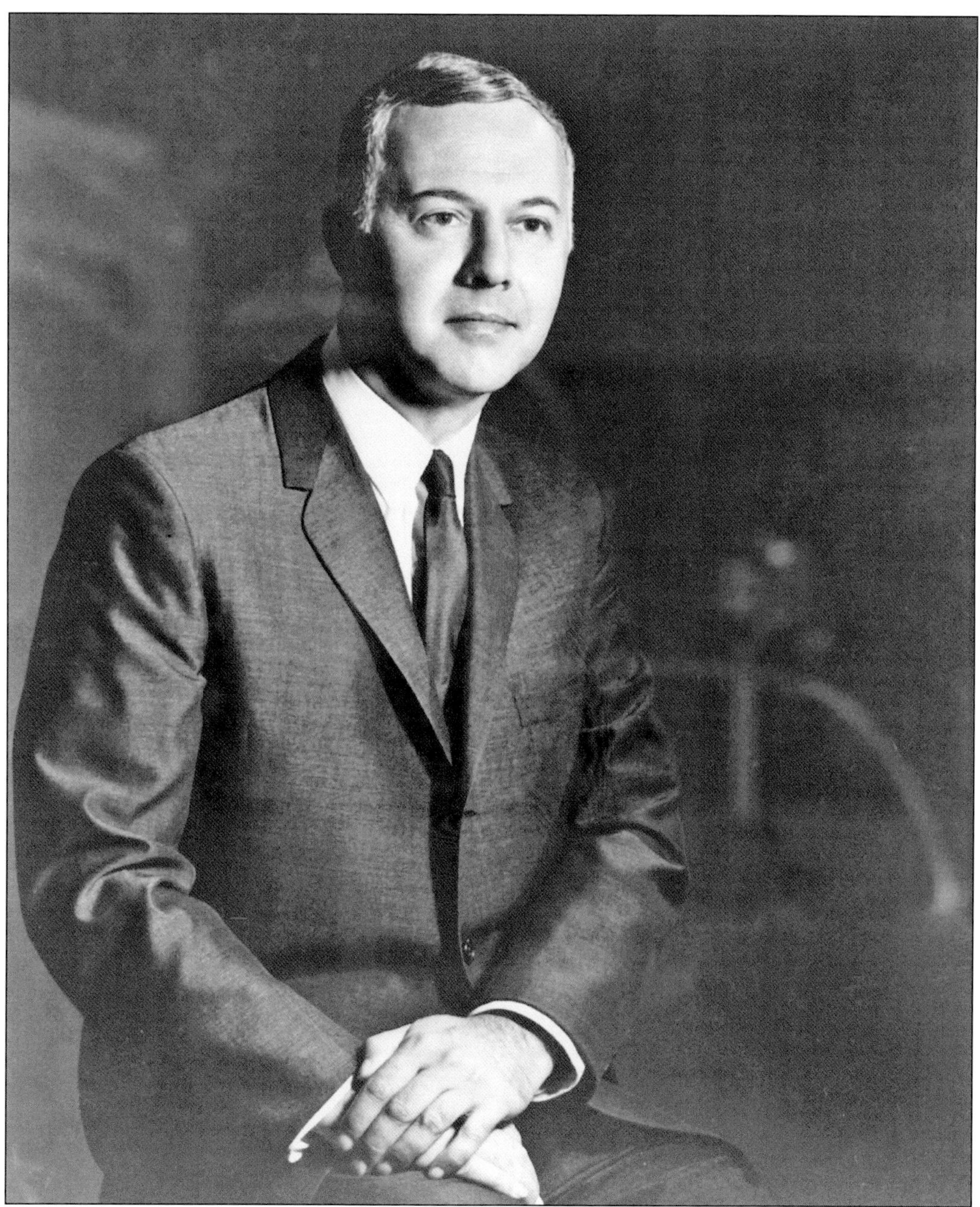

DR. BRAGE GOLDING. The independent campus selected its first president in 1966. During Dr. Brage Golding's six-year tenure, the campus grew to include a gymnasium, student dormitories, a library, and the Creative Arts Center. In addition, four colleges and a graduate school were established. Under Dr. Golding's tutelage, the university achieved full accreditation.

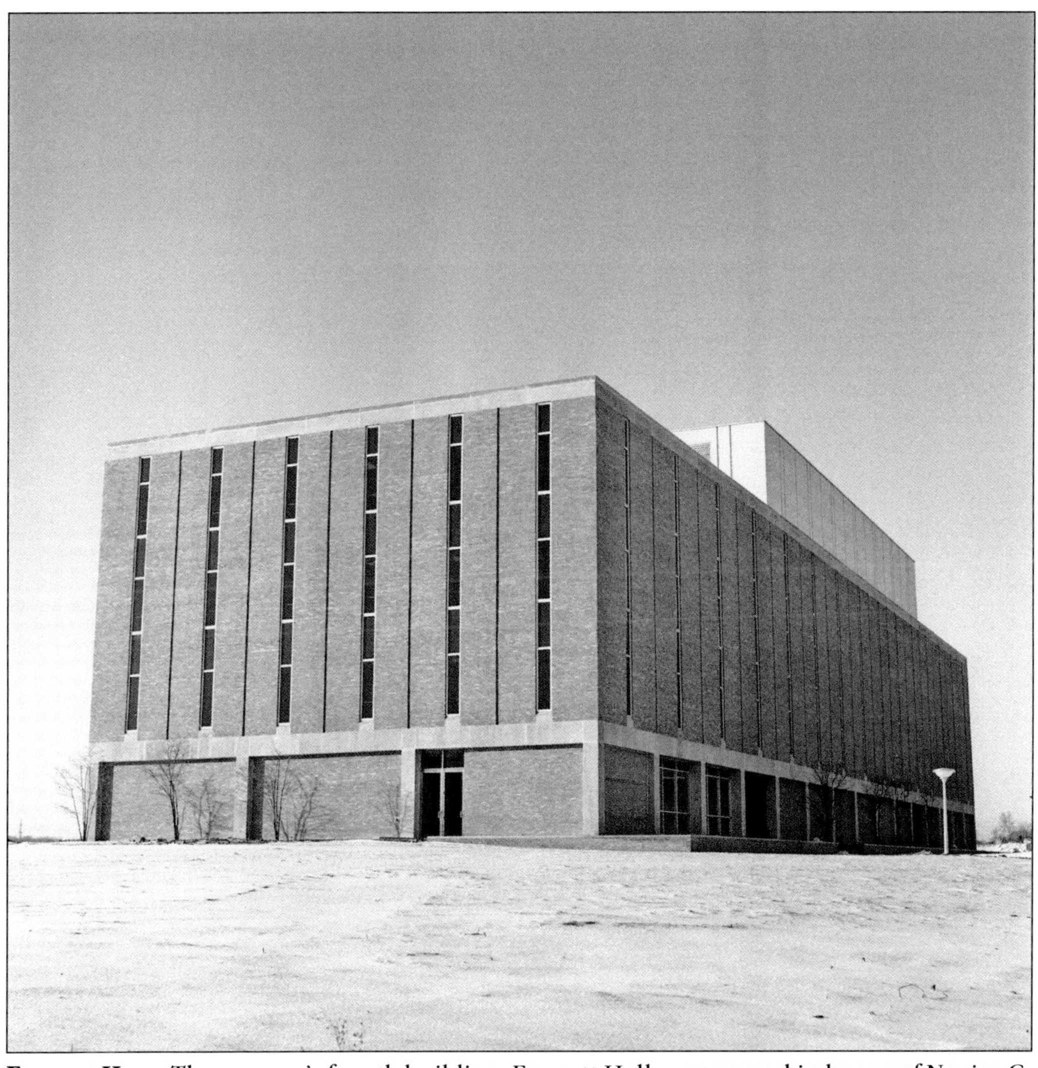

FAWCETT HALL. The campus's fourth building, Fawcett Hall, was named in honor of Novice G. Fawcett, the president of Ohio State University and a key figure in making sure that the new project would be successful. Completed in 1967, Fawcett Hall was a multipurpose instructional facility. Fawcett Hall is the final building to make up the Founders' Quadrangle.

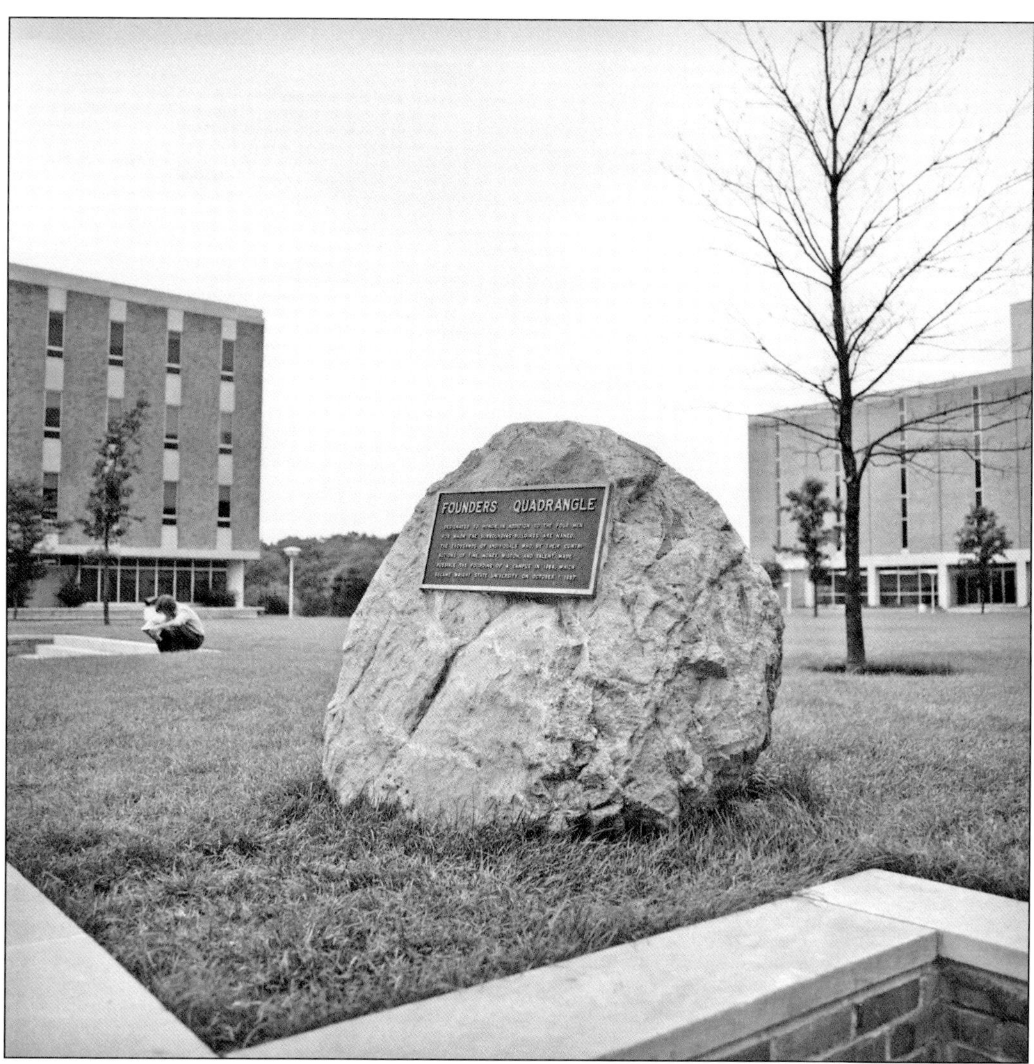

FOUNDERS' QUADRANGLE. The Founders' Quadrangle, also known as "the Quad," is comprised of the first four buildings, named after the four men who played critical roles in the founding and establishing of Wright State University. The buildings making up the Quad are Allyn Hall, Oelman Hall, Millett Hall, and Fawcett Hall. A plaque at the northwest corner of the Founders' Quadrangle commemorates their hard work and vision.

Two

INDEPENDENCE

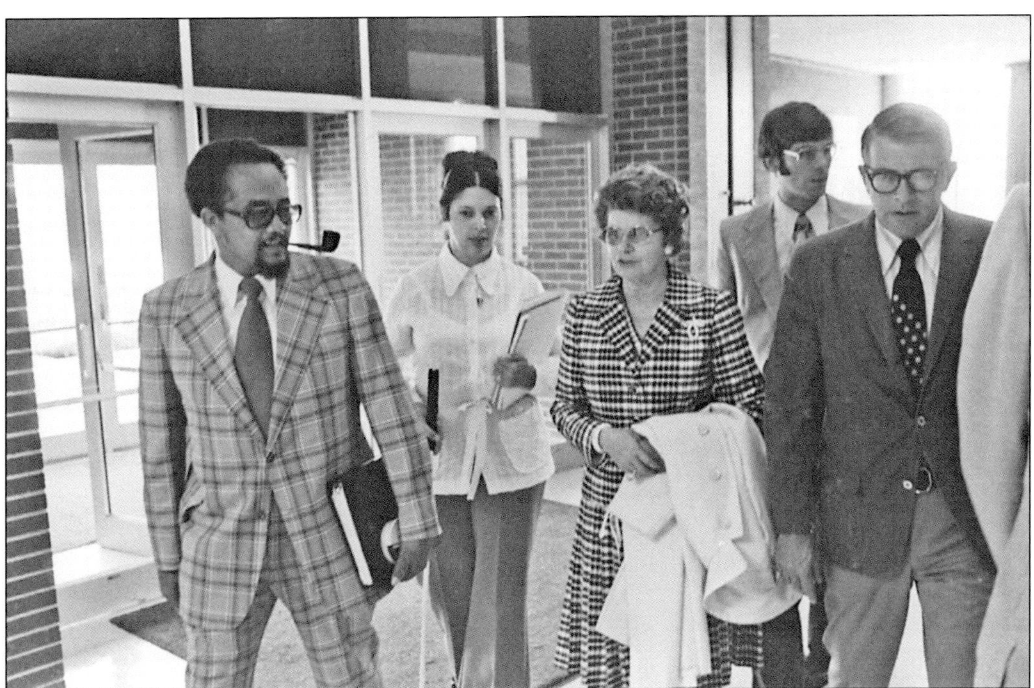

CLARA E. WEISENBORN. Clara E. Weisenborn (center) was born in Dayton in 1907. She was elected to the Ohio House of Representatives in 1952 and the Ohio Senate in 1966, serving until 1974. She cosponsored the bill that established Wright State University. She was also instrumental in the development of the medical school at the university.

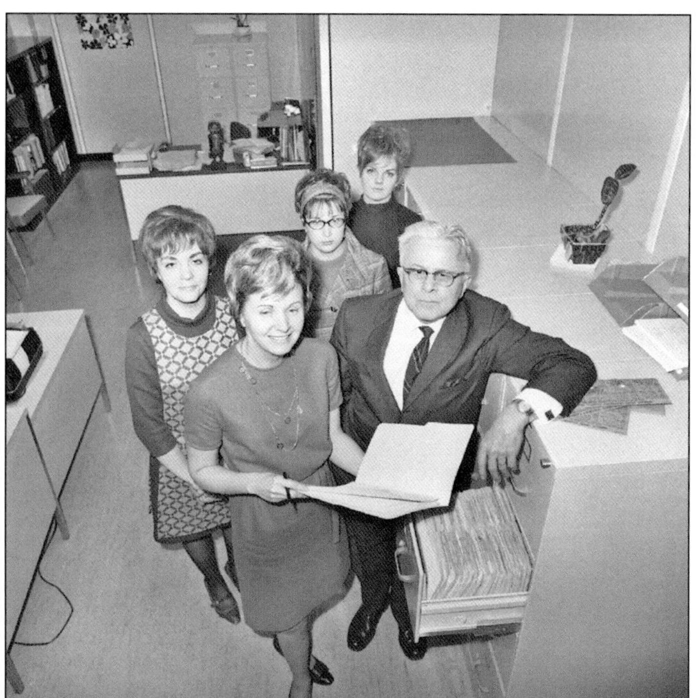

SCHOOL OF GRADUATE STUDIES. The School of Graduate Studies was established in 1967. Offering over 60 master's degrees and seven doctorates, the School of Graduate Studies strives to provide students with a quality education to make them competitive in their prospective career fields. To help offset education costs, students are encouraged to apply for graduate, teaching, or research assistantships.

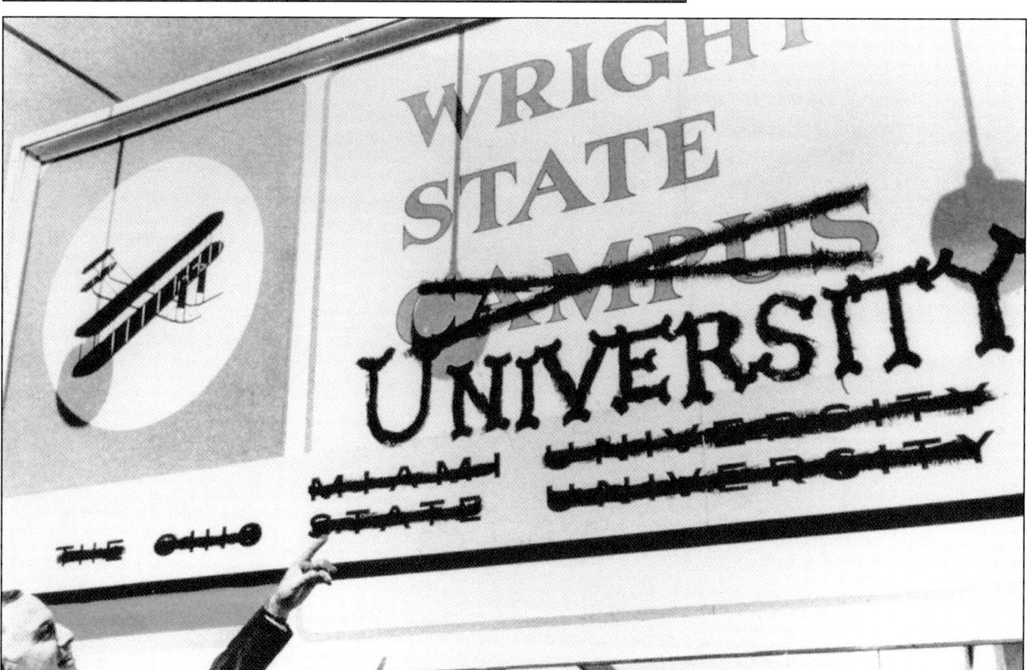

INDEPENDENCE. Dr. Golding faced mounting pressure from different sources pushing the branch campus to sever ties with Ohio State and Miami University and become independent. Senate Bill No. 210 stated that the university could become independent when enrollment reached 5,000 but not before July 1, 1967. On October 1, 1967, the university became independent. The university could establish extracurricular activities, student services, housing, adequate food service, and recreational facilities.

Naming the University. When the university reached independent status, the next mission was to name it. The goal was to disassociate from the University of Dayton and separate its identity from Ohio State and Miami University. The Sigma Tau Epsilon fraternity set up a contest to name the university. It attracted suggestions such as Wright Brothers University, Martin Luther King University, and Whatsamatta University. The Ohio General Assembly decided on Wright State University.

THE DAYTON DAILY NEWS

James M. Cox, Publisher 1898-1957

PAGE 2 SUNDAY, DECEMBER 20, 1964 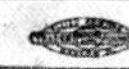

Once Again: Why Not Wright Bros. University?

Now that a new discussion has started on a name for the new divisional university here, perhaps it is timely to renew a suggestion made on this page a year or so ago.

As many people have recommended, why not call the new institution "Wright Brothers university?"

Of all the illustrious people who have lived in Dayton, none has affected the pattern of humanity and of human life to a fraction of the degree that both were changed by Orville and Wilbur Wright and their flying machine.

Powered flight brought the aviation age and, behind it, the new era of space travel. It reduced the size of the earth. It made all mankind neighbors. To be the home of such an invention is a distinction known to only a few spots in the world.

The new university is linked with aviation. It is almost physically a part of the Wright-Patterson complex. It is tied closely to aviation research and to the creativity and invention that were the hallmarks of the Wrights.

The spirit of discovery and invention is uniquely the spirit of the Dayton community and of the university that will become a major community resource.

Tie all this to the fact that, Wright Field aside, the name of the Wrights is virtually uncommemorated here and you have a compelling case for an appropriate and fine-sounding name: Wright Brothers university.

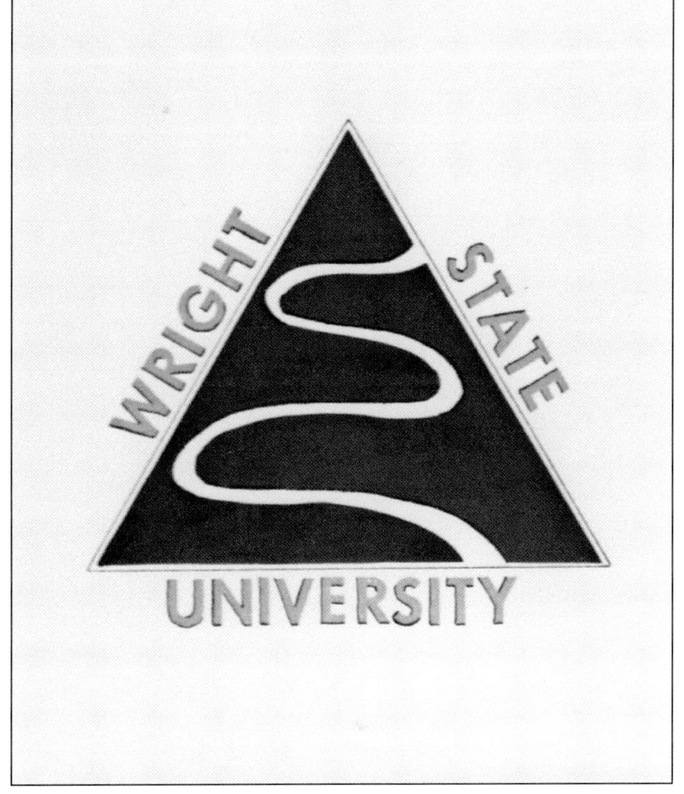

Triangular Emblem. In 1968, the fraternity collected suggestions for an emblem. The triangular emblem chosen employs contemporary symbolism and shows a meandering river. The river is identified as the area's Mad River. The stable shape of the triangle represents academic discipline; the river, constantly changing its general direction in search of the sea, represents academic freedom in search of truth.

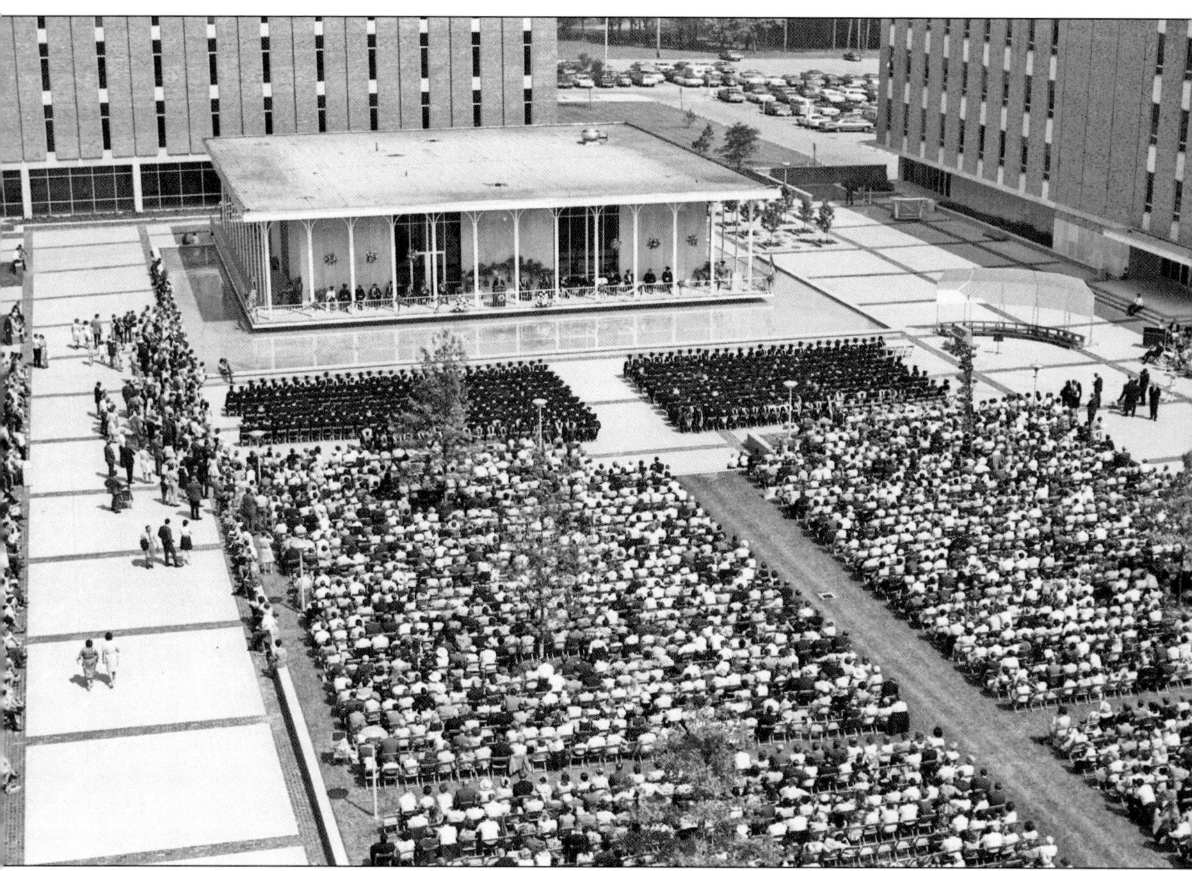

FIRST COMMENCEMENT. The first commencement ceremony was held on the Founders' Quadrangle on Sunday, June 23, 1968. Three hundred and fifty-six students received degrees from the university's graduate school and the Colleges of Business and Administration, Education, Liberal Arts, and Science and Engineering. The message to the graduates centered on adjusting to rapid changes within their individual lives as well as within their communities.

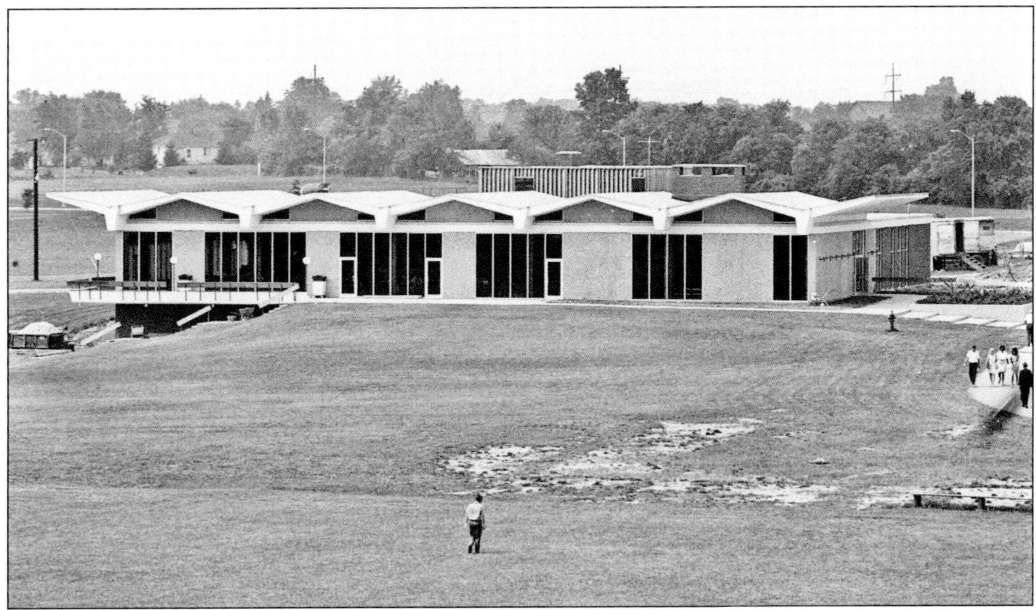

University Center. For the first few years, students did not have a place they could lounge, nor did they have adequate food service. This changed in 1969 with the opening of the University Center. The University Center provided students with food facilities, a bookstore, a recreational area, conference rooms, and lounges. The center underwent expansion in 1970 to include more dining areas, a larger bookstore, and additional meeting rooms.

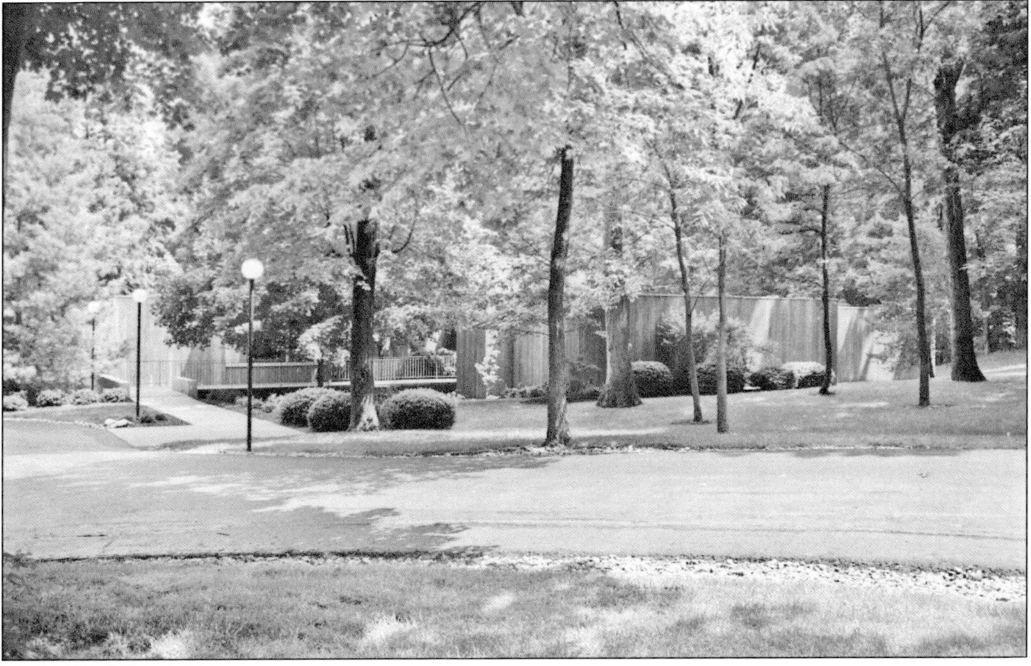

Rockafield House. Completed in 1969, the Rockafield House was established as permanent housing for the university's president. Located in a secluded area on campus, the house was funded by donations and gifts from Dayton residents and from the state. Today, the house is used for visiting alumni and is a housing option for future presidents.

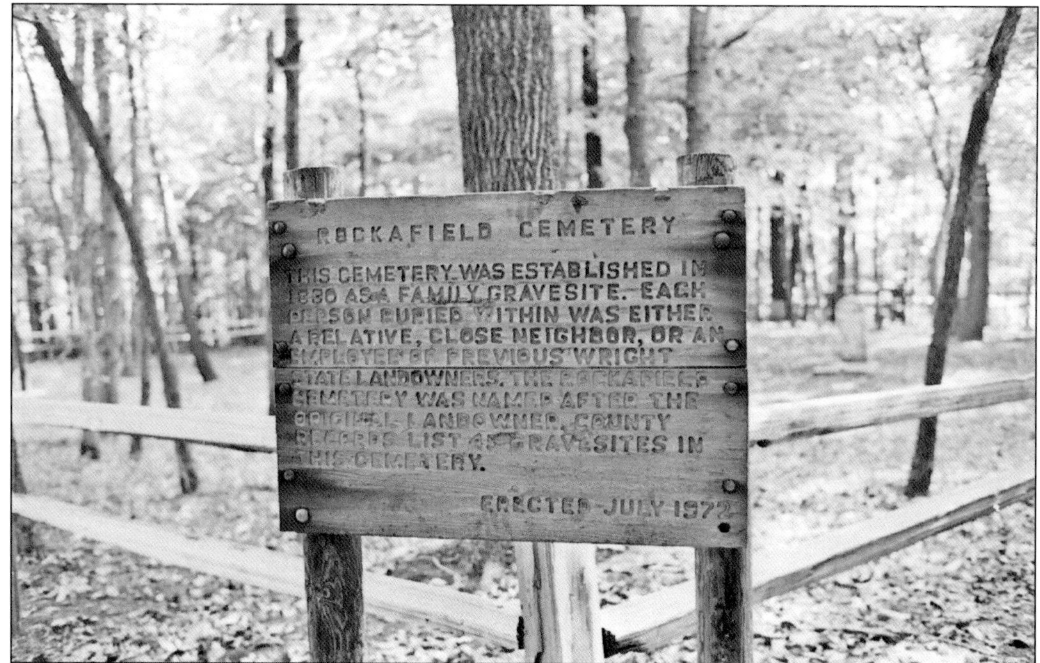

CAMPUS ROCKAFIELD CEMETERY. The Rockafield Cemetery was part of the 1964 land acquisition for the Dayton campus. Located on land owned by Joe Roger, the cemetery had been established around 1825. Any donor to the Anatomical Gift Program may be buried here.

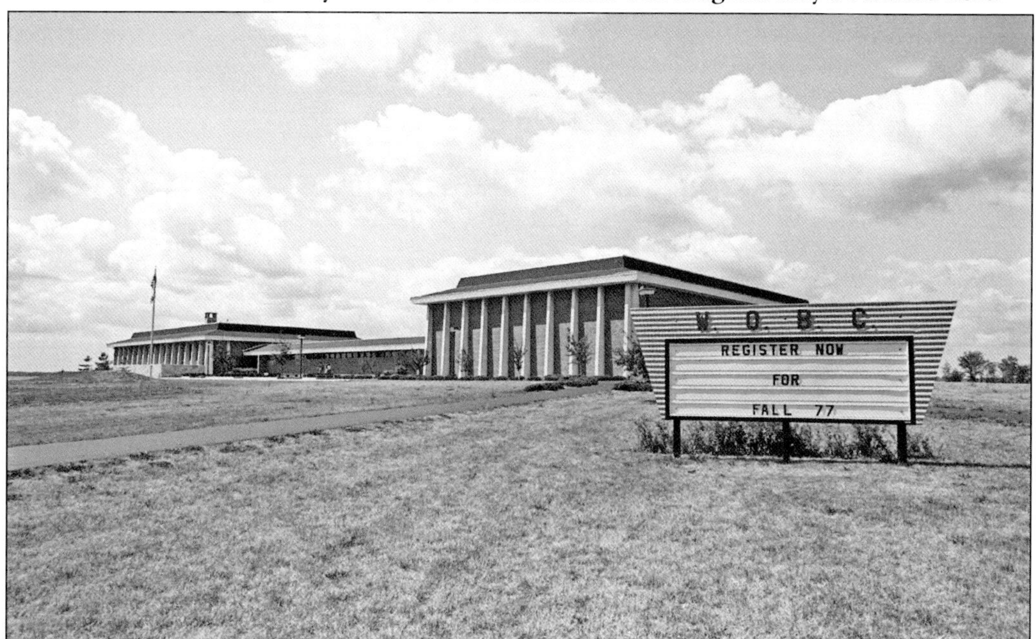

LAKE CAMPUS. The Lake Campus was created in response to a growing need for residents in counties around Celina, Ohio. The Western Ohio Education Foundation fundraising efforts led to the acquisition of a 173-acre site for the new campus. In 1969, the Western Ohio Branch Campus became Wright State University's first branch campus. In 1986, it was renamed the Wright State University–Lake Campus.

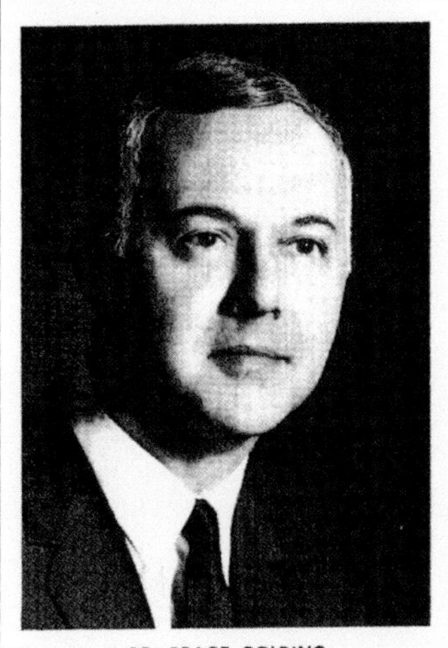

DR. BRAGE GOLDING

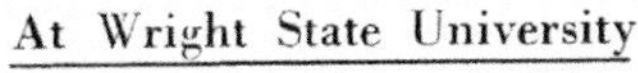

At Wright State University

The Potential Is Unlimited

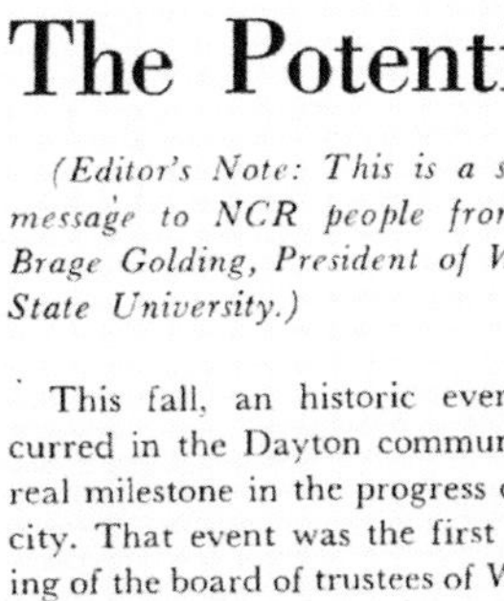

(Editor's Note: This is a special message to NCR people from Dr. Brage Golding, President of Wright State University.)

This fall, an historic event occurred in the Dayton community, a real milestone in the progress of this city. That event was the first meeting of the board of trustees of Wright State University, on October 5, signifying the independence — the "coming of age"—of Wright State. At that meeting, NCR Chairman Robert S. Oelman was elected chairman of the Wright State board of trustees.

As Mr. Oelman expressed it at that time, "We have come a long way in a short period of time. It was only five and one-half years ago that a number of Dayton citizens were discussing whether it would be feasible to start a project of this magnitude. . . .

"Yet we meet here today in a firmly established university, in the midst of an impressive campus. . . ."

We have indeed come a long way. Five and a half years ago, Wright State was only a persistent thought in the minds of a few. Yet, because of men like Mr. Oelman, and thousands of other Dayton community residents like you at NCR, Wright State University is here today.

Those years have been extremely active. It was in the spring of 1962 that the community put together $6,000,000 for higher education, half of which was to help expand the University of Dayton, the other half to start "the Dayton Campus," a permanent home for the many programs Miami and The Ohio State universities had been offering locally for a number of years. Within months following the successful completion of that unprecedented fund-raising effort, momentum increased: a 618-acre campus was purchased; a master plan developed; and ground broken for the first building. It was obvious that Dayton and Daytonians wanted this university!

That first building was named in honor of Stanley C. Allyn, who, with Mr. Oelman, was so instrumental in making the new campus a reality.* For more than a year, Allyn Hall was a complete university in one building —an "instant campus." Since then, state funds have made possible three more buildings: one principally for science studies, one for engineering, and the largest of the group, the library-classroom building, primarily for liberal arts, business, and education. All are sturdily constructed, air-conditioned, and well equipped. The new student center is now under way, and at the first meeting of the board of trustees, we took steps toward construction of twin dormitories to house some 200 students. Still more buildings are in the planning stage at this time.

Progress has by no means been confined to the building phase, however visible and dramatic such progress is. While the bulldozers and bricklayers were at their jobs, an equal effort was being made to build a strong faculty, to gather an aggressive administrative team, to expand and sharpen our curriculum, to stock our library, to recruit a student body, and to prepare for independence from Miami and Ohio State universities, of which we had been a branch since the beginning.

**A plaque in the building reads: " . . . named in honor of Stanley C. Allyn, industrialist and civic leader . . . dedicated to the thousands of citizens, industries, foundations, and the U.S. Air Force whose generous contributions to the Combined University Building Fund in 1962 created this new campus for higher education. . . ."*

Leadership Needed. The newly independent university needed leadership. From 1970 to 1971, Dr. Golding created and filled key positions. In June 1970, Frederick White was appointed as the first vice president. In August, O. Edward Pollock was chosen as the vice president and director of student services. In September, Andrew Spiegel was appointed at the provost and vice president. In July 1971, Dean Robert Kegerreis was selected as the vice president and director of administration.

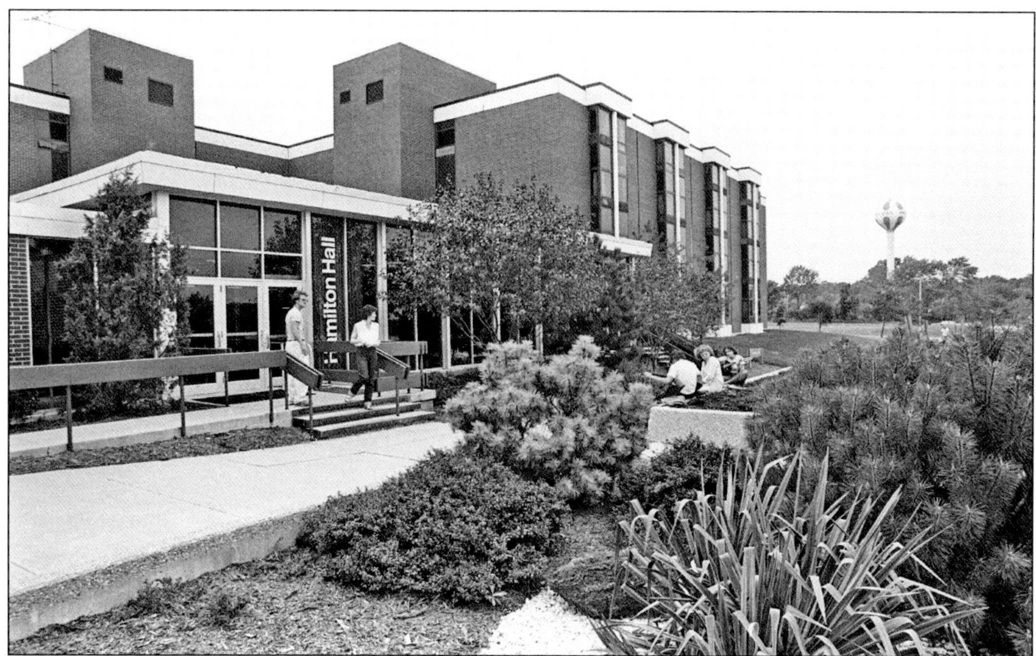

Hamilton Hall. In 1970, the first on-campus housing became available for students. Hamilton Hall, a traditional dormitory-style residence hall, provided housing for over 300 students. The 1980s brought on the first phase of multi-complex housing communities demonstrating the university's focus on attracting residential students. Today, campus housing includes apartments for graduate students, nontraditional students, and students with families.

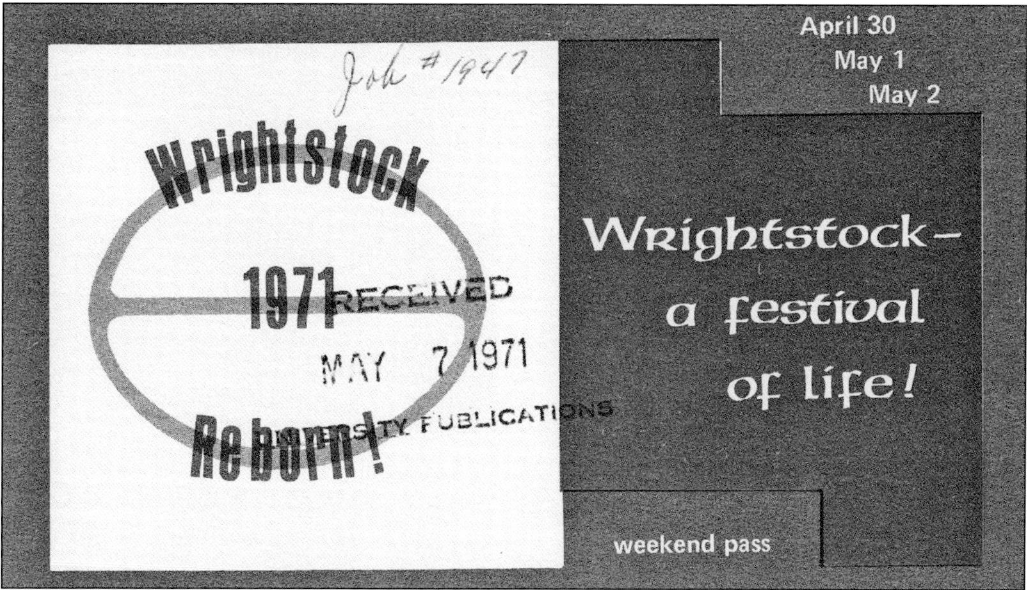

WrightStock Music Festival. Sponsored by the Student Caucus, the WrightStock Music Festival, modeled after the famous Woodstock Music Festival, took place in 1969 on Achilles Hill on the east side of campus. Also referred to as the "festival of life," WrightStock hosted thousands of people from varying distances regardless of there being no big-name entertainers performing.

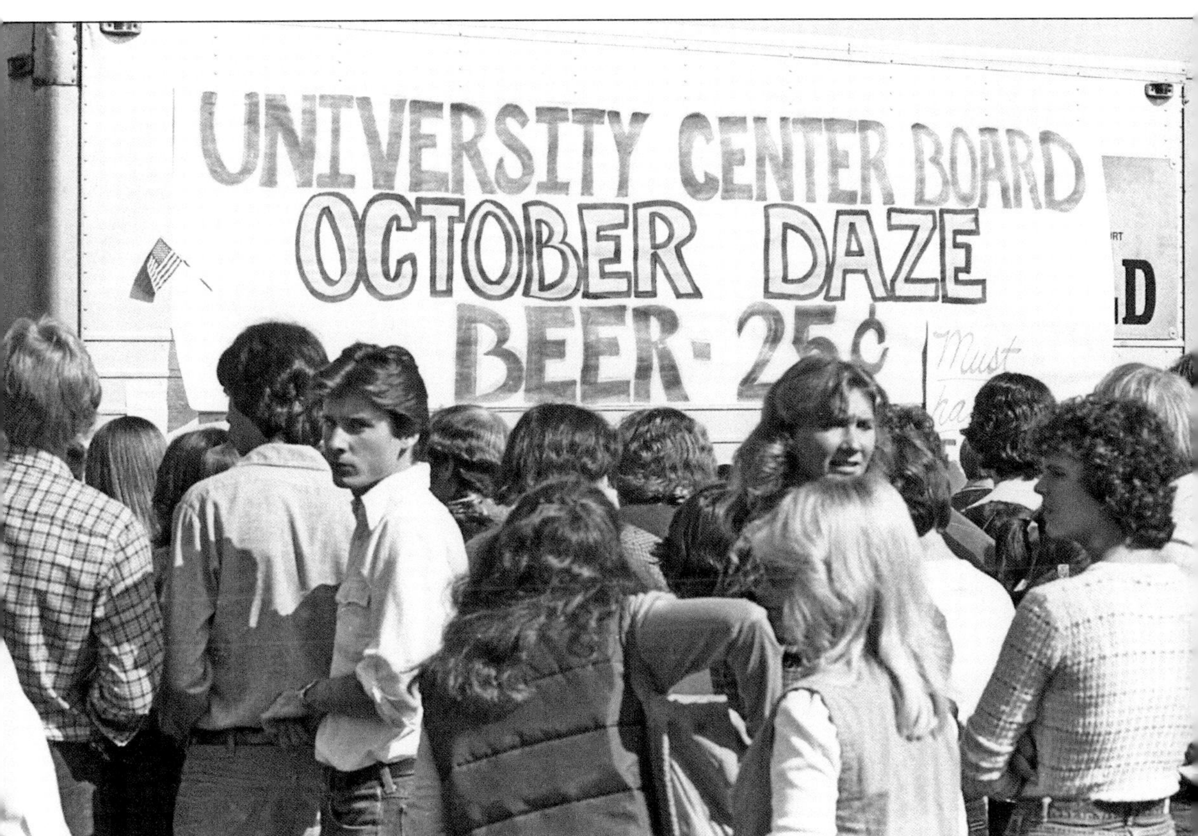

October Daze. October Daze was a three-day festival that included carnival-style rides such as a Ferris wheel; students also enjoyed helicopter rides. There was a battle of the bands as well as nightly film classics. The event changed names over the years. Prior to the fall of 2012, when the university was under the quarter system, students participated in May Daze; now the one-day event is referred to as April Craze.

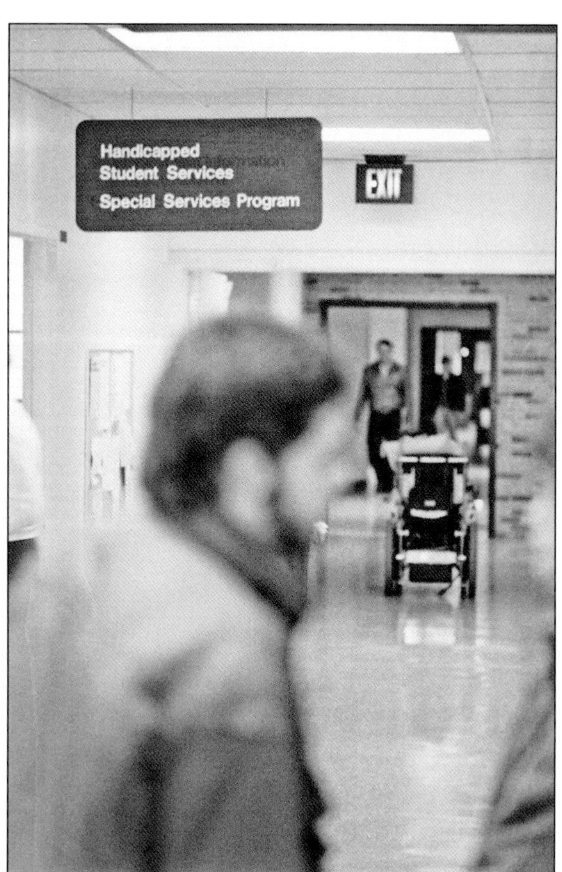

Handicapped Student Services Office. In 1970, twenty years prior to the Americans with Disabilities Act, Wright State University actively engaged in making the campus barrier-free through its architecture and support services for students, faculty, and staff. Wright State University established the Handicapped Student Services Office six years before federal regulations required such actions. Today, Wright State University is 100 percent accessible. The former Handicapped Student Services Office is now the Office of Disability Services.

Bolinga Center. Opening on January 15, 1971, the Bolinga Black Cultural Resource Center is a tribute to Dr. Martin Luther King Jr. The purpose of the Bolinga Black Cultural Center is to address the concerns of black students while offering a space for persons interested in black history. The center has hosted numerous presentations and lectures from professionals around the nation.

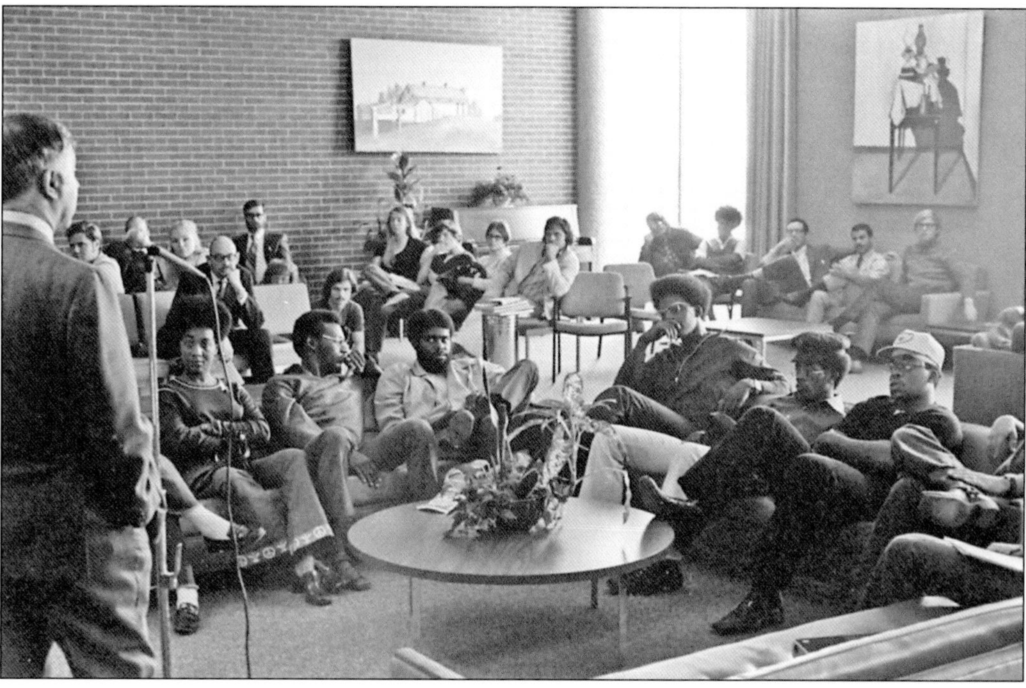

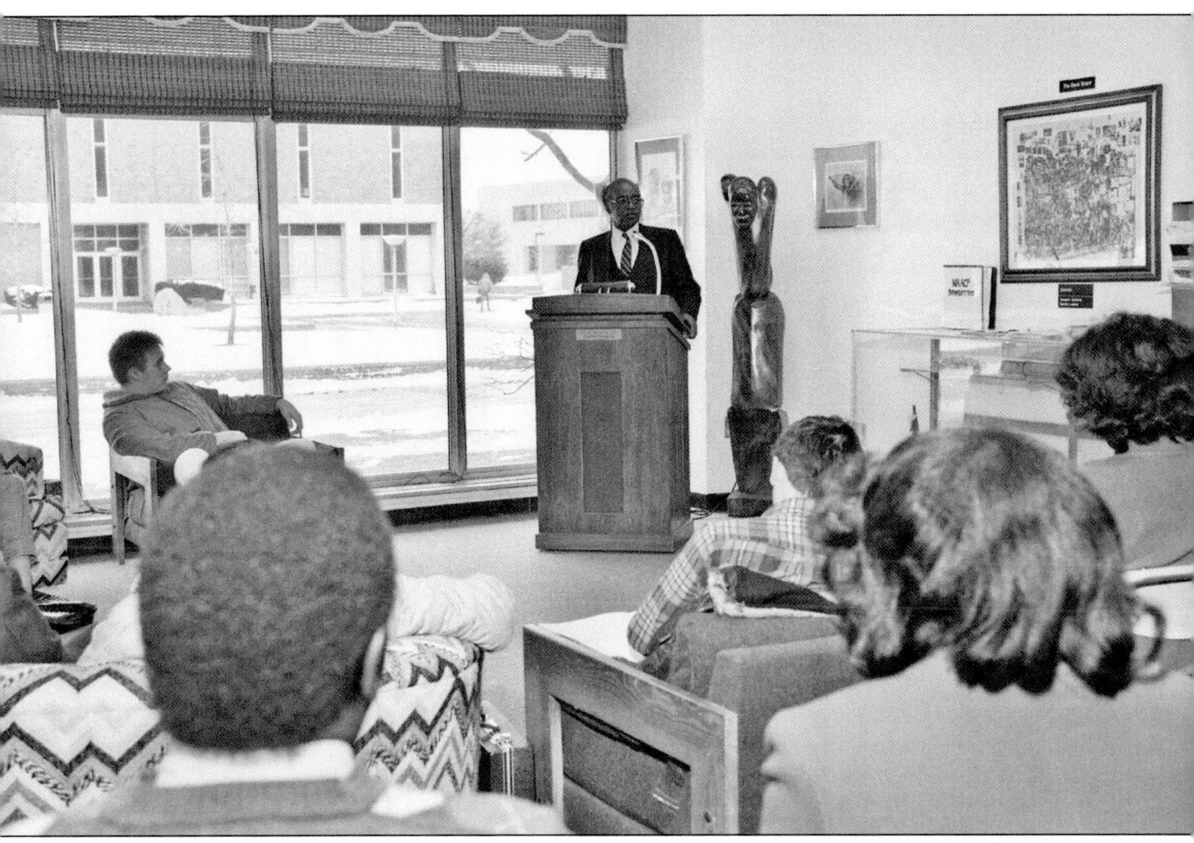

C.J. McLin. The Ohio Democratic Party's Clarence Joseph McLin Jr., also known as C.J. McLin, was an African American politician who ran for state representative in 1966 following Dayton's race riots. After winning the election, he went on to serve 11 consecutive terms. He was instrumental in funding the Paul Laurence Dunbar House and the National Afro-American Museum, located in Wilberforce, Ohio.

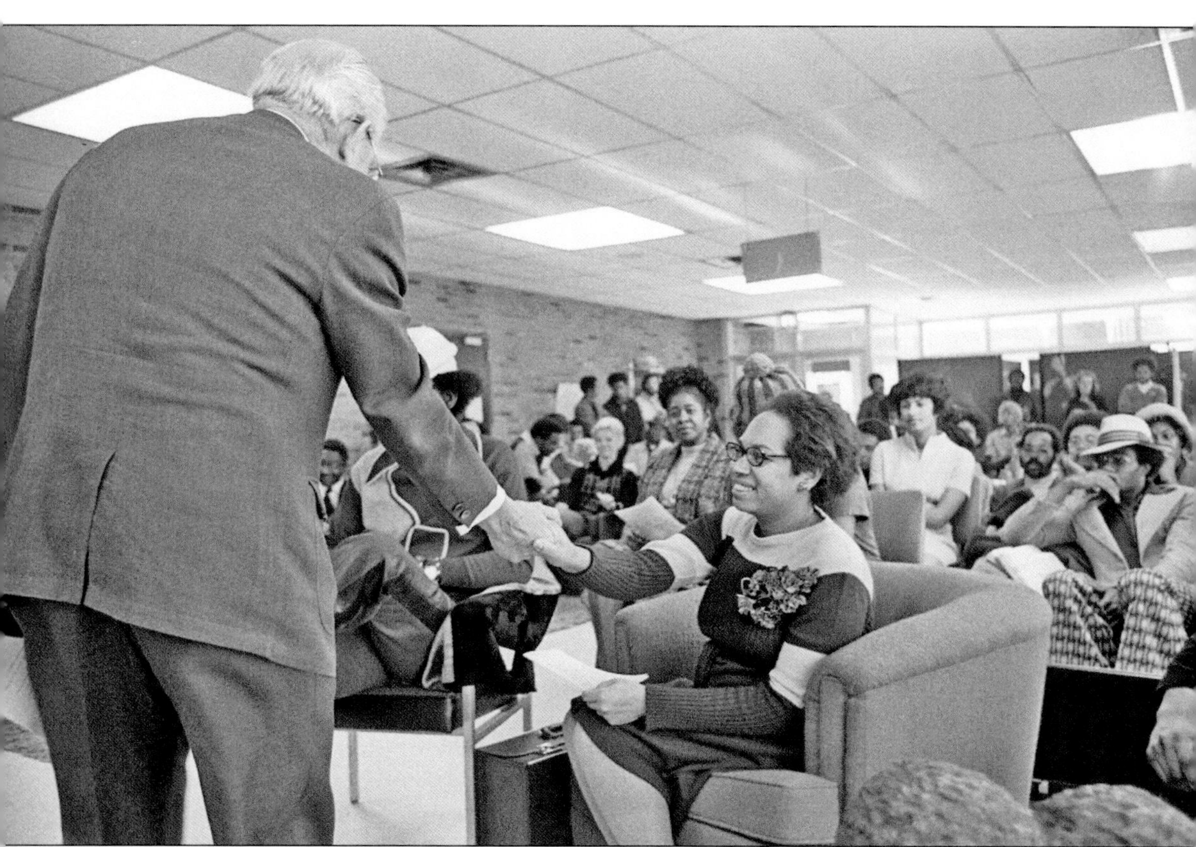

Dr. Yvonne Seon. Dr. Yvonne Seon is the founding director of the Bolinga Black Cultural Resources Center. Dr. Seon is a prolific scholar with great achievements such as being the first African American woman ordained in the Unitarian Universalist Church and the first African American and youngest woman to be appointed to a major US delegation (US Delegation to 14th General Assembly, UNESCO, in Paris, France).

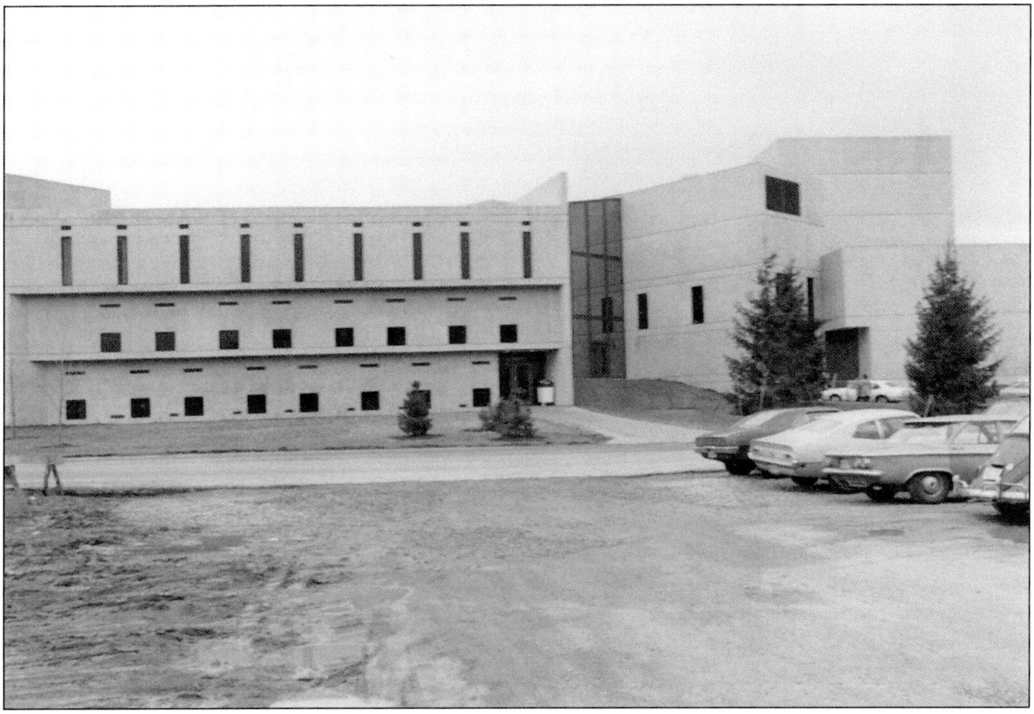

Creative Arts Center. The Creative Arts Center was completed in 1973 with significant expansion in 1990. The center is home to the Theatre, Dance, and Motion Pictures Department and the Art and Art History Department. It also houses the Robert and Elaine Stein Galleries, the Benjamin and Marian Schuster Concert Hall, the Festival Playhouse, and the Herbst Theatre.

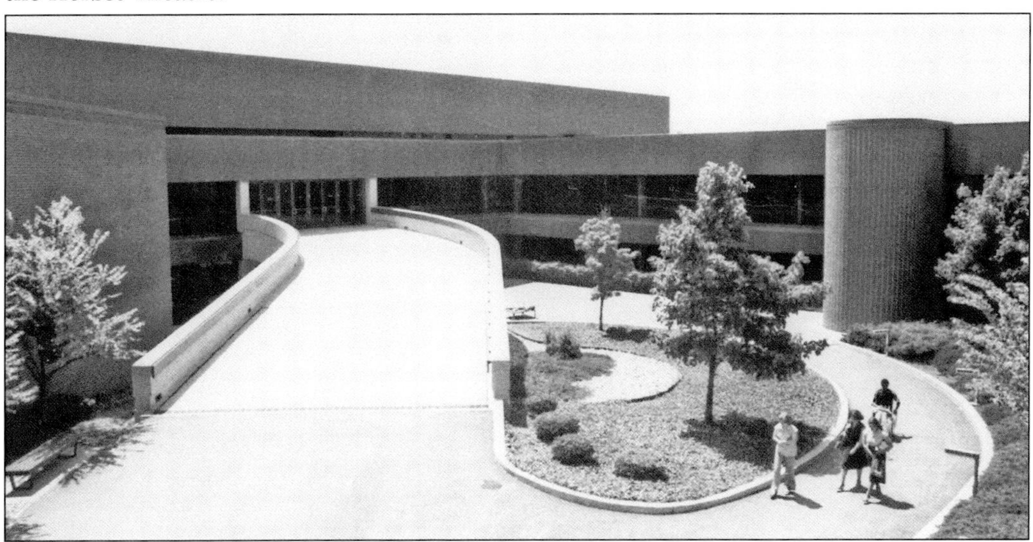

P.E. Building. The James A. Rhodes Physical Education Building was completed in 1973. It was a part of the student complex that also consisted of student housing in Hamilton Hall and the University Center. Robert J. Kegerreis, the university's second president, was inaugurated here in November 1973. In 1994, the physical education building and the University Center were combined to form what is now the Student Union.

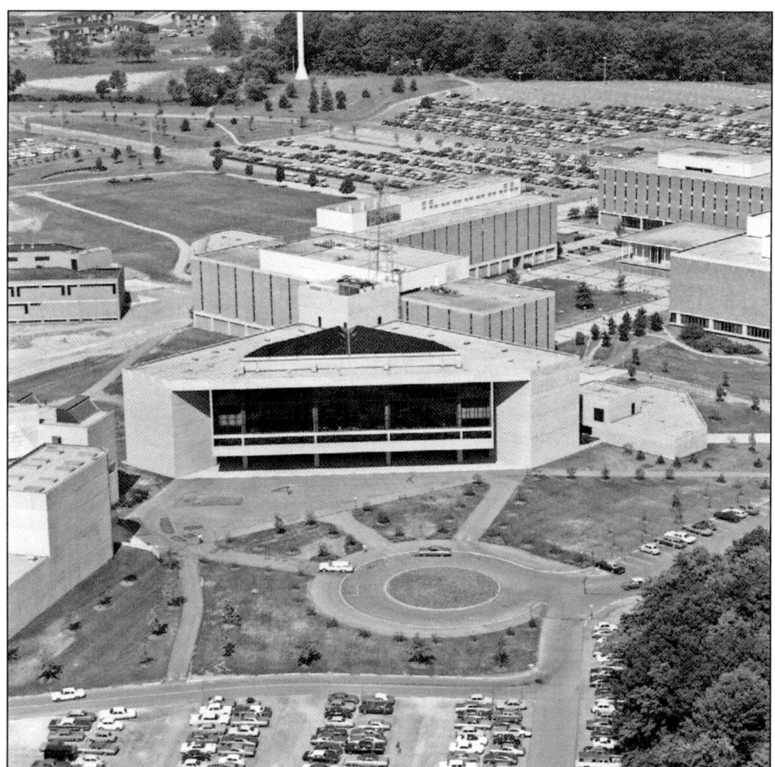

University Library. The university completed its library building in 1974. In the next few years, the University Library merged with the Medicine Library to become the University Libraries. This architectural beauty is different from the traditional brick buildings in that it is a triangular poured-concrete structure. On the inside is a four-floor atrium with skylights over the second-floor reading room.

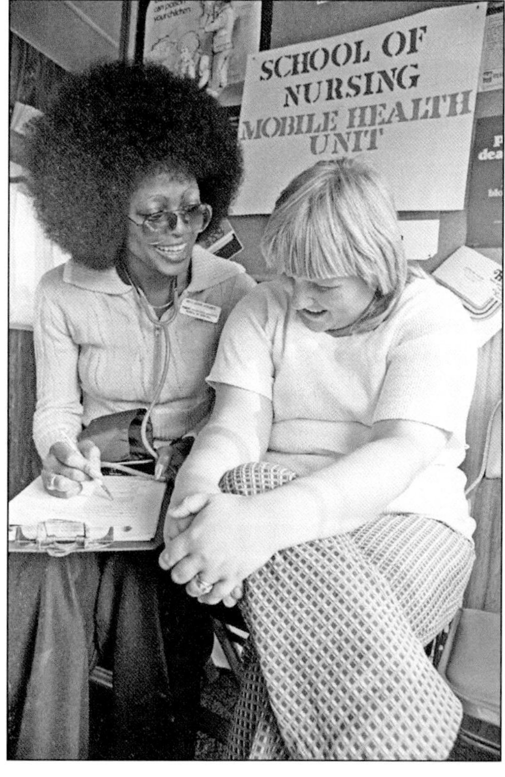

College of Nursing and Health. The Wright State University–Miami Valley College of Nursing and Health, located in University Hall, seeks to be a community leader as it provides its students with innovative education programs that will serve not only the Dayton community but also communities its graduates, faculty, and staff will influence in the present and beyond.

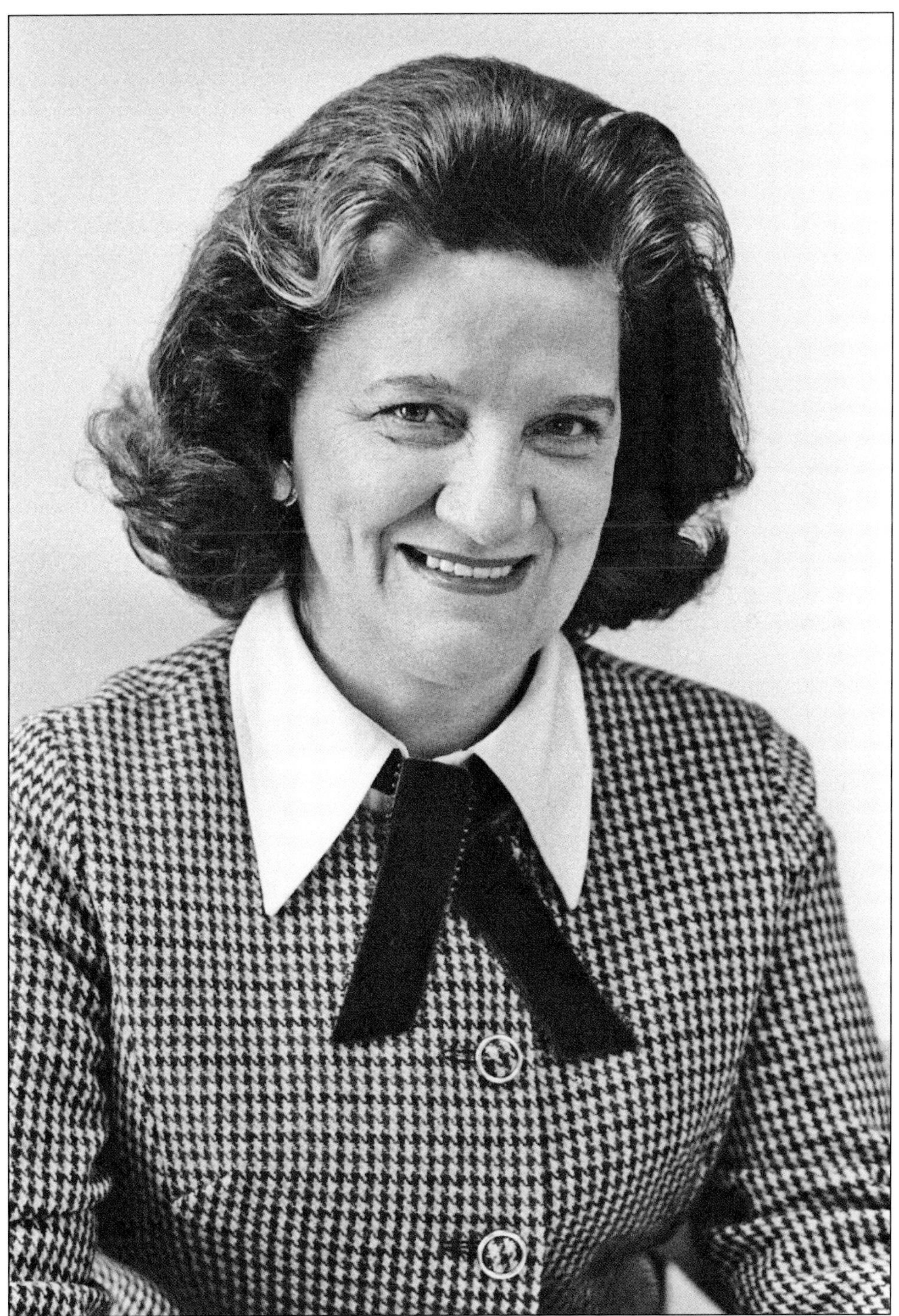

Elenore Koch. Elenore Koch served as a counselor as well as an administrator for student support services before she became the university's first female vice president. As the vice-provost of student affairs, she was in charge of a number of services such as admissions, registrations, and departments like food services and the University Center.

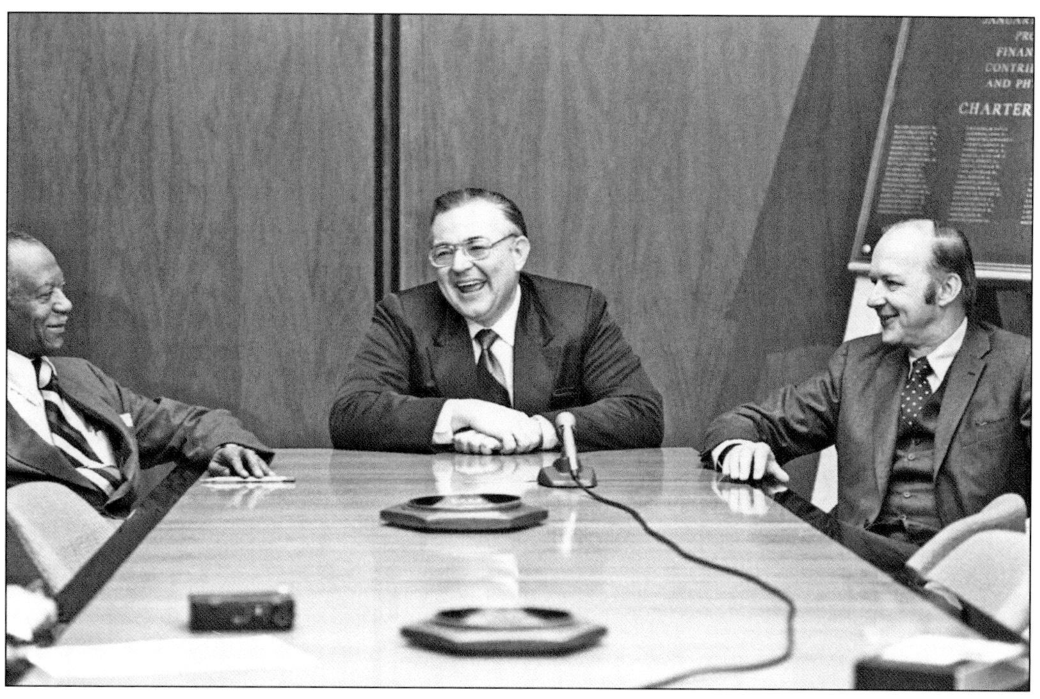

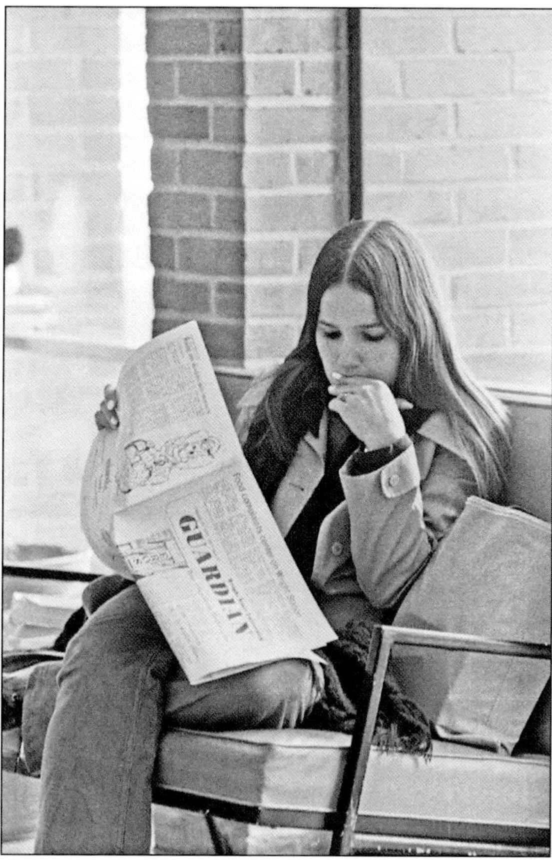

Medical Sciences. The idea to establish a medical school at Wright State University came from area physicians and community leaders who understood that using local hospitals and clinical resources would be cost-effective for medical education. In 1972, Congress passed the Teague-Cranston Act, which provided financial support for five new US medical schools, including Wright State University. In 2005, the name was changed to the Boonshoft School of Medicine to recognize Oscar Boonshoft.

The *Guardian* Newspaper. The official newspaper of the university is the *Guardian.* The mission of the newspaper is to present current, unbiased news for the Wright State University community. Published every Wednesday throughout the school year, the paper can also be found in digital form on its website. Furthermore, the paper's readers can also find videos and podcasts with the latest information about the campus and the Greater Dayton region.

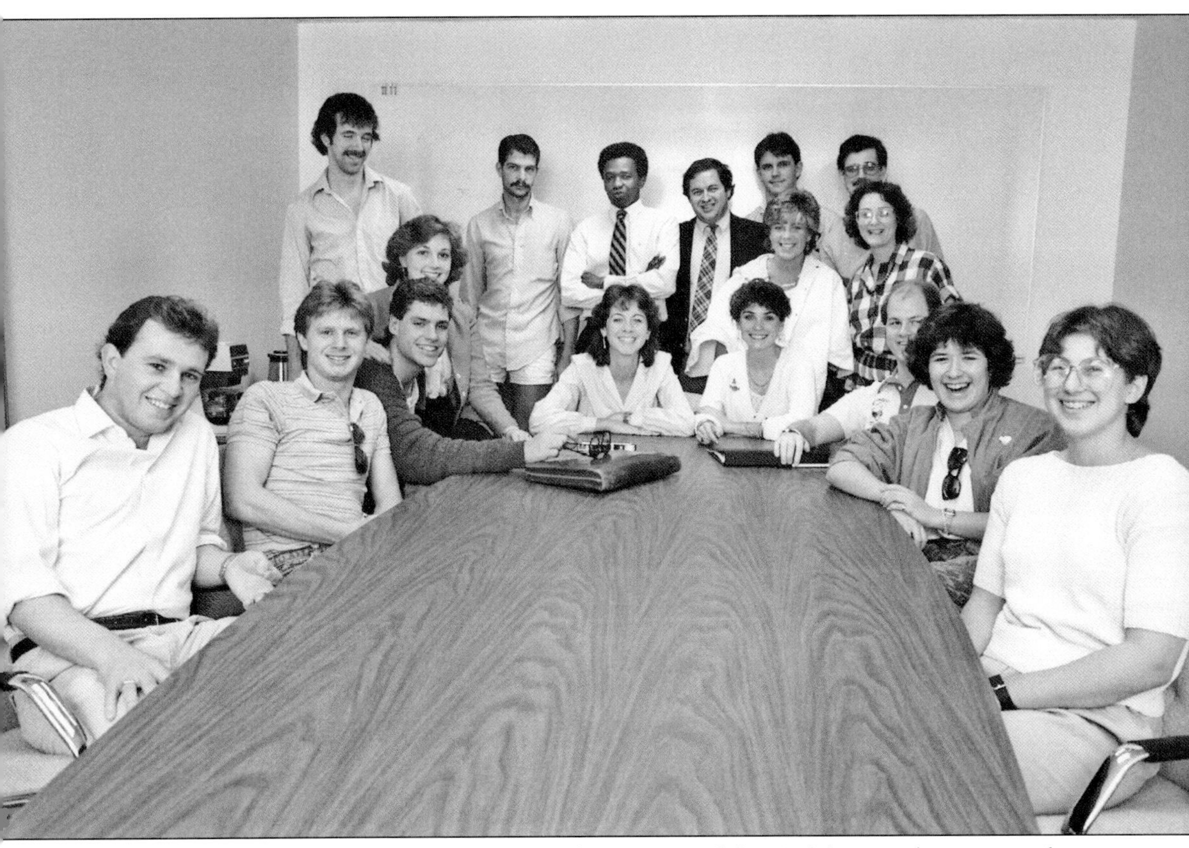

National Model United Nations. The Wright State Model UN delegates have earned top honors at the National Model United Nations Conference for over 30 years. This streak is unmatched by any other university. The Model UN team meets in the fall and spring and prepares by researching and participating in regional practice stimulations. In the spring, the delegation travels to New York City, where it spends a week representing a country on various topics and issues.

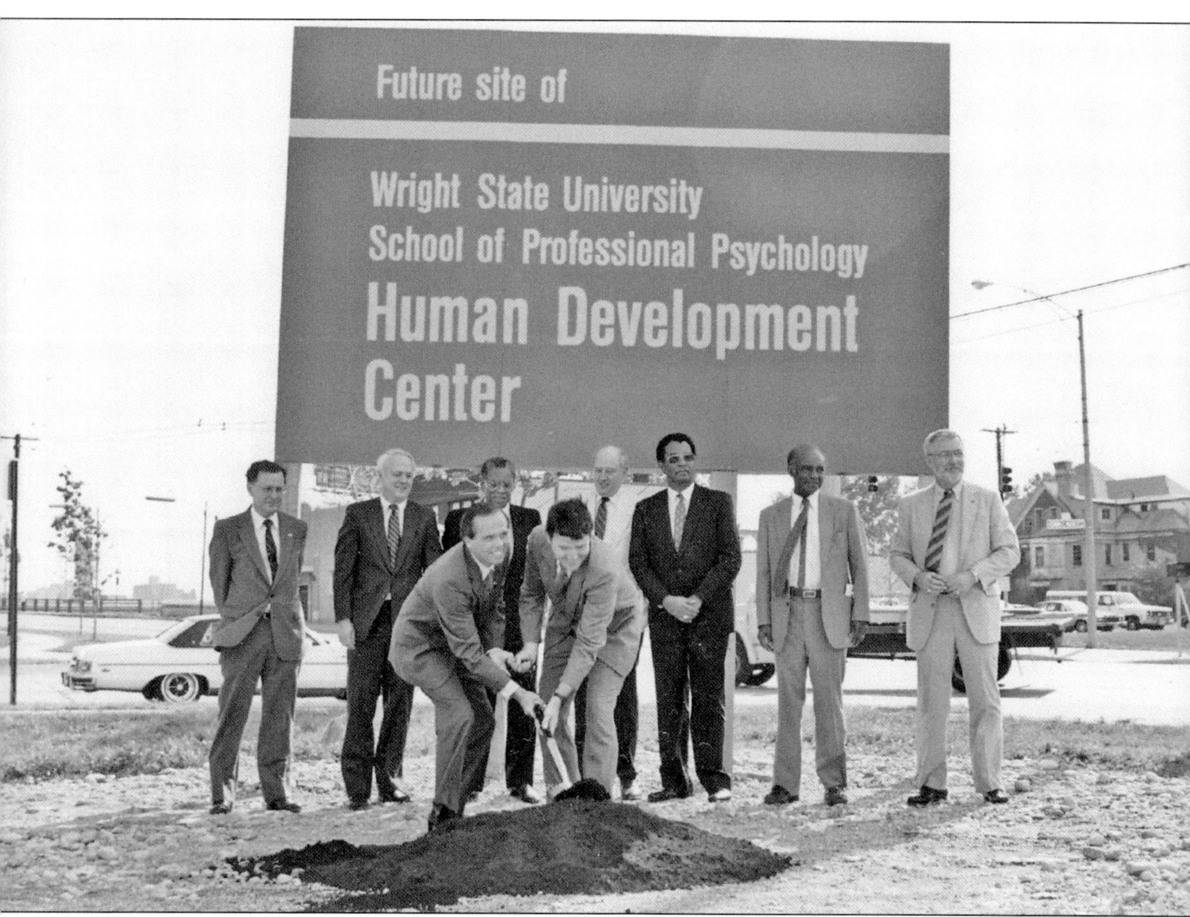

School of Professional Psychology. The School of Professional Psychology functions as a separate school within the larger campus community. It was one of the first doctoral programs in the country to establish a practitioner model program and offer a doctorate in psychology. The school takes pride in its multifarious faculty and students who seek to promote diversity and cultural sensitivity.

Three

Rapid Growth and Expansion

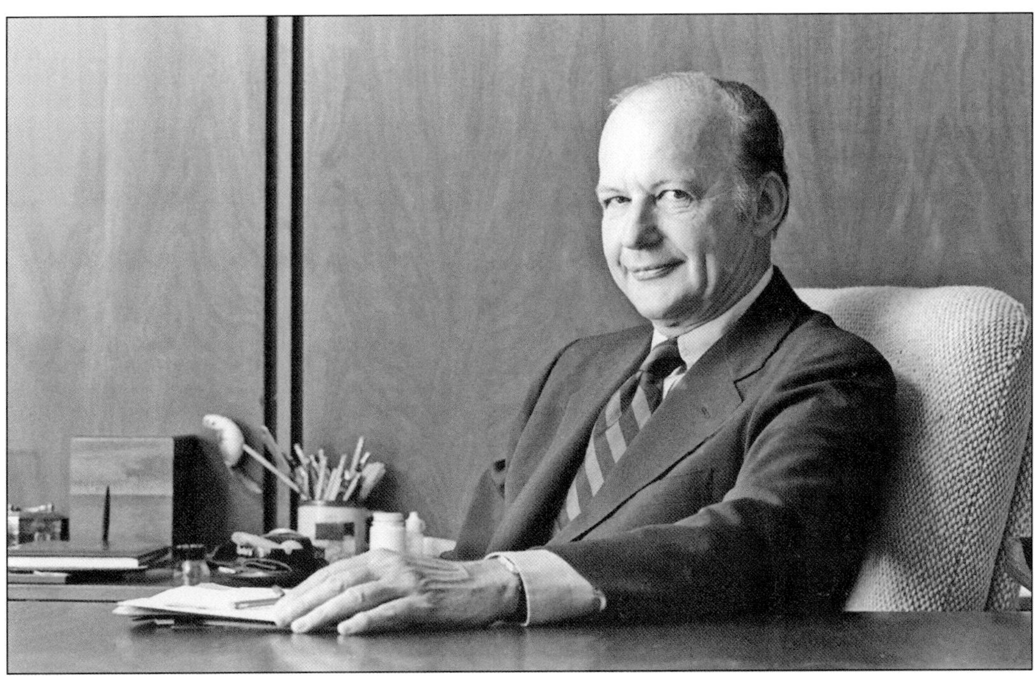

Pres. Robert Kegerreis. Named the university's second president in 1973, Robert Kegerreis had been with the school as a faculty member since 1969. His administration is credited with raising the school from adolescence to adulthood as its infrastructure and curriculum grew. It was under his administration that the Schools of Medicine, Nursing, and Professional Psychology and the Biomedical Sciences program were created in addition to eight new structures being built.

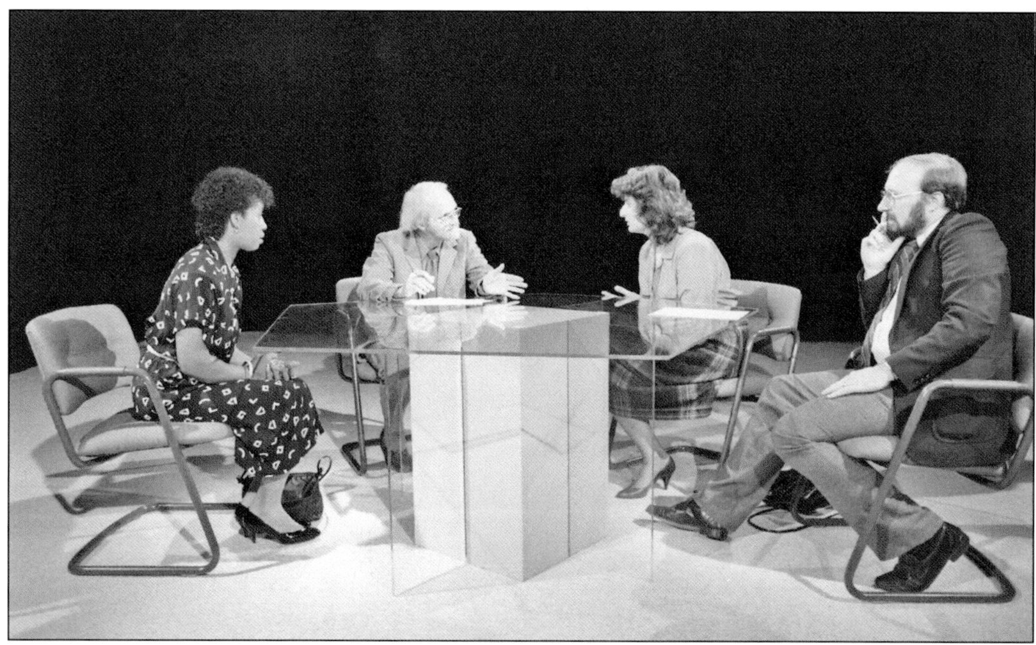

TELEVISION CENTER. Opening in 1973, the Television Center originally offered location and studio recording as well as closed-circuit television. Today, the Computing and Telecommunications Services (CaTS) calls the Television Center home. It now offers service and support for university video productions, digital video streaming, campus satellite, and cable television systems, as well as the university's Educational Access Channel 21.

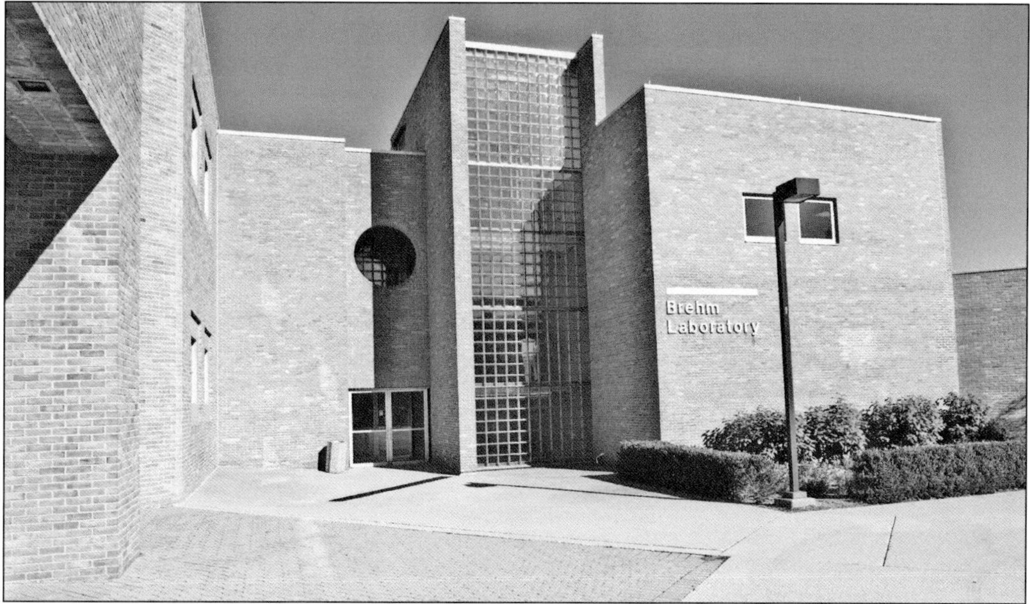

BREHM LAB. The Brehm Laboratory building was completed in 1973 as an addition to Oelman Hall. The Department of Chemistry is situated here. The building also contains chemistry labs, research facilities for the Department of Earth and Environmental Sciences, student lounges, and a unique teaching facility for the science teacher program. The Department of Chemistry offers degree-granting programs at the undergraduate and master's levels.

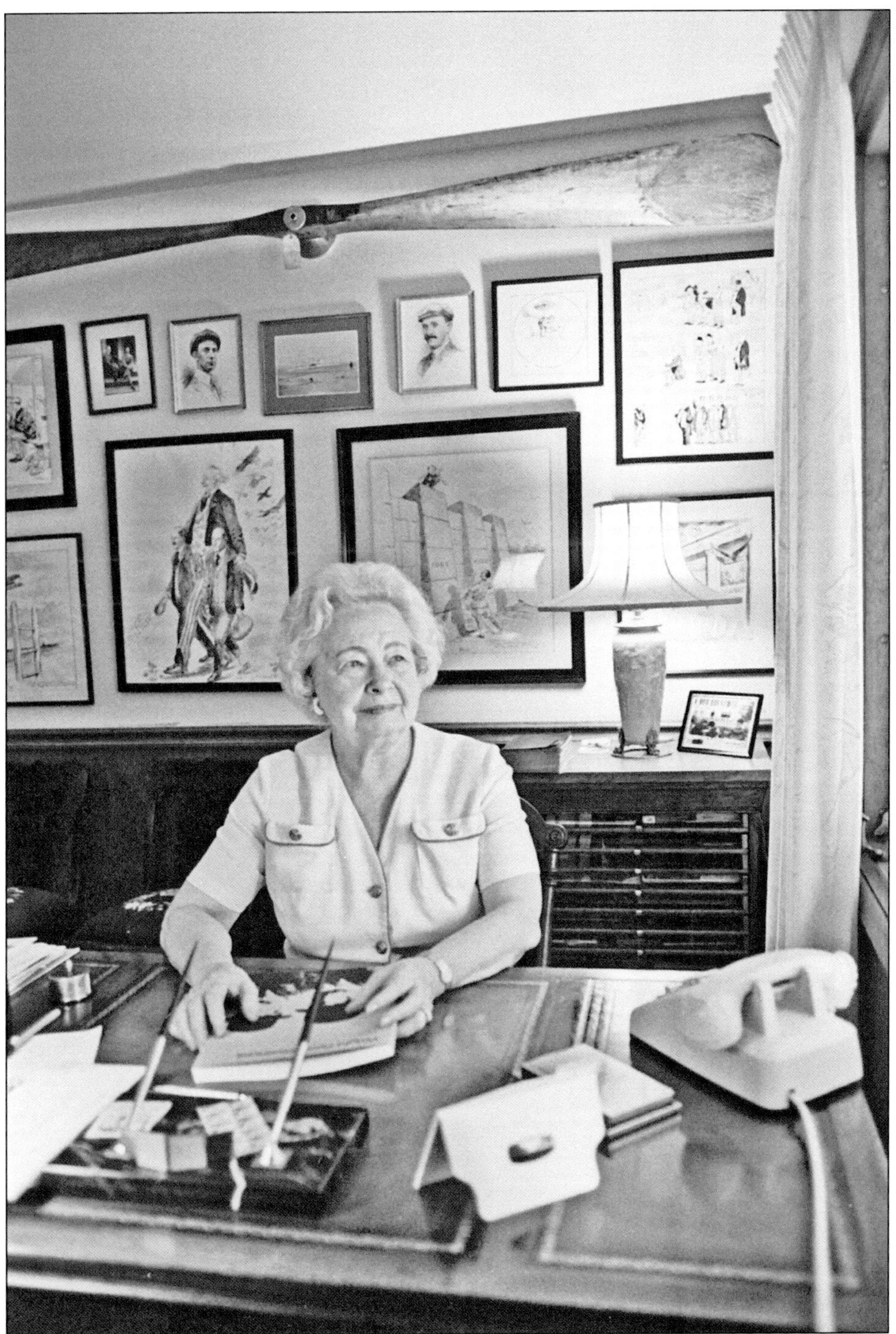

Ivonette Wright Miller. In 1973, the niece of Orville and Wilbur Wright donated the brothers' rare collection of documents including photographs, books, papers, and other materials to the university's library. Now housed in the Special Collections and Archives in the University Libraries, the collection documents the brothers' pioneering work in aviation.

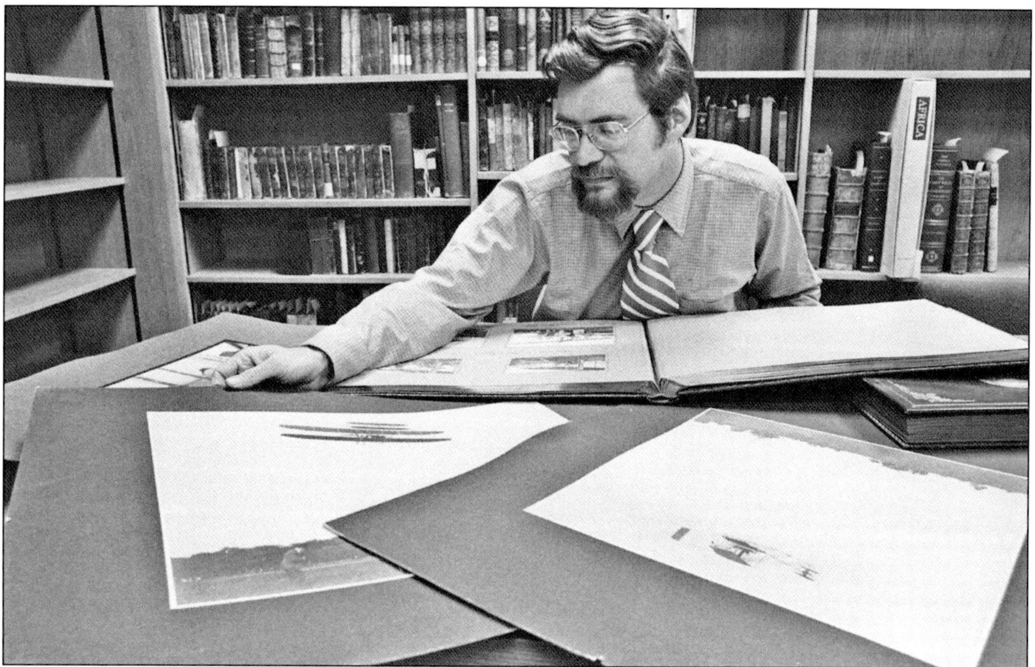

ARCHIVAL ADMINISTRATION AND HISTORICAL ADMINISTRATION. In 1975, the school established a graduate program in archival administration and historical administration—the first of its kind in Ohio as well as one of only a few in the country. The training students receive prepares them for various career fields, such as museum, archival, library, and a plethora of other career opportunities. As of today, the program is the master's in Public History Graduate Program.

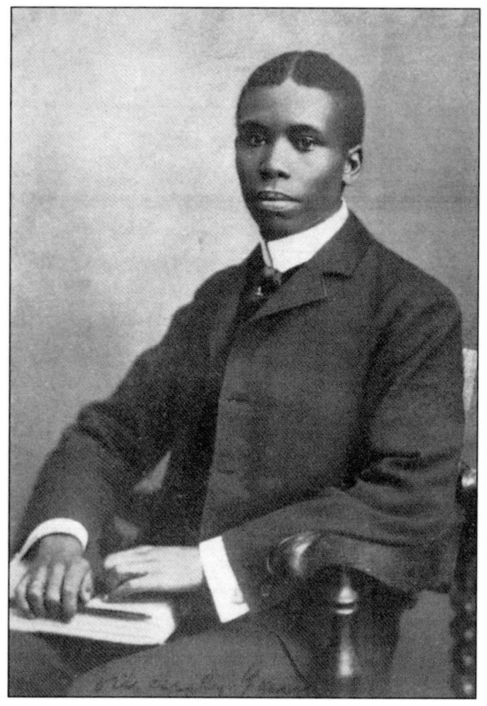

PAUL LAURENCE DUNBAR COLLECTION. In 1975, the University Library acquired another rare collection. The materials of Dayton native Paul Laurence Dunbar were donated to the library by William Shepherd, an engineer in Dayton. The collection included a nearly complete set of autographed first editions of Dunbar's works. Shepherd promised that he would purchase the remaining two volumes for the University Library.

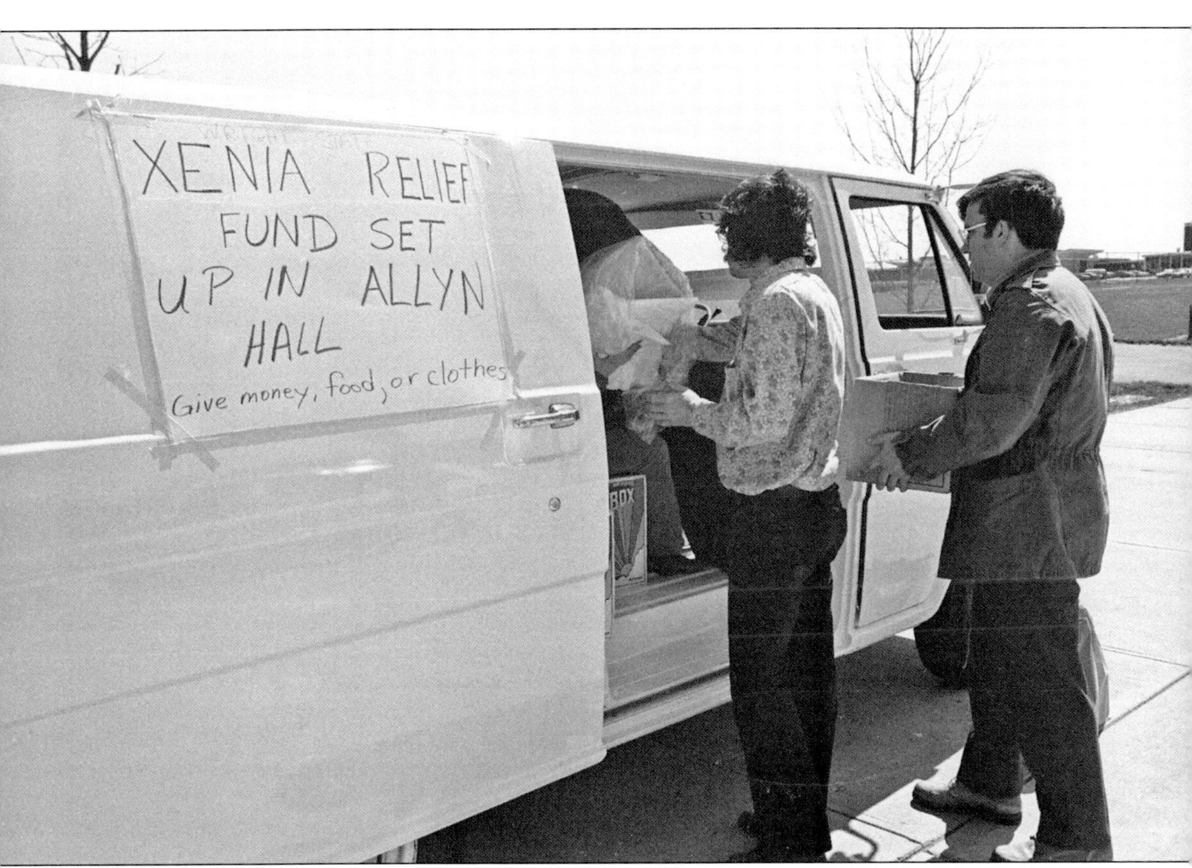

Xenia Tornado Relief. After an F5 tornado tore through Xenia, Ohio, on April 3, 1974, killing 33 people, injuring 1,300, and causing damage to 1,400 building, students at the university organized a drive, raising funds and collecting food, clothing, blankets for those in need. These efforts resulted in more than $3,000 being raised and 69 vanloads of goods collected.

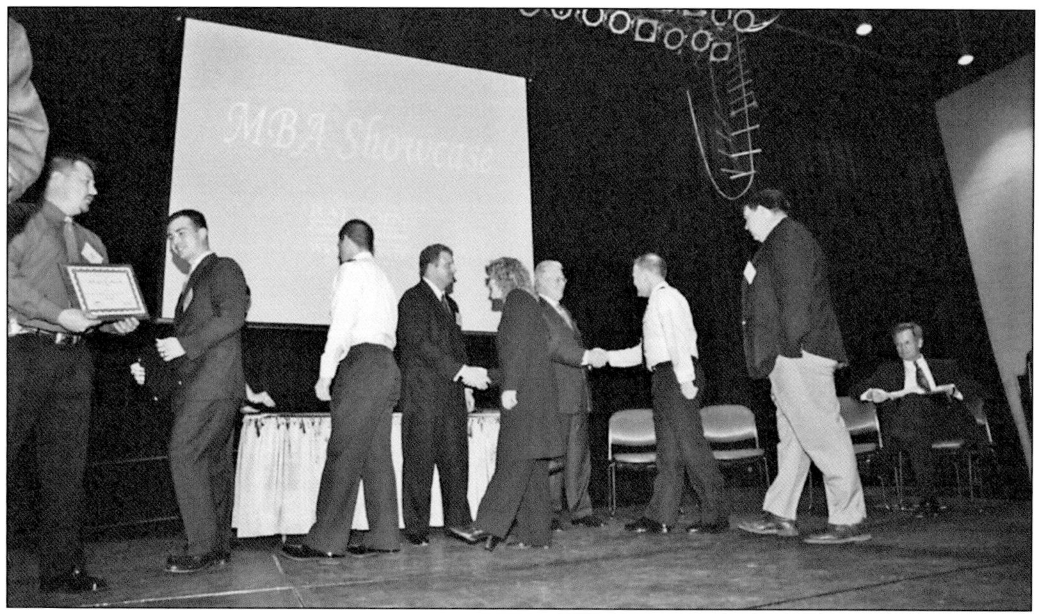

MBA Program. In 1974, Wright State's master's of business administration program became the first in the Dayton region to be accredited by the Association to Advance Collegiate Schools of Business (AACSB International). Only 28 percent of the 1,400 business programs in the United States have met this rigorous standard.

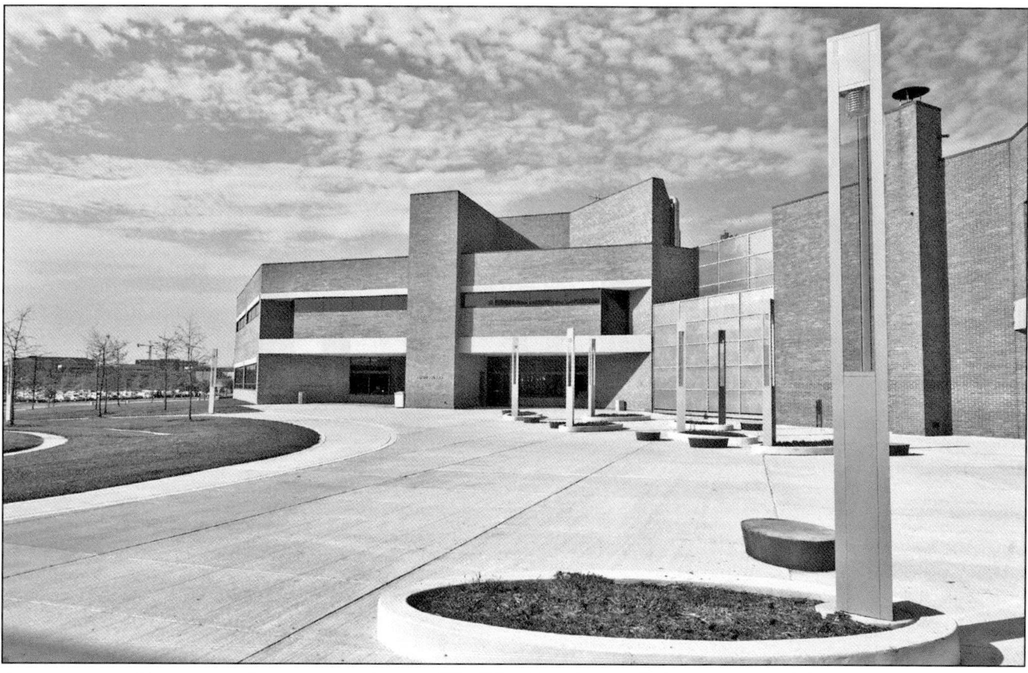

Biological Sciences Buildings I and II. The Biological Science Buildings I and II were constructed in 1975, undergoing renovations in 2009. The Biological Science Building I holds the Departments of Biological Sciences, Biomedical Sciences, and Clinical Laboratory Science. The Biological Science Building II is home to the Department of Neuroscience, Cell Biology, and Physiology as well as offices and laboratories.

CONTROVERSY ON CAMPUS. In 1976, students requested that the controversial film *Deep Throat* be shown on campus. In 1977, university established a landmark policy that dealt with obscene materials. That same year, Bob Woodward spoke at the university about the Watergate scandal and the film *All the President's Men*. In 2005, Roger Wilkins, who wrote editorials for the *Washington Post* during the Watergate scandal, spoke at the university. Woodward and Wilkins won Pulitzer Prizes alongside one another.

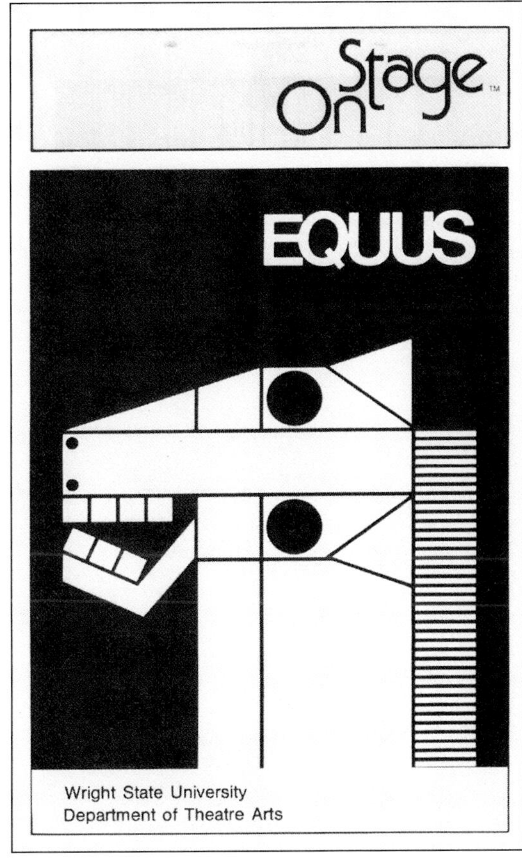

FELS INSTITUTE. The university collaborated with the Samuel S. Fels Institute of Philadelphia during the summer of 1977 to create the Fels Institute located in Yellow Springs, Ohio, which is a study of human growth and development. Today, the Fels Institute concentrates on a number of things like risk factors for heart disease and obesity, body composition, growth, bone maturation, and aging.

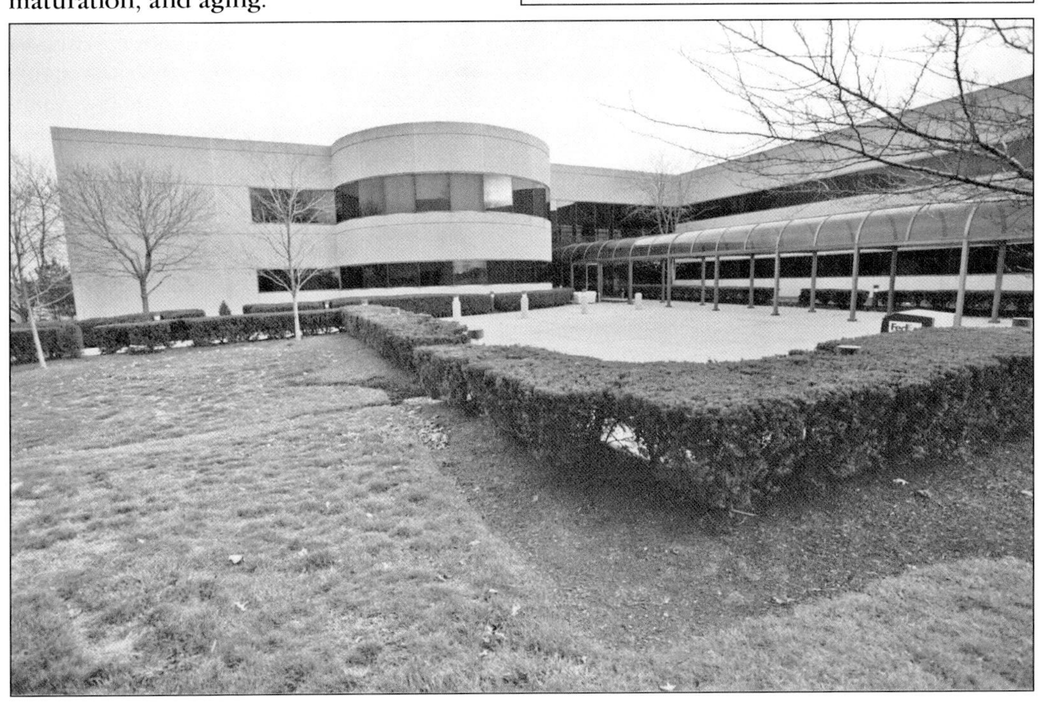

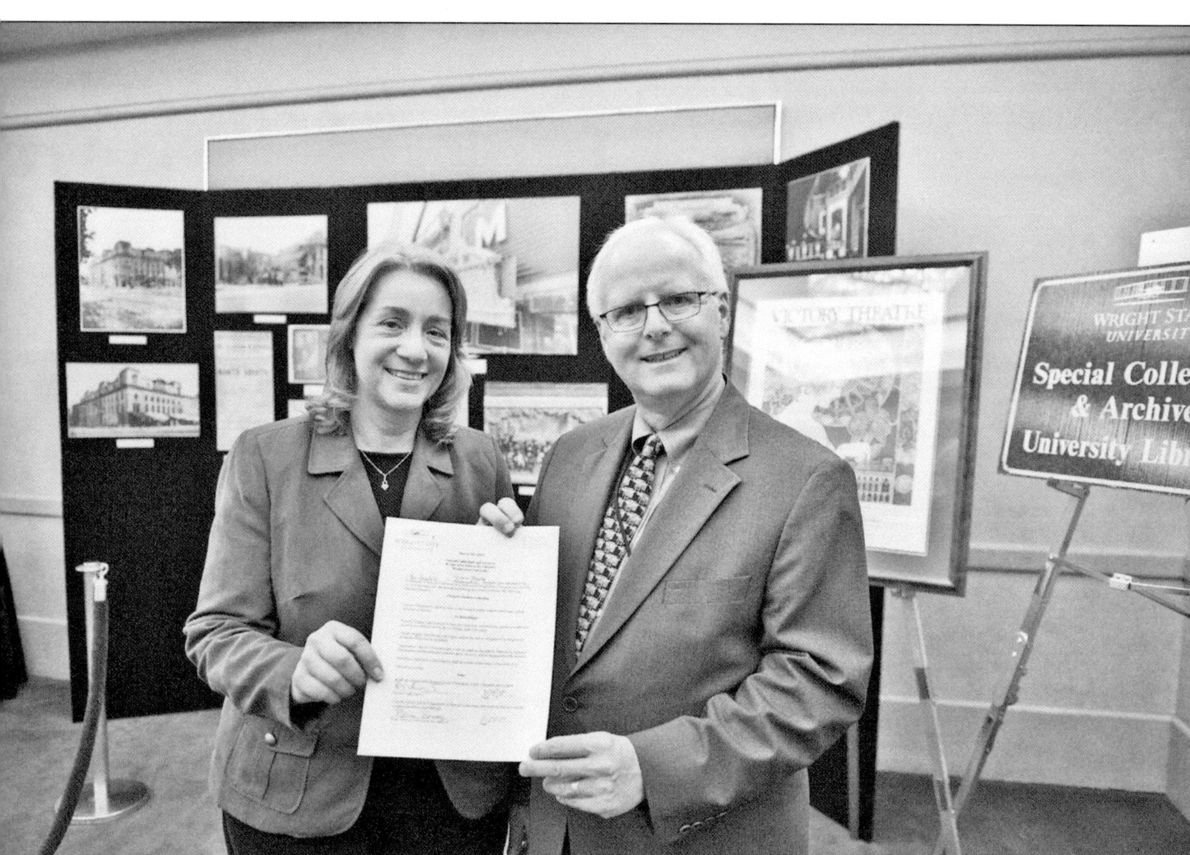

SPECIAL COLLECTIONS AND ARCHIVES. The Special Collections and Archives is home to the most complete Wright brothers collections in the world, the Paul Laurence Dunbar materials, the *Dayton Daily News* archives, and hundreds of others collections that document the history of aviation, people, events, and the landscape of Dayton as well as the Miami Valley. The Special Collections and Archives is a resource for Wright State's Public History Graduate Program.

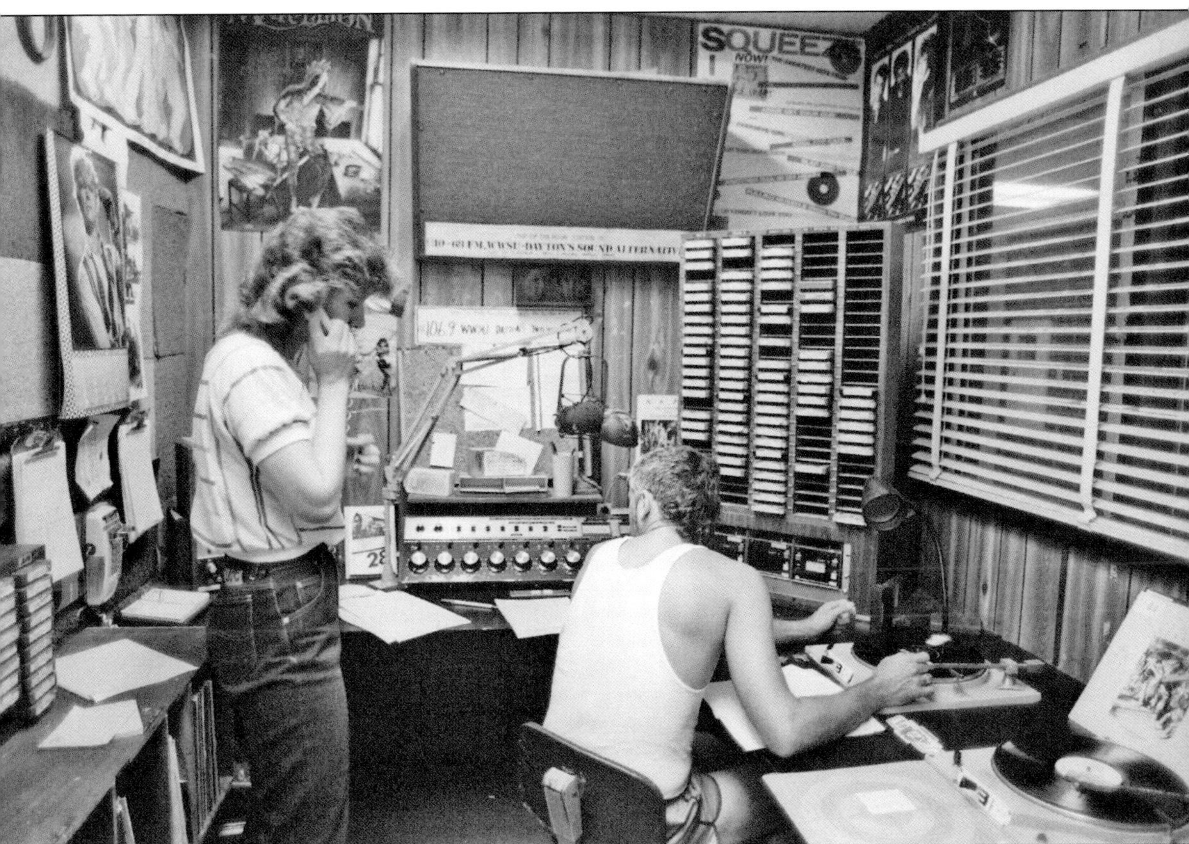

WWSU 106.9 FM. On April 4, 1977, the university launched its own radio station. The programming aired every day from 7:00 in the morning until midnight. When it first went on air, the station's schedule included public service programs and musical genres like folk, jazz, rock, and classical music. The station continues to be staffed by student volunteers.

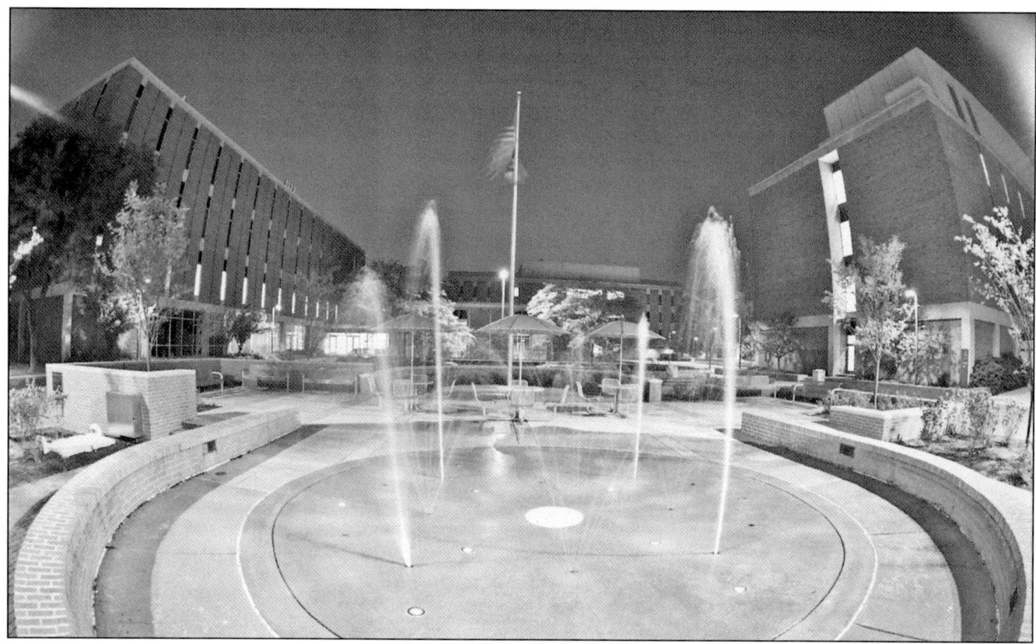

Trustees' Plaza. At the northwest corner of the Founders' Quadrangle is the Trustees' Plaza. The dedication ceremony took place on April 22, 1977, with Henry Ford II, chair of the Ford Motor Company and longtime friend of Robert S. Oelman, delivering the keynote address. The plaza remains a popular site for outdoor ceremonies and student gatherings between classes.

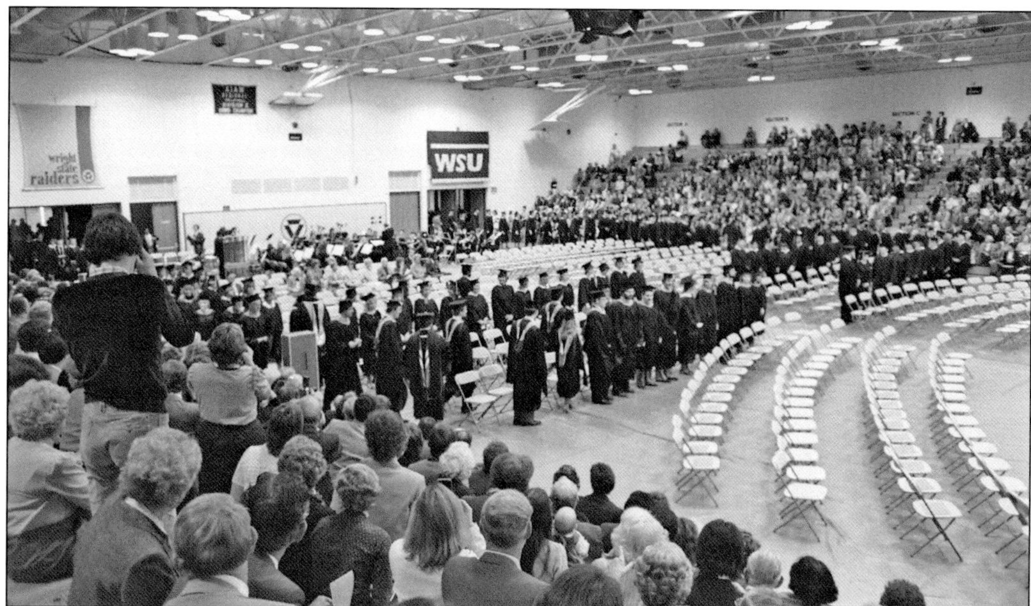

Commencement, June 11, 1977. The commencement ceremony on June 11, 1977, remains a special memory for the community since the number of graduating students had reached historic levels, causing the ceremony to be held at the University of Dayton's athletic arena. Among the 1,823 graduating students, a majority of the degrees went to those in the graduate school.

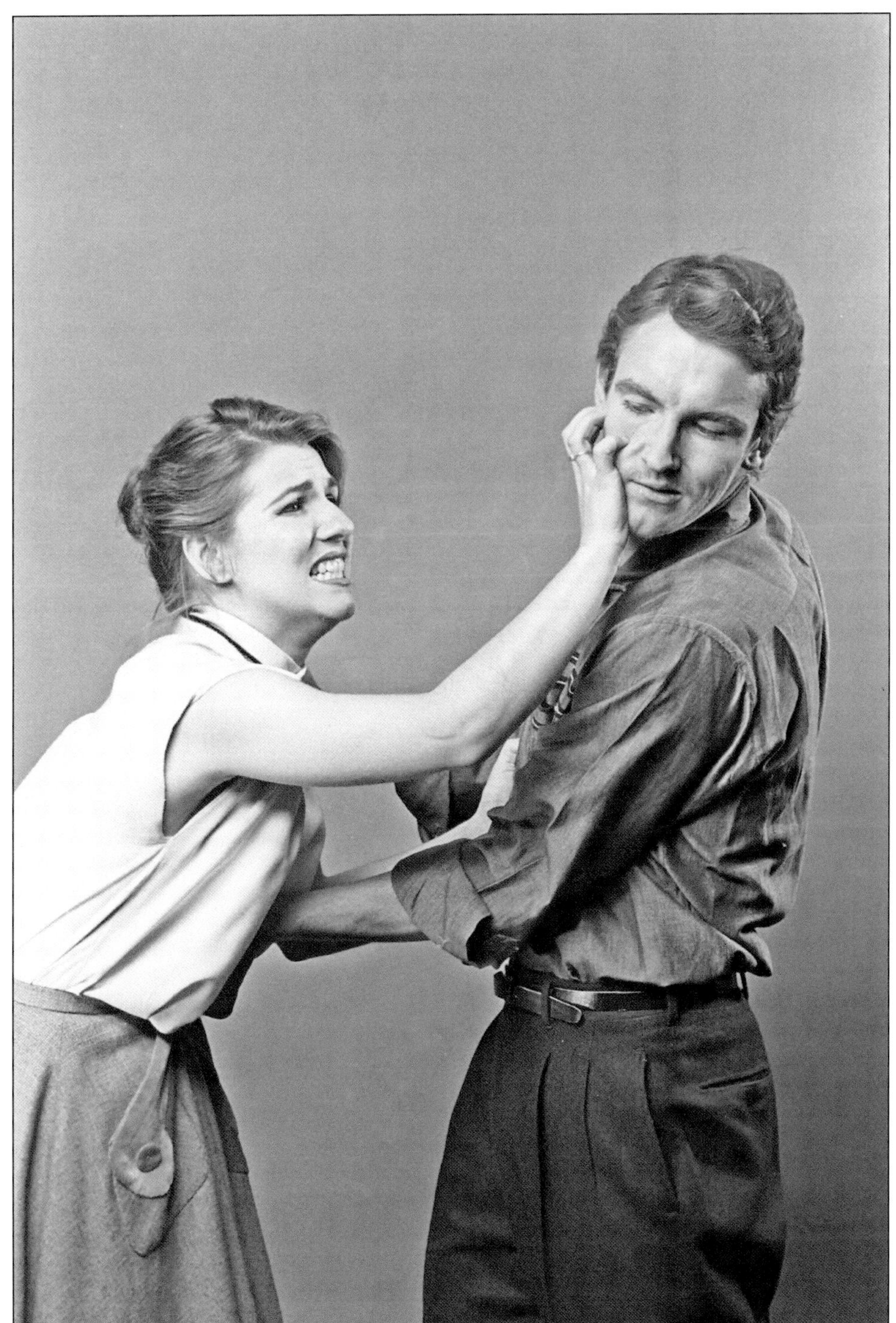

***Look Back in Anger* Production.** Wright State University was one of 10 colleges to perform in the American College Theatre Festival in the spring of 1979 in Washington, DC, and its production of *Look Back in Anger* was selected for a production at the Kennedy Center for Performing Arts. Directed by Robert Britton, the play was performed on April 16 and 17.

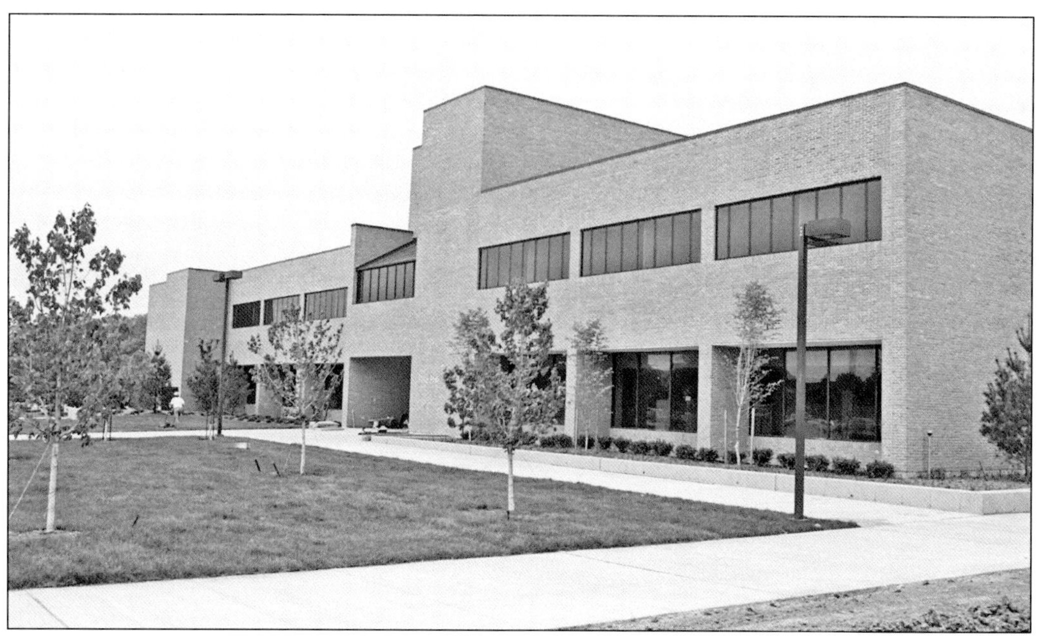

Rike Hall. Rike Hall was named after Dayton-area business and civic leader David L. Rike, retired chairman of Rike's Department Store. He also served on the Wright State Board of Trustees from 1969 to 1973. Rike Hall was completed in 1981. It is home to the Raj Soin College of Business. The building underwent renovations in 2007 including 22 additional classrooms with updated technologies and the nationally recognized Soin Trading Center.

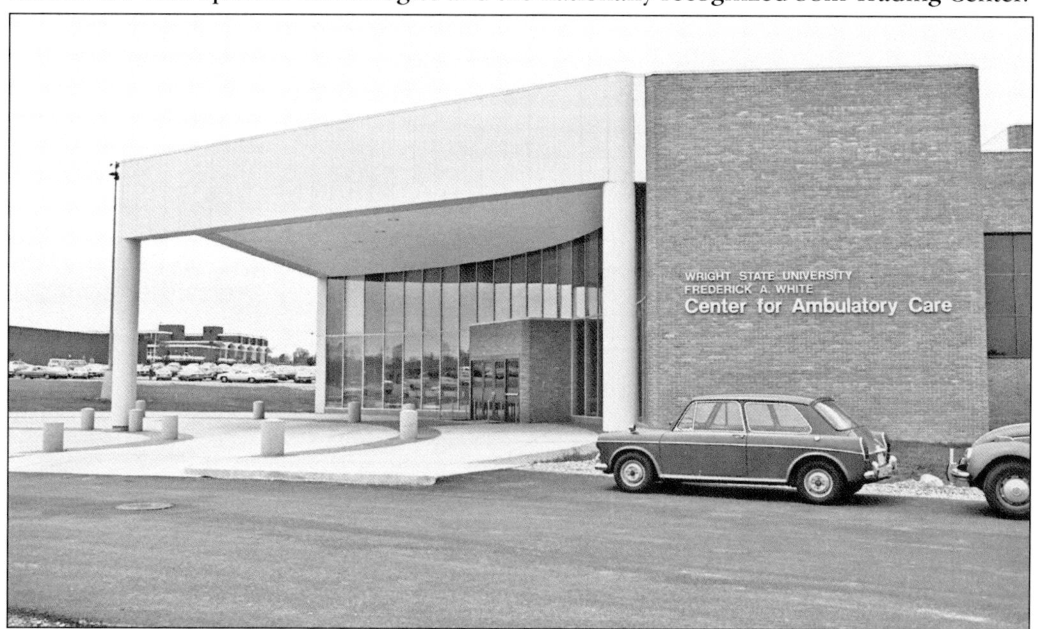

Frederick White Center. The Frederick A. White Center for Ambulatory Care was dedicated in September 1981. The center provided medical students and faculty with a facility where they could engage in office practice. In 2008, the building was renovated, rededicated, and renamed. Known as White Hall, it is the hub of the Boonshoft School of Medicine and includes a state-of-the-art medical center, a 150-seat auditorium, and an anatomy learning center.

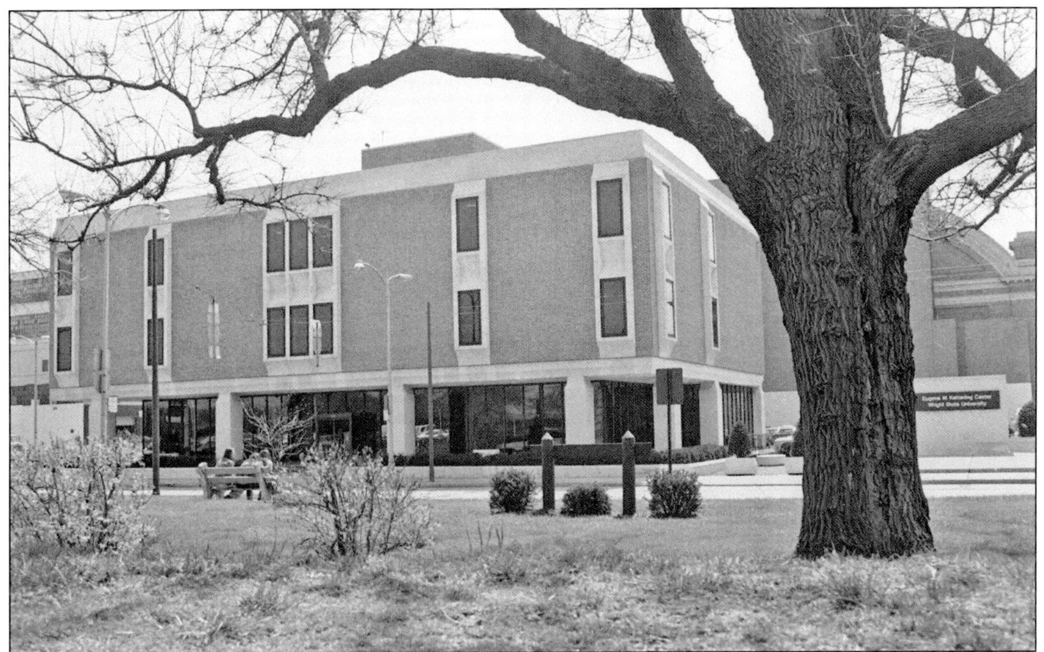

Kettering Center. The Kettering Center, once housed in the College of Continuing and Community Education in downtown Dayton, was a nonprofit foundation for engineering students. Sometime later, the Kettering Center was leased to Wright State University, which later purchased it as a permanent continuing education center. The Kettering Center closed its doors in 2009.

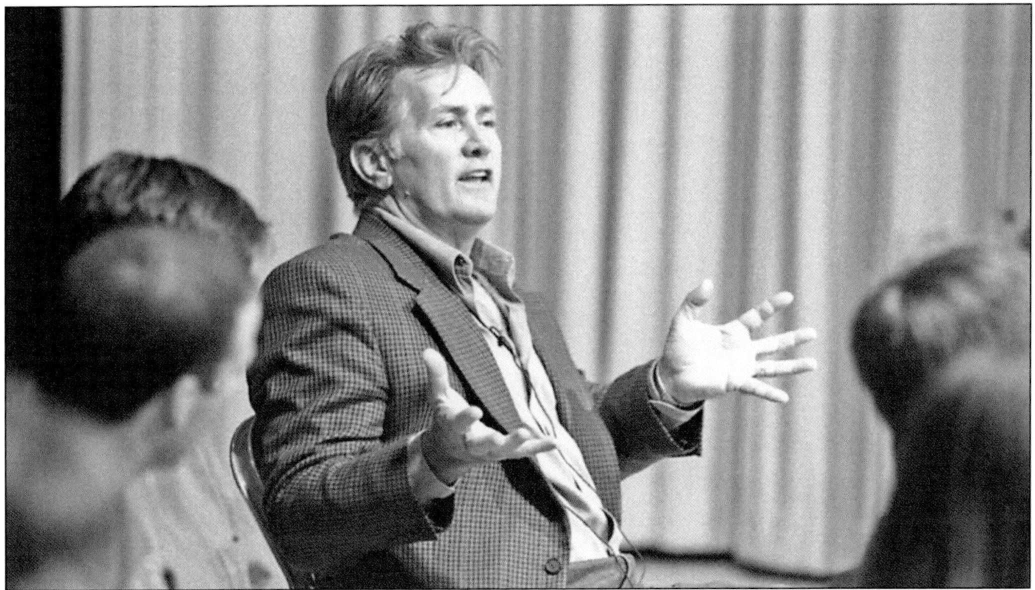

Artist Series. Wright State has always been a major supporter of the arts. The 1979–1980 Artist Series featured prominent artists such as opera soprano Beverly Sills, concert pianist Bela Szilagyi, jazz trombonist Phil Watson, and actor Martin Sheen (pictured). Since then, the Artist Series has become tradition. The event continues to draw renowned artists from around the world.

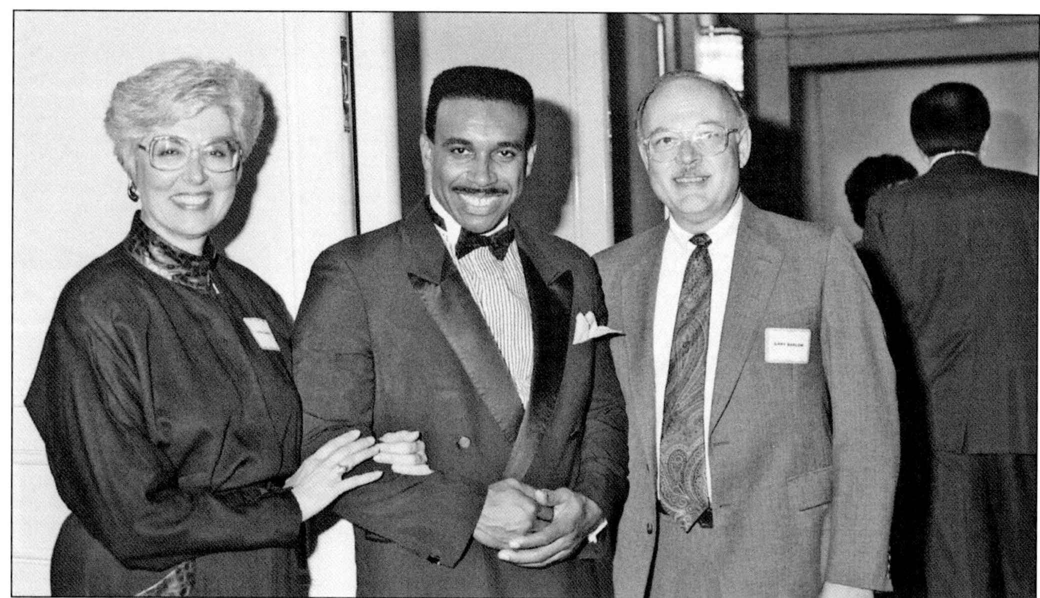

Commitment to Public Service. Wright State University has always made commitments to public service through promotions or cosponsoring of artistic talent in the region. The historic 19th-century Victory Theatre, now called the Victoria Theatre, hosts such performances in its restored building. The theater has booked renowned talent like the Alvin Ailey American Dance Theatre and the James Tatum Jazz Trio.

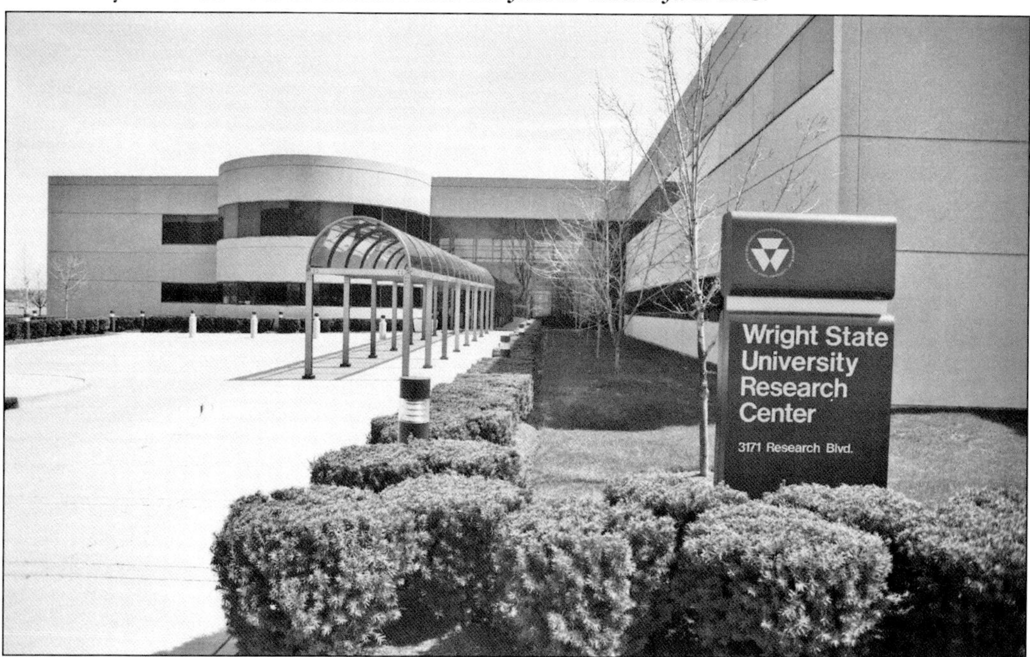

Miami Valley Research Park. The Miami Valley Research Park was created as a response to the decline in the manufacturing industry during the 1970s. Regional institutions such as Wright State University, the University of Dayton, Sinclair Community College, and Central State University collaborated to establish this facility, which is now a 1,250-acre campus home to employers in the field of technology.

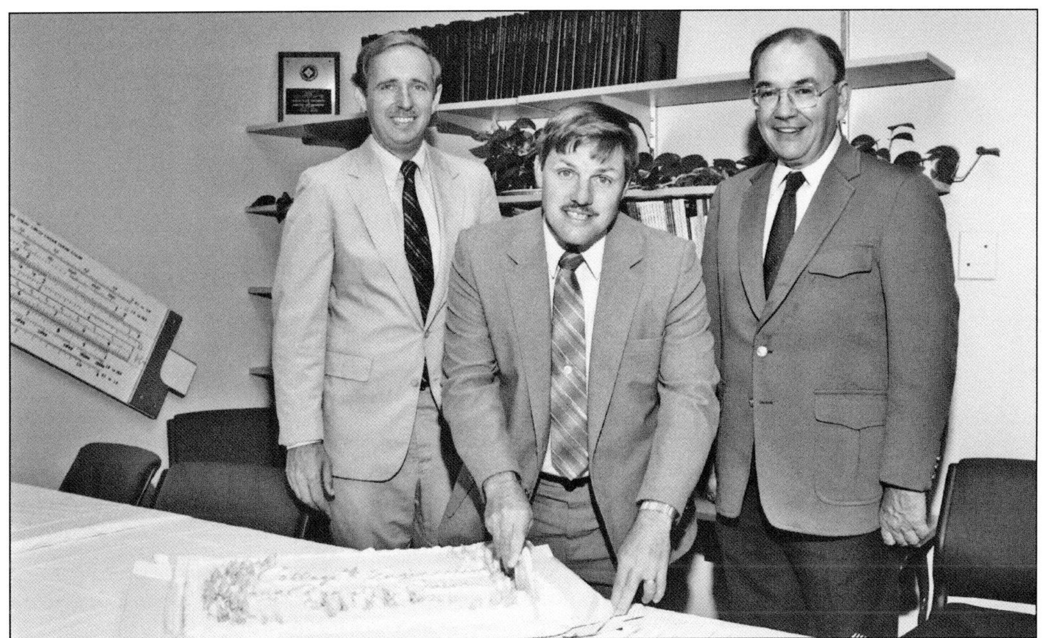

College of Engineering and Computer Science. The renowned College of Engineering and Computer Science is home to several departments, such as the Departments of Biomedical, Industrial and Human Factors Engineering, Computer Science and Computer Engineering, Electrical Engineering, and Mechanical and Materials Engineering. The college offers degrees at the undergraduate, master's, and doctoral levels as well as certifications.

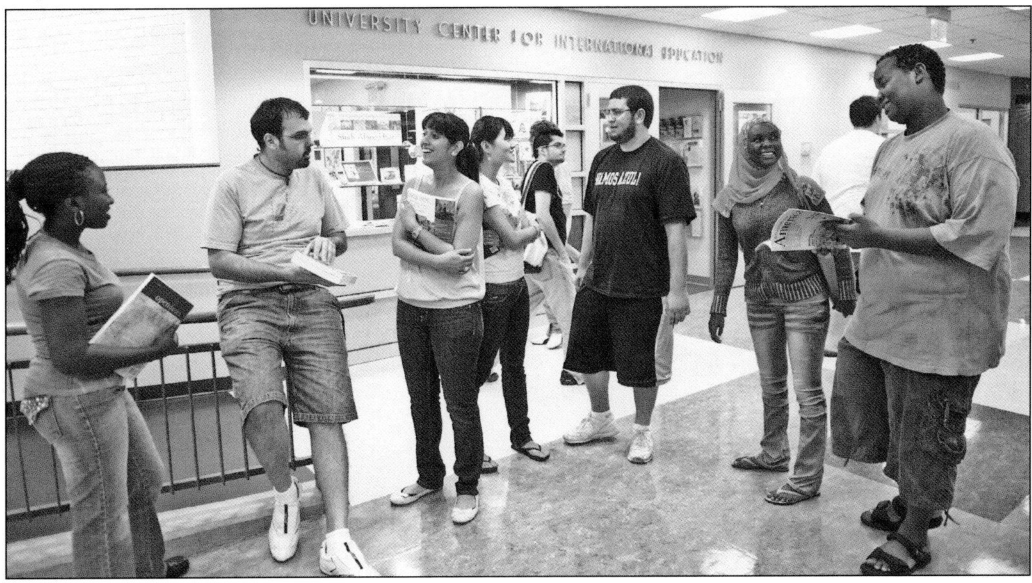

University Center for International Education. The University Center for International Education provides international students with support services. It also provides students, faculty, and staff with opportunities to gain international understanding through learning and experience. The center offers programs and services such as faculty-led Ambassador Study Abroad programs, overseas teaching through the University Study Abroad Consortium and partner exchange programs, and the Study Abroad Faculty Development Program.

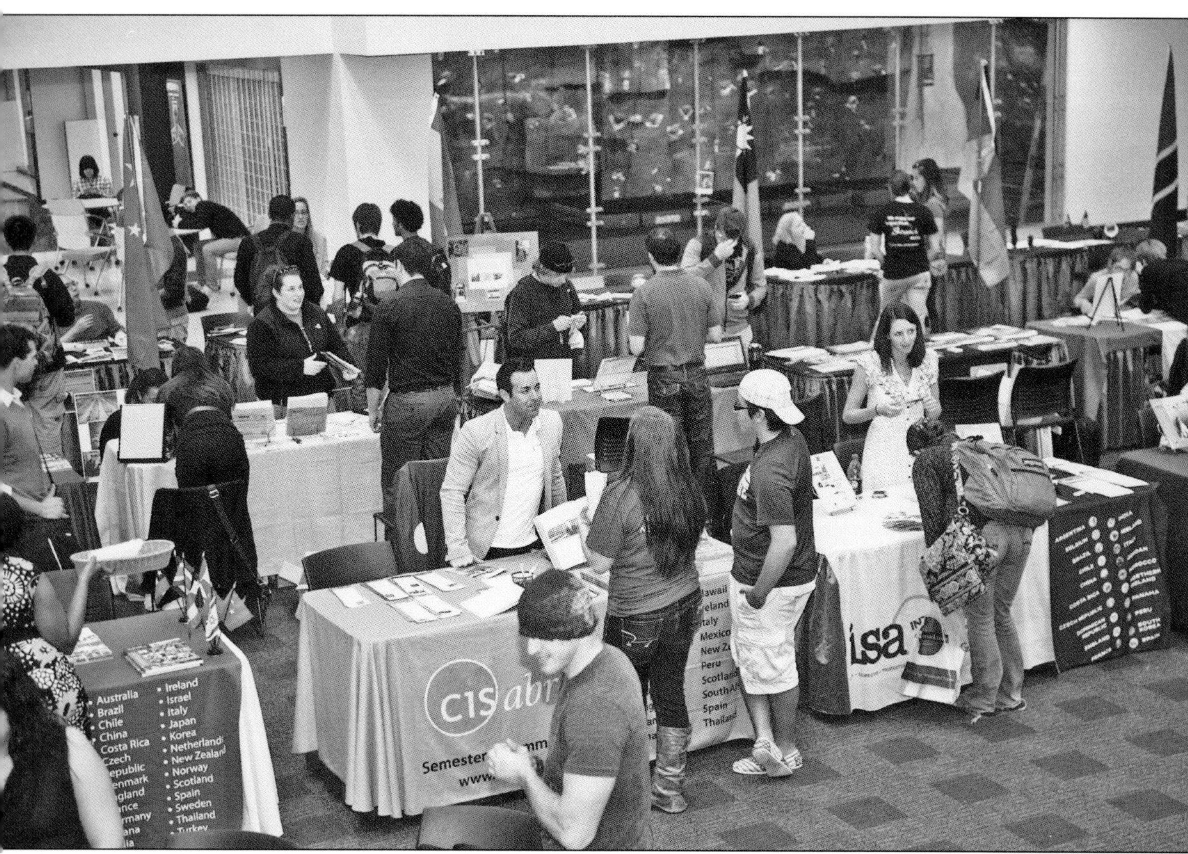

Study Abroad Programs. Wright State offers three types of study abroad programs. Ambassador programs are faculty-led and allow students to study abroad for short periods while earning credit during summer sessions. Exchange programs allow students to travel to WSU partner institutions for a semester or a full year. Third-party provider programs are offered by professional organizations and allow students to study for a semester or full year.

Four

Service and Leadership

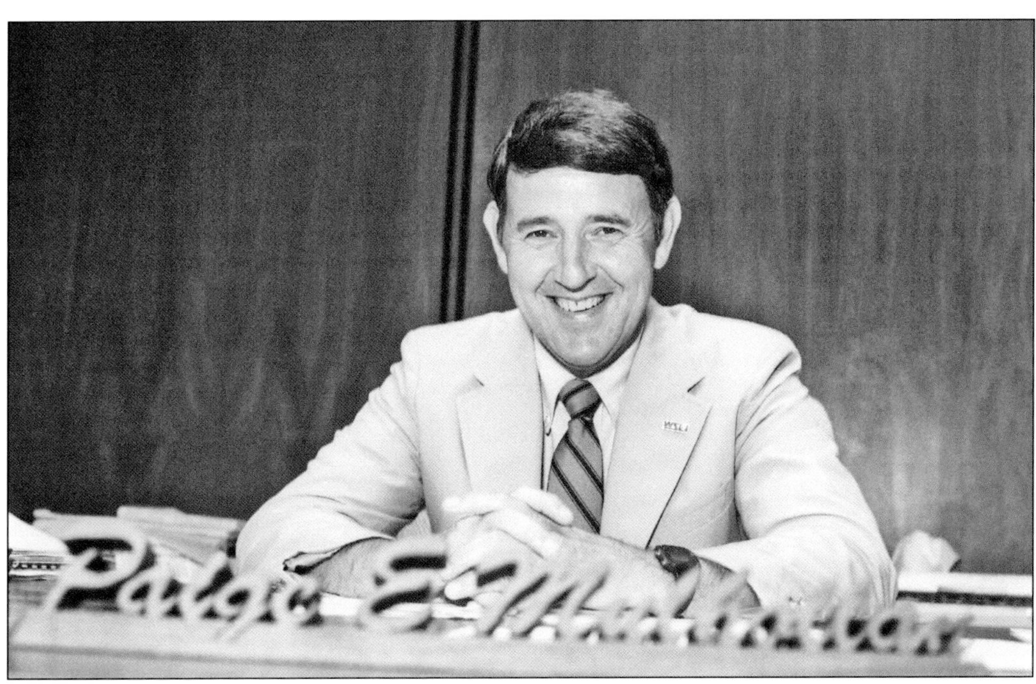

Dr. Paige Mulhollan. The university named its third president in 1985. Dr. Paige E. Mulhollan is credited for transforming the school into a metropolitan university where leadership and service in the Dayton area are important to its mission. During his administration, the campus expanded to add more departments and buildings like the Nutter Center, the Russ Engineering Center, and a new Student Union.

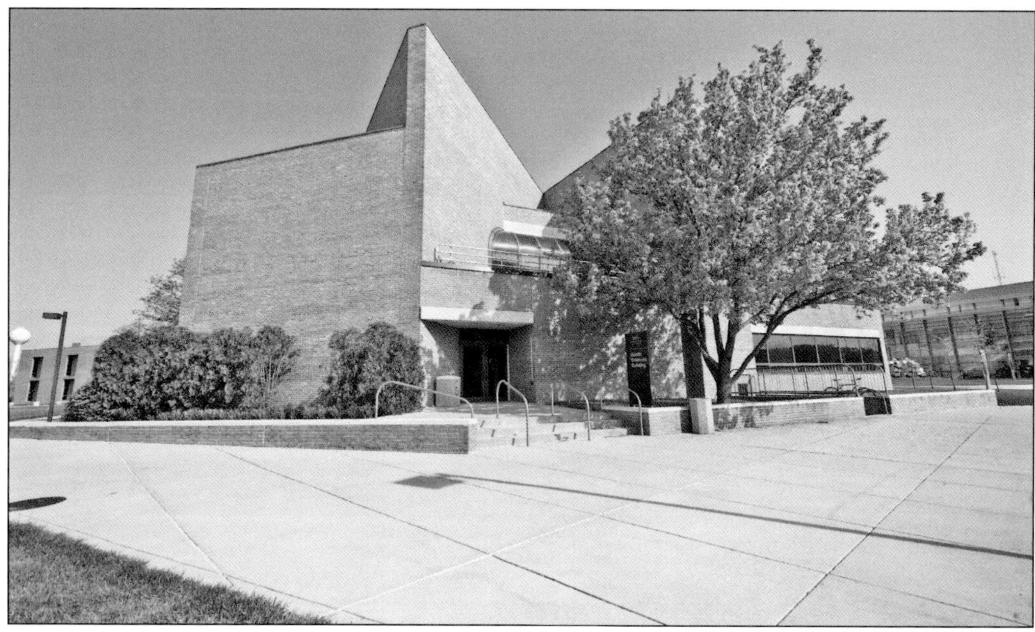

Health Sciences Building. The Health Sciences Building was completed in 1986. It gives the campus an added visual appeal with its irregular shape and angles. The School of Professional Psychology and the Department of Pharmacology and Toxicology call this building home. It also houses several other departments and programs, research laboratories, and classrooms.

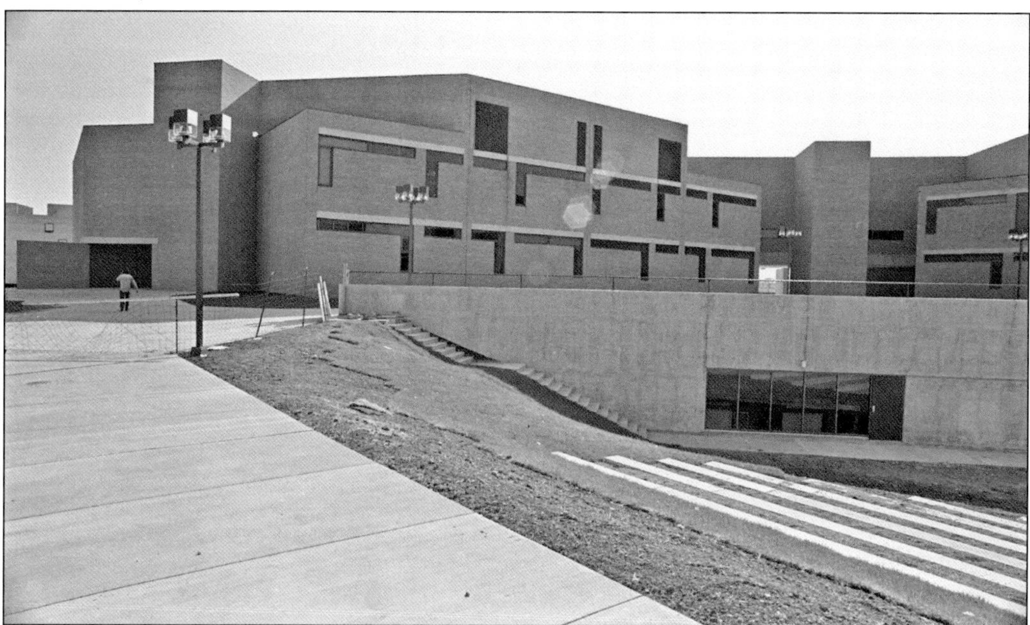

Mathematical and Microbiological Sciences. Completed in 1986, the Mathematical and Microbiological Sciences Building is full of classrooms, offices, and computer labs. The Department of Mathematics and Statistics is situated here. It was the original site of the College of Computer Science and Engineering before the Fitz and Delores Russ Engineering Center was created and the college moved in.

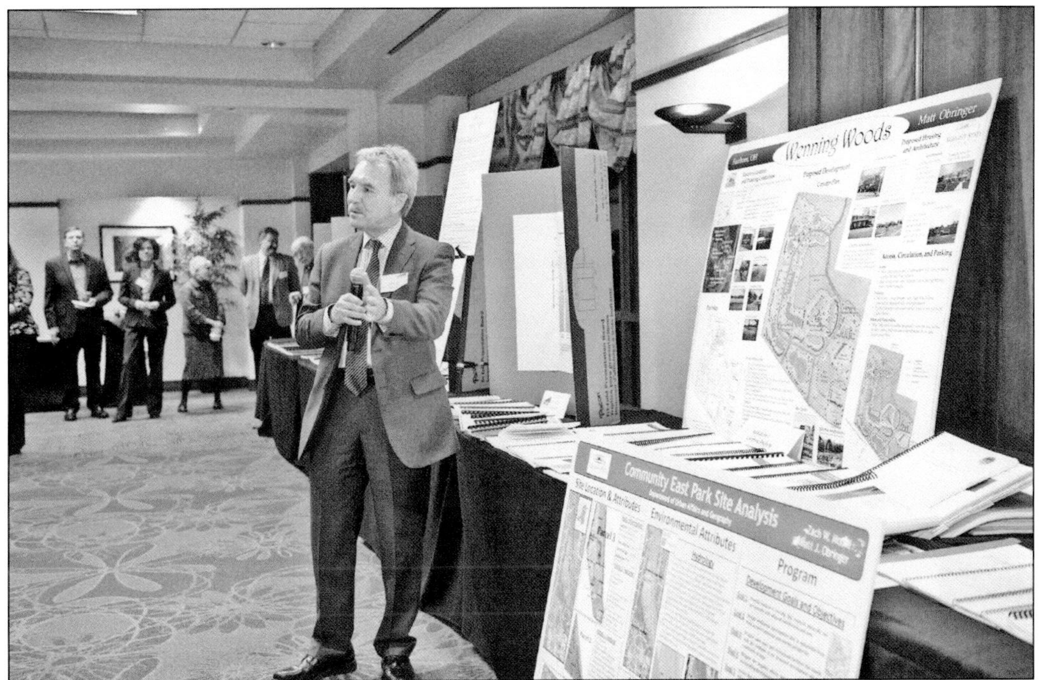

Center for Urban and Public Affairs. In 1986, the Center for Urban and Public Affairs (CUPA) was created to support and address issues pertaining to urban, suburban, and rural areas. The center's research focuses on data collection and analysis, policy evaluation, and planning.

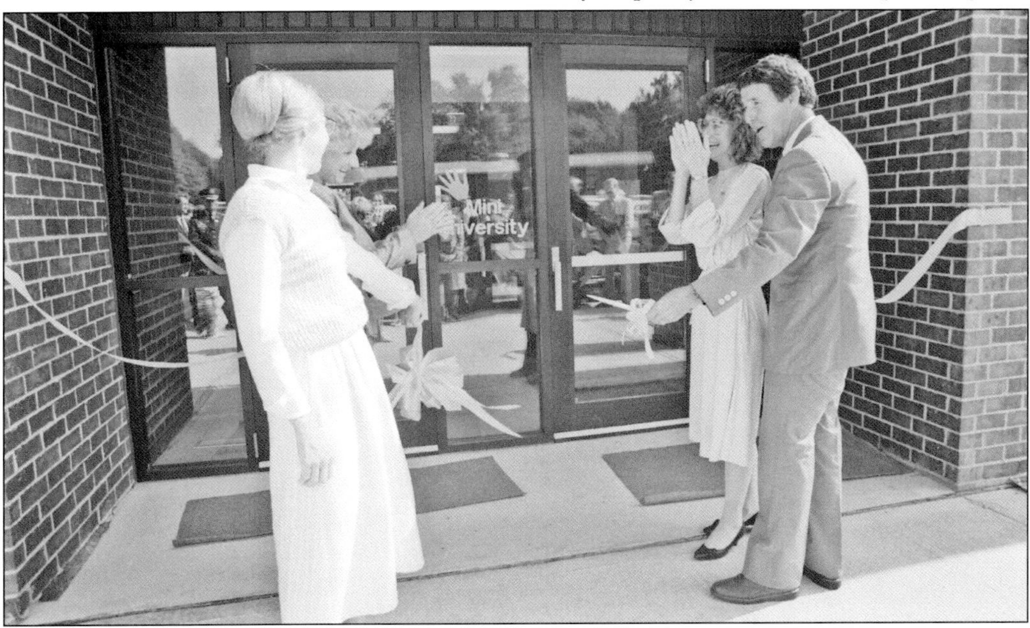

Mini University, Inc. The Child Development Center is the Mini University on the campus. It started in the Warner House. It offers early childcare and education for children from six weeks to 12 years of age. The center was founded in 1987 and was accredited by the National Association for the Education of Young Children in January 1990. It was the first early childhood center in Greene County to attain this accreditation.

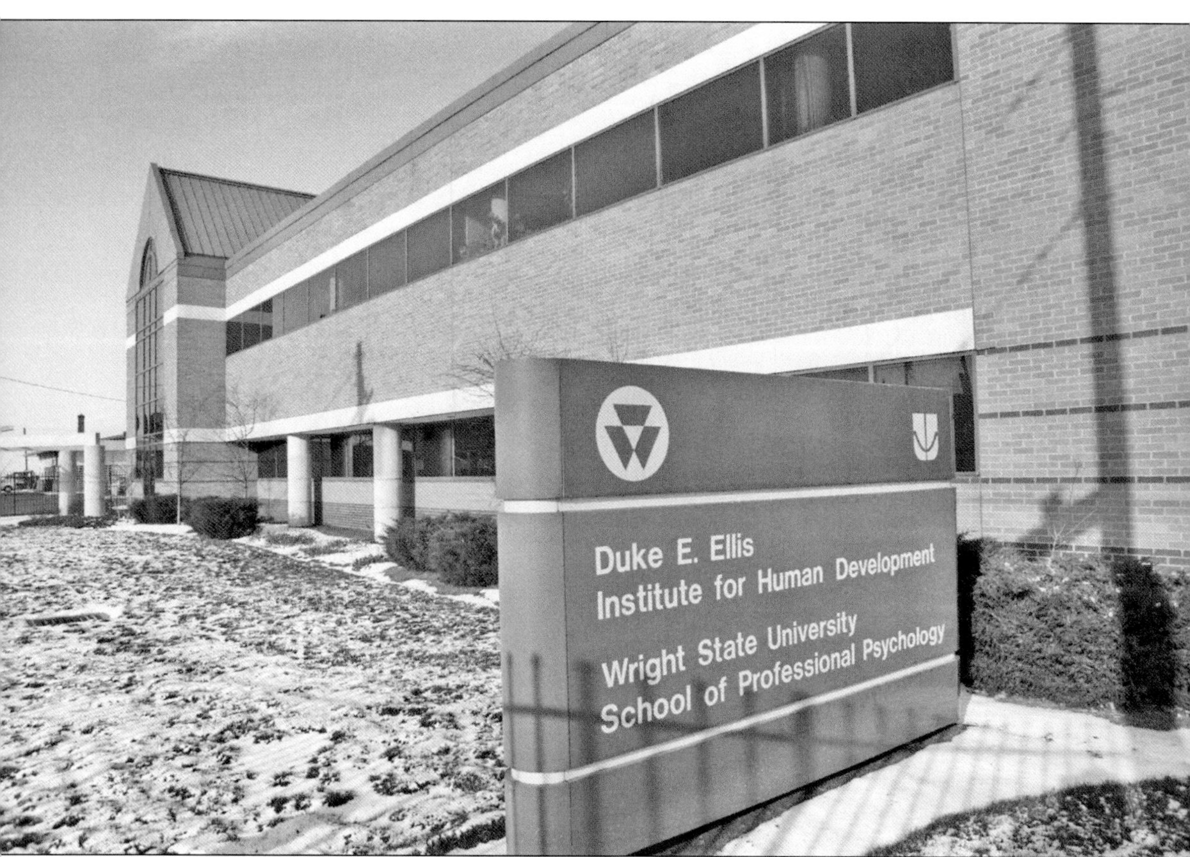

Duke Ellis Human Development Institute. Opening in the fall of 1989, the Duke E. Ellis Human Development Institute is an extension of the School of Professional Psychology (SOPP). As the SOPP in conjunction with the institute trains the next generation of professional psychologists, the institute seeks to address the needs of the community while promoting human health and effectiveness.

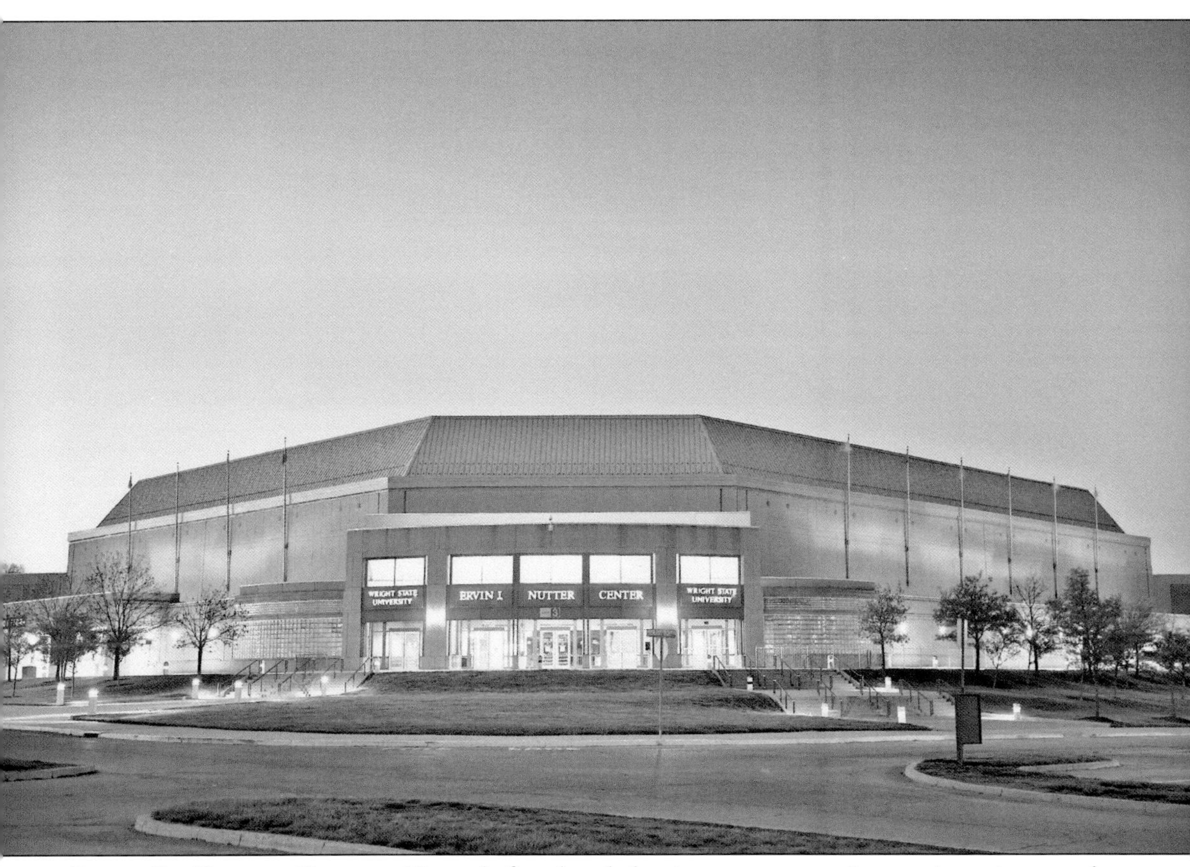

Ervin J. Nutter Center. Named for local businessman, engineer, inventor, and philanthropist Ervin J. Nutter, the Nutter Center was built in 1990. The women's and men's basketball teams as well as the women's volleyball team call the center home. The center's Berry Room is a common conference and meeting space. The McLin Gymnasium serves as a practice facility and also a place for the university's and local high schools' commencement ceremonies.

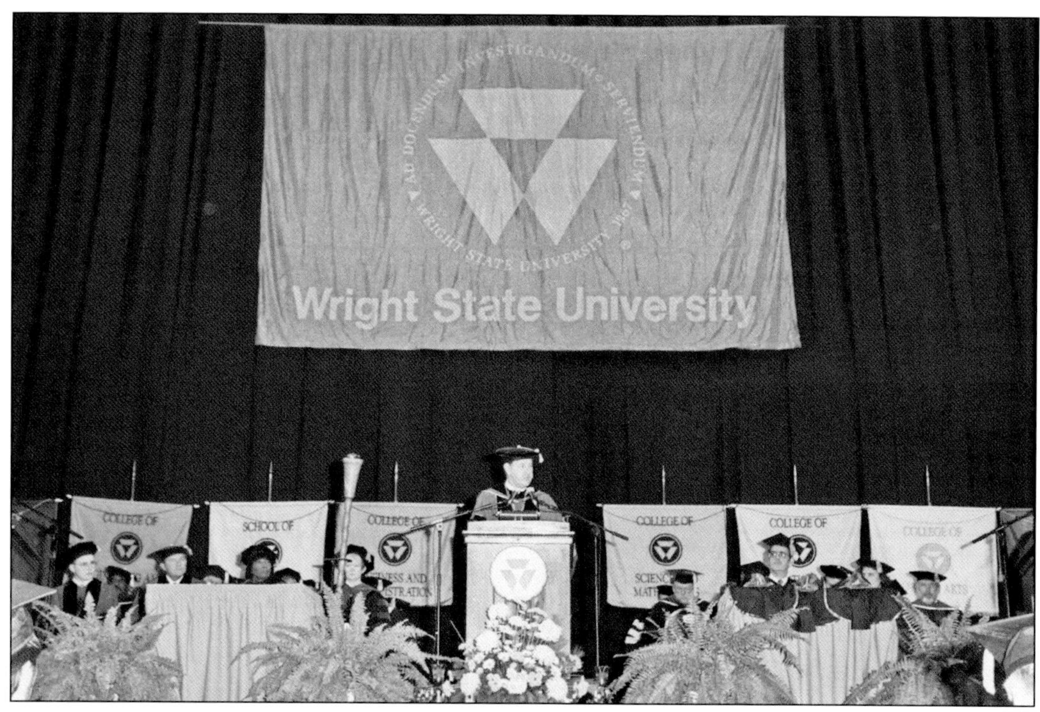

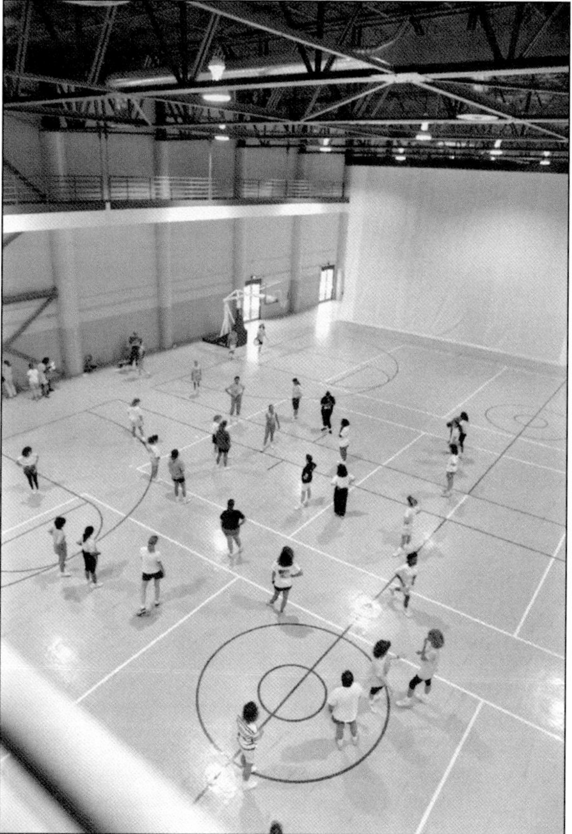

NUTTER CENTER'S FIRST COMMENCEMENT. For the first time in the school's history, commencement was held in an on-campus building when the Nutter Center's first commencement took place in 1990. Area high schools like Beavercreek, Fairborn, Centerville, Miamisburg, and Fairmont also utilize the McLin for their annual commencement ceremonies.

C.J. MCLIN GYMNASIUM. Located across the hall from the main arena of the Nutter Center is the McLin Gymnasium, named after C.J. McLin. Since 1991, the Lady Raiders volleyball team has played here. In 1998, the Midwestern Collegiate Conference took place in McLin. This was also the site of the 2006 Horizon League Championship.

Center for Healthy Communities. Established in 1991 as Partners for Community Health, the initiative now known as the Center for Healthy Communities is dedicated to improving the health and overall well-being of the Dayton community. Collaborating with organizations like Wright State University, Sinclair Community College, and the Kellogg Foundation, the center educates health professionals to achieve its goal of community health.

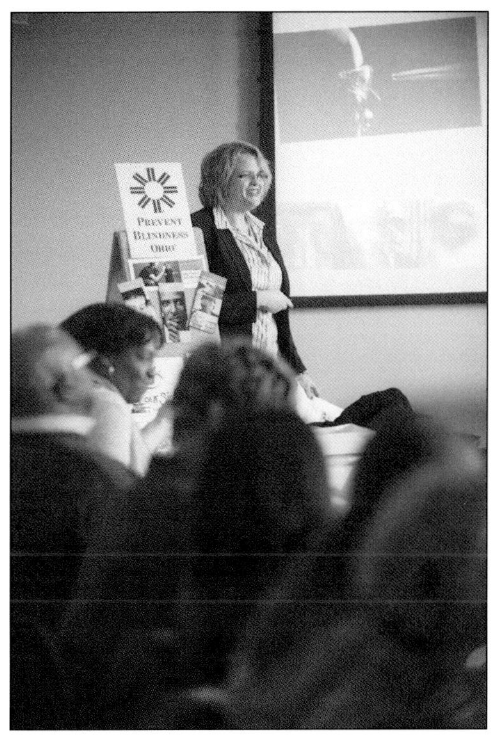

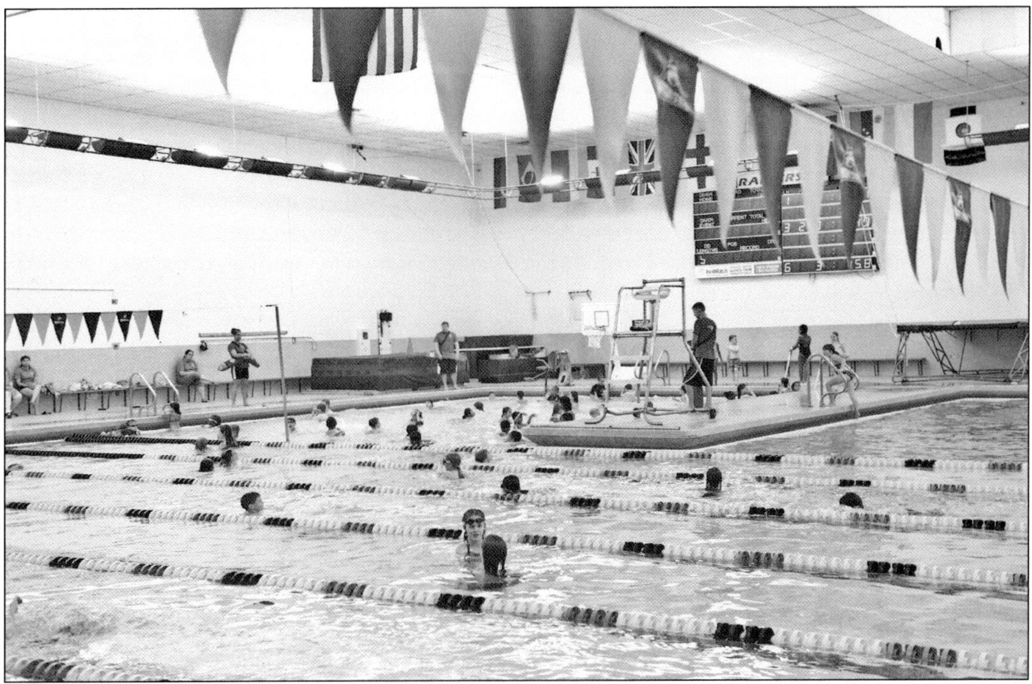

Wright State University Natatorium. Located on the first floor of the WSU Student Union, the pool is home to the women's and men's swimming and diving teams. Competing in Division I since the 1991–1992 season, these women and men's teams have gone on to win 18 conference titles, 228 individual awards, and 77 relay events.

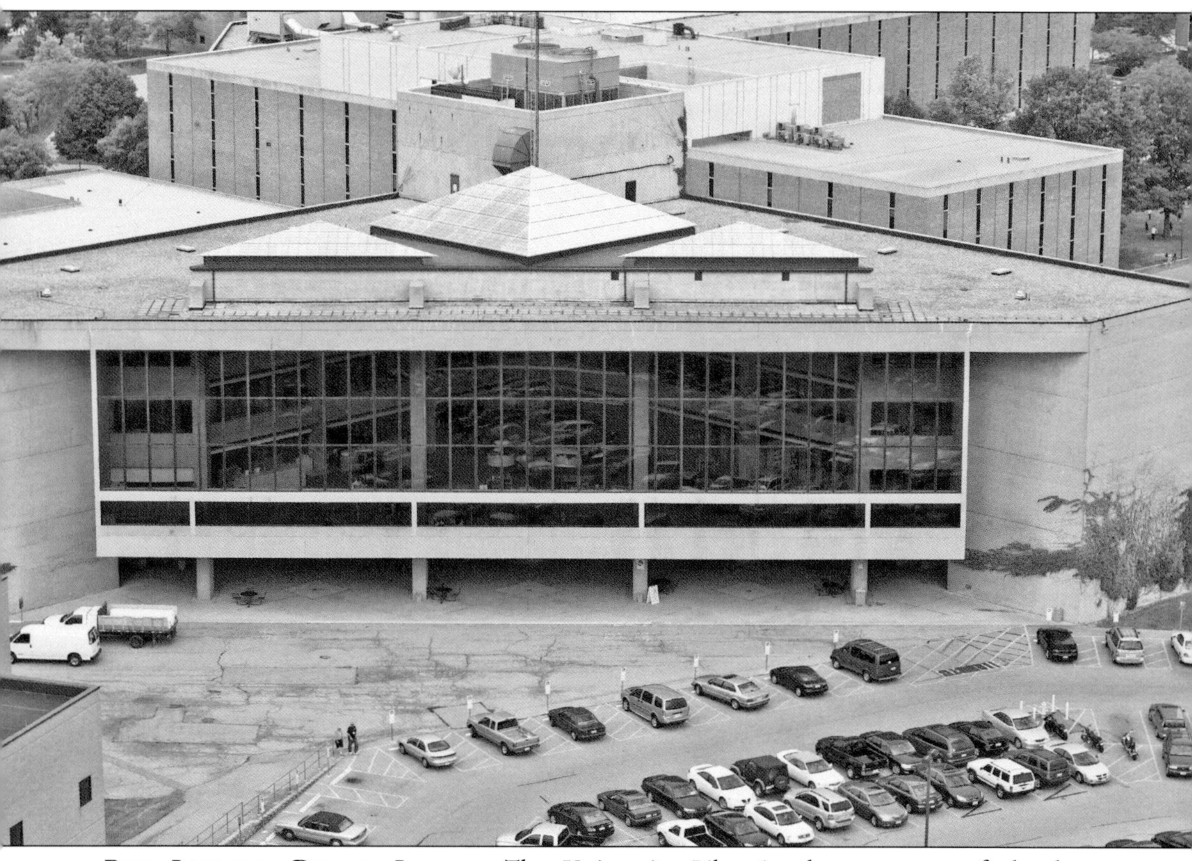

Paul Laurence Dunbar Library. The University Libraries house some of the largest collections in Dayton. The libraries are a member of OhioLINK, a network that provides access to materials in academic libraries. The Student Technology Assistance Center provides students with technologies and multimedia platforms to create original works. In 1992, the main library was named the Paul Laurence Dunbar Library, recognizing the acclaimed poet's importance to Dayton, his significant works, and his friendship with the Wright brothers.

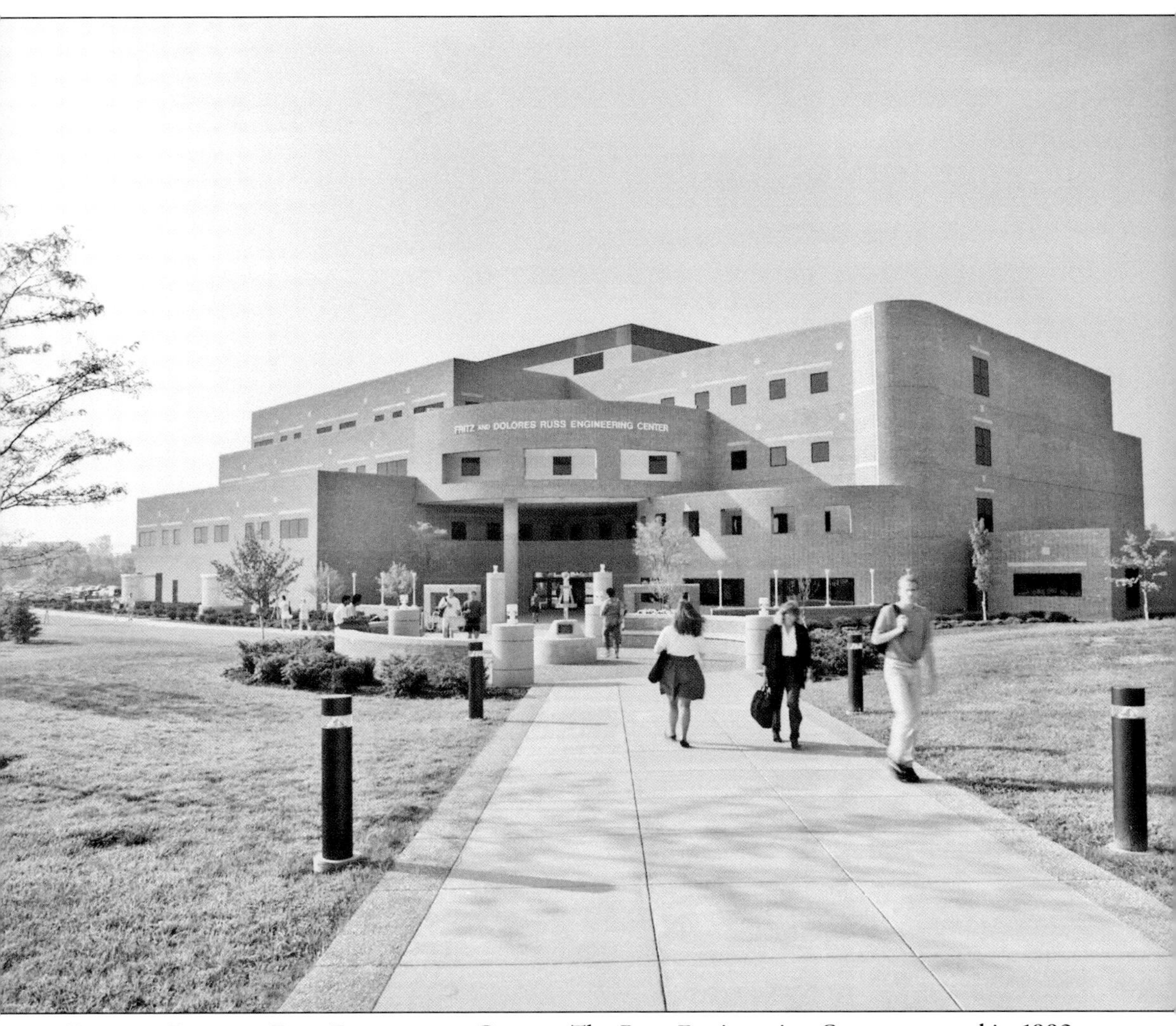

FITZ AND DOLORES RUSS ENGINEERING CENTER. The Russ Engineering Center opened in 1992. It is named for Fitz and Delores Russ, the founders of Systems Research Laboratories, Inc. The center is the largest academic building on campus. It houses the College of Engineering and Computer Science and serves the students, faculty, and staff at Wright State as well as industrial partners throughout the Miami Valley.

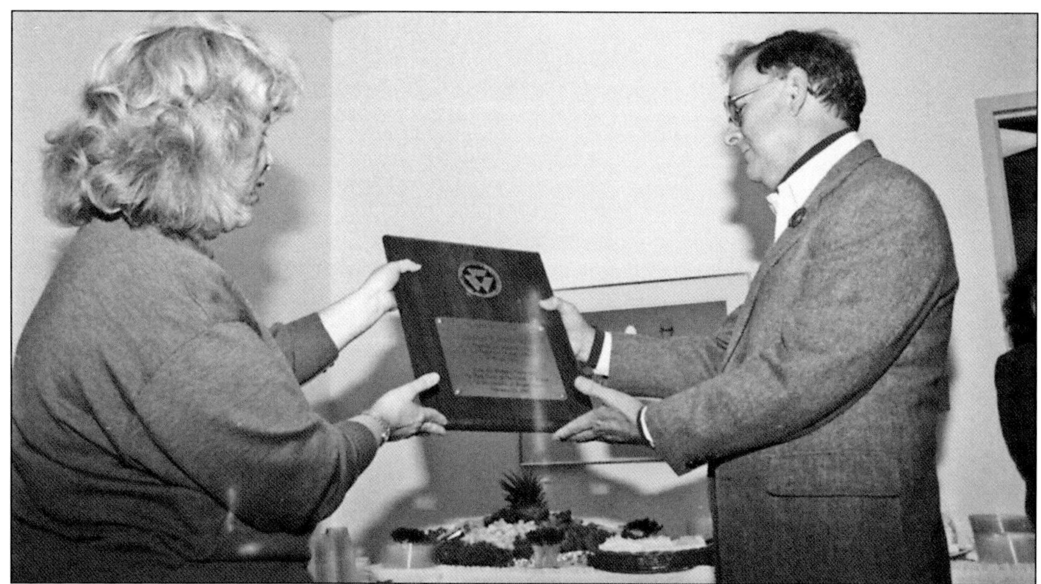

The Women's Center. The Women's Center has worked to serve women on campus since 1993. It also works with the surrounding area by providing resources and facilitating connections for all people. The center strives to create an environment where women are supported, encouraged, and not marginalized. It provides services in four main areas: community and leadership, programs and events, resources and information, and institutional and individual advocacy.

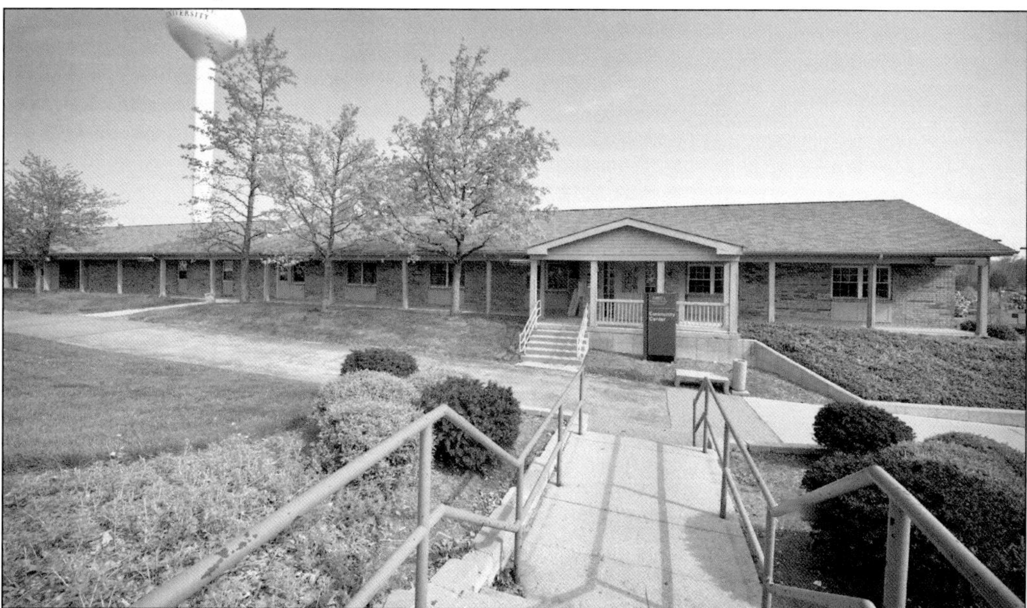

Residence Life and Housing. The Residence Life and Housing office is located under the Wright State water tower. The office helps incoming and returning students secure housing in the many residential communities. The dormitory communities are Hamilton Hall, the Woods, and the Honors Community. The apartment complexes are Forest Lane, University Park, College Park, and the Village. The office is also the package pickup location for on-campus students.

The Village Residential Community. The Village residential community has offered housing to on-campus students since 1993. The Village apartments are open to juniors, seniors, graduate and professional students, students with families or partners, or students at least 23 years of age. The complex consists of three buildings, a picnic shelter area with a grill, and a playground.

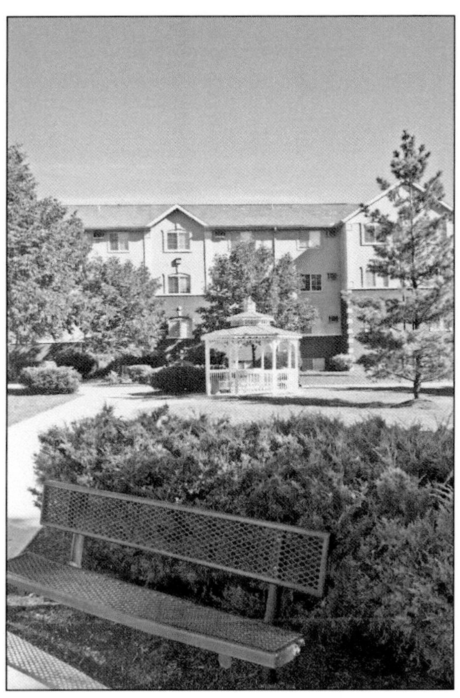

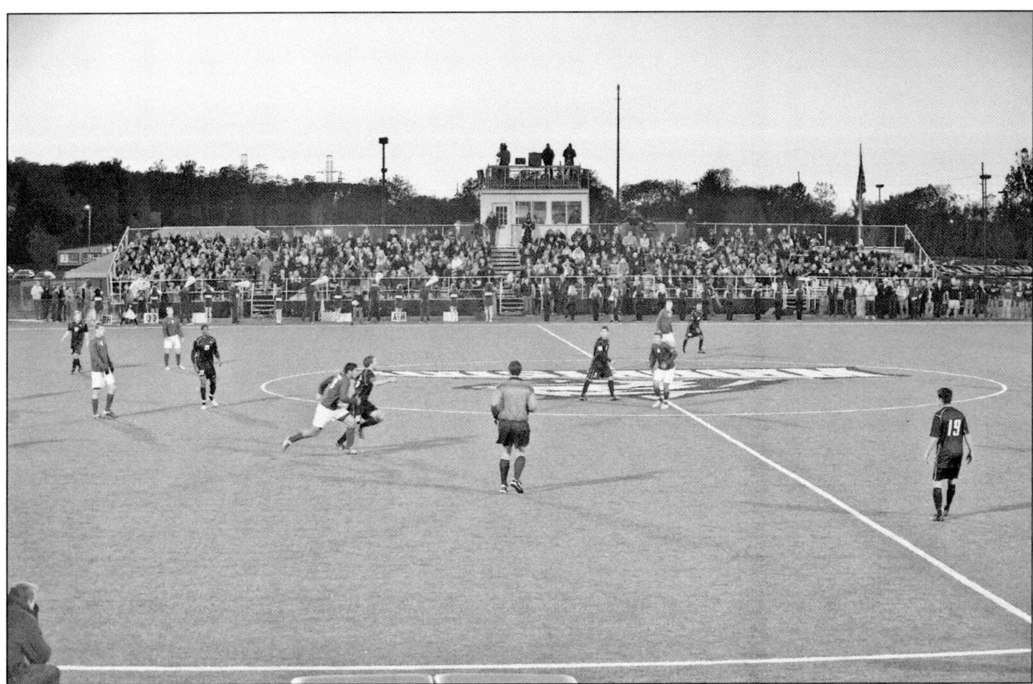

Division I Raider Athletics. The intercollegiate athletic teams at Wright State University compete in the NCAA Division I Horizon League. There are seven men's sports teams, competing in basketball, baseball, cross-country, swimming and diving, tennis, soccer, and golf. The women compete in eight sports, including basketball, tennis, cross-country, track and field, volleyball, soccer, swimming and diving, and softball. The Raiders have won many league titles and have advanced to NCAA tournaments.

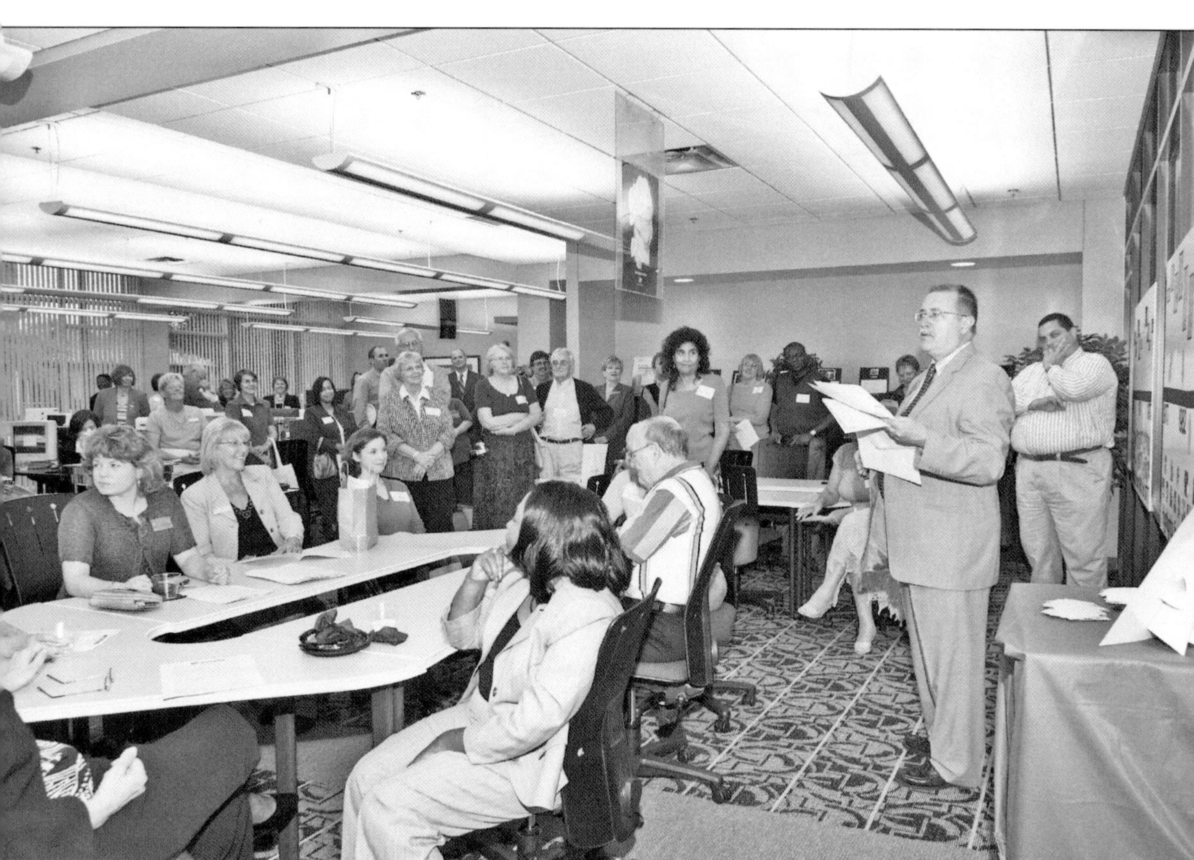

College of Education and Human Services. The College of Education and Human Services is one of 39 out of 50 teacher-preparation institutions in the state of Ohio accredited by the National Council for the Accreditation of Teacher Education. The department offers undergraduate, graduate, and doctoral degrees and licensure and endorsements in over 40 programs. The college takes pride in the difference it has made in the lives of former and current students.

Five

Maturity and Transformation

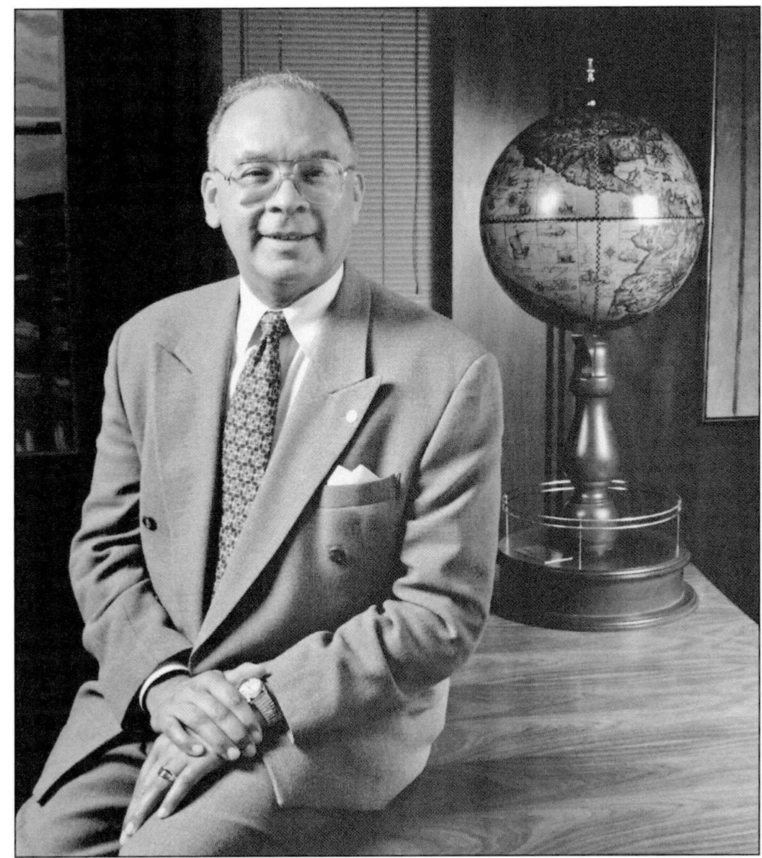

Dr. Harley E. Flack. In 1994, the university appointed its fourth president. Dr. Harley E. Flack was the university's first African American president and the first African American president of a major metropolitan university in the state of Ohio. During his administration, he stressed the importance of community building and collaborative efforts on campus and throughout the Dayton community, as evident in his relationships with Dayton Public Schools.

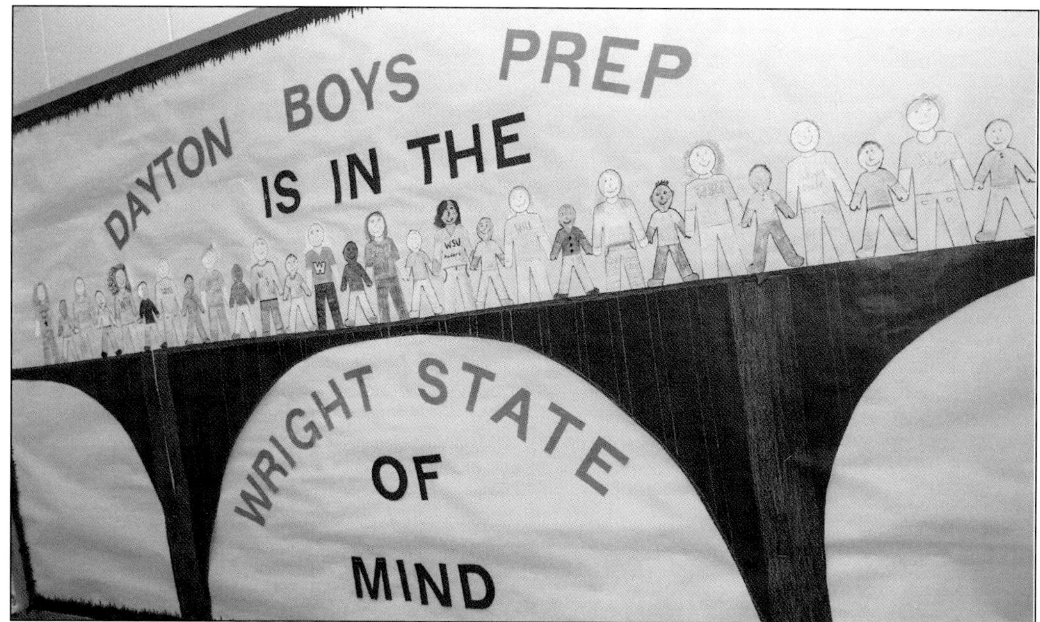

Public School Partnerships. Since 1994, the university's College of Education and Human Services has agreed to partner with 10 local public school districts to create opportunities for professional preparation, schools, and community agencies. The districts are Bellbrook-Sugarcreek Local Schools, Dayton Public Schools, Dayton Regional STEM School, Fairborn City Schools, Huber Heights City Schools, Milton-Union Exempted Village, Ripley Union Lewis Huntington School District, Trotwood-Madison City Schools, Troy City Schools, and West Carrollton City Schools.

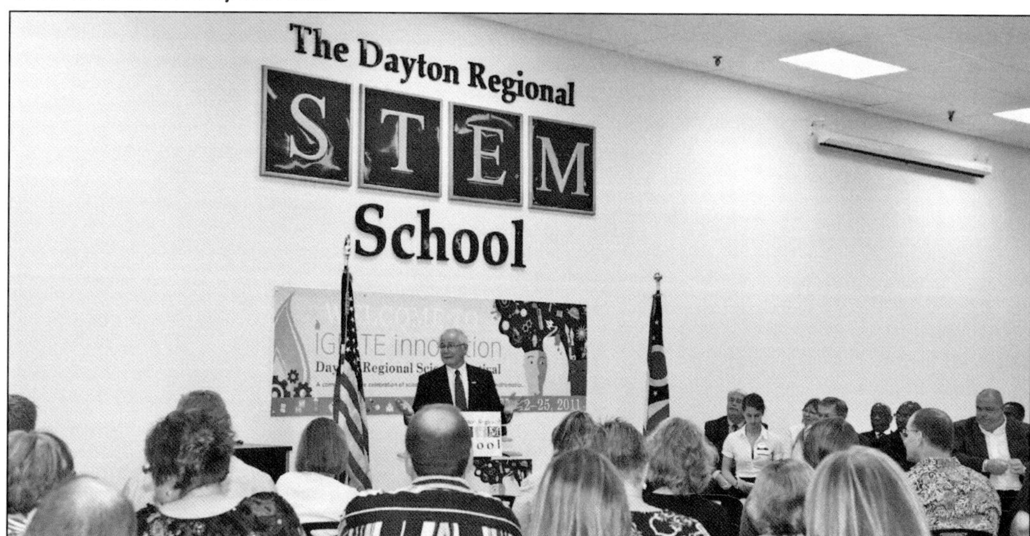

Dayton Regional STEM School. The university is a founding partner in the creation of the Dayton Regional STEM School. Since 2009, Wright State has supported the school and its model of offering students a relevant, real-world educational experience. The STEM school is a part of the university's College of Education and Human Services. Many of the university's faculty members serve on the governing board of the STEM school to facilitate ties between the school and the university.

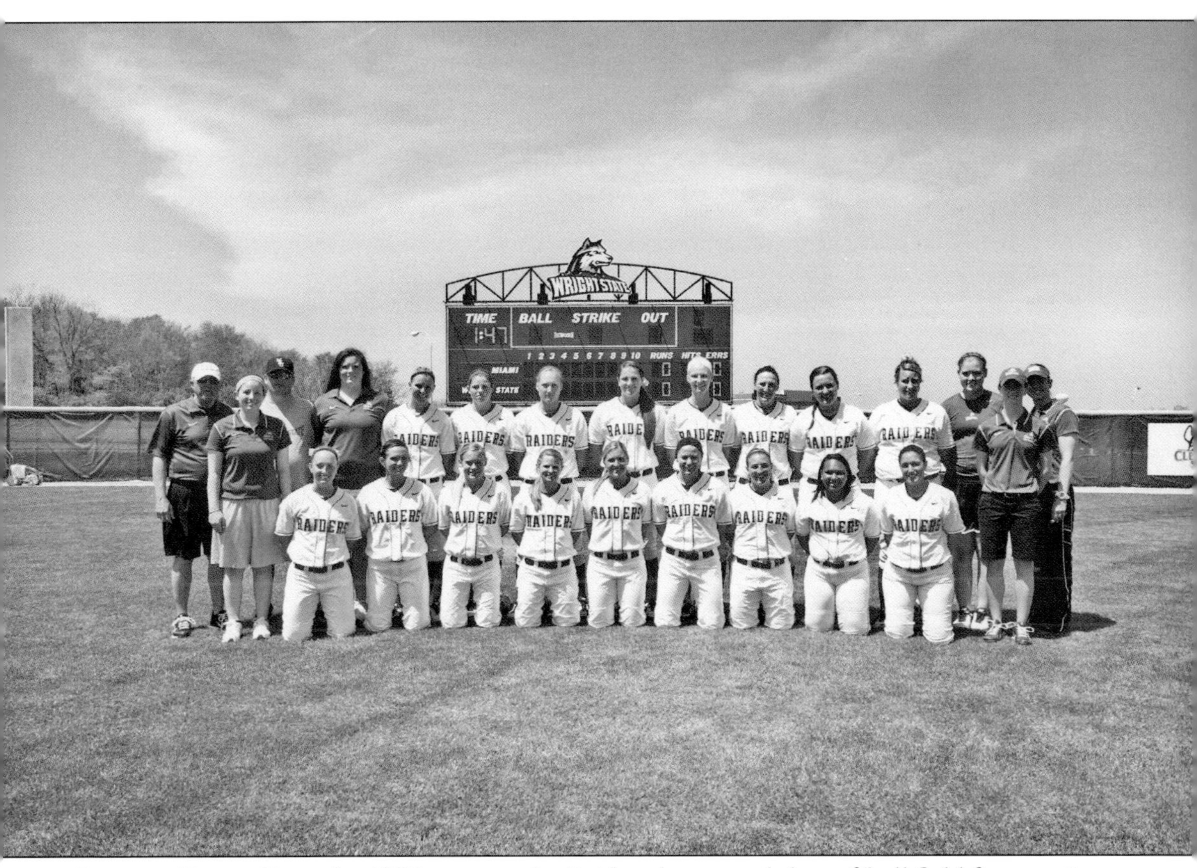

Softball Field. Since the 1995 season, the Raiders have used the softball field for practice and home games. Other uses for the field include tournaments for the Ohio High School Athletic Association (OHSAA). The field has since undergone renovations to build a press box, concession stands, dugout, restrooms, and a state-of-the-art sound system. New lights were added in 2012, allowing night games to take place.

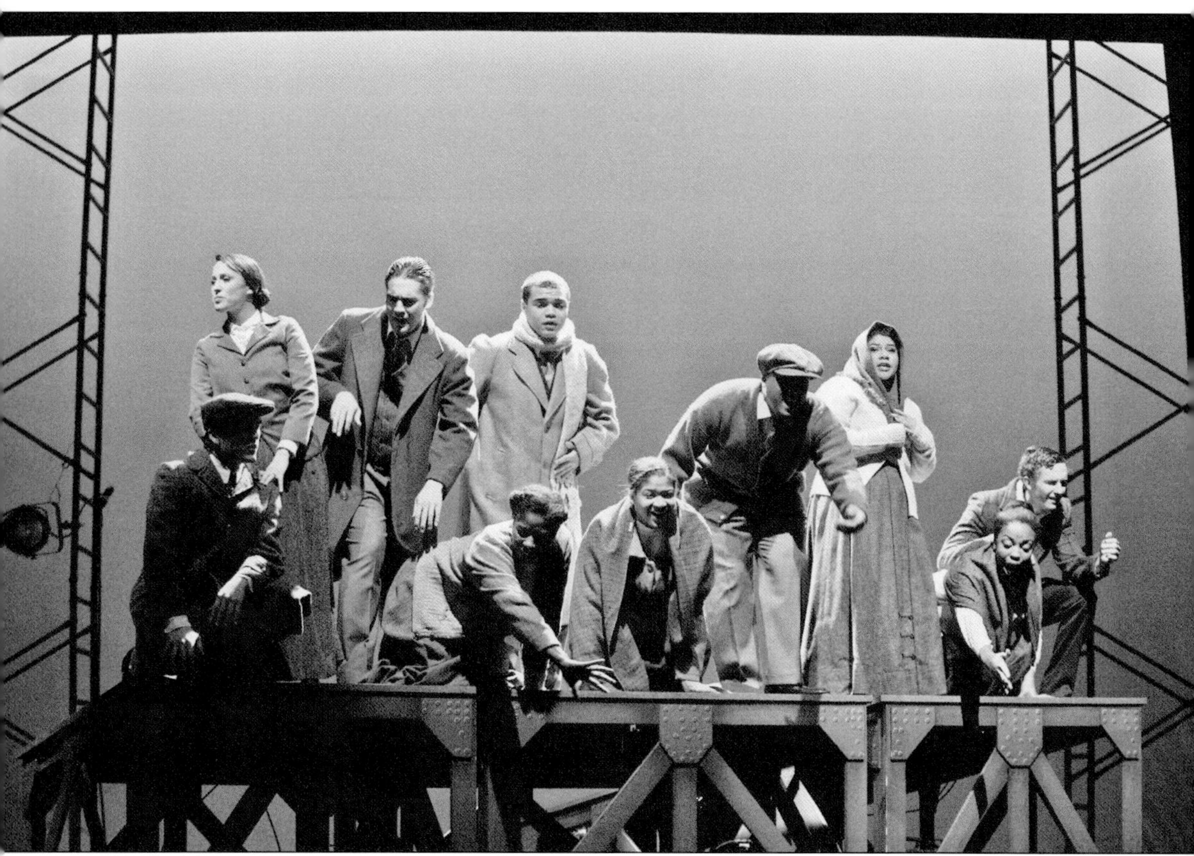

1913: The Great Dayton Flood. The Department of Theatre, Dance and Motion Pictures original *1913: The Great Dayton Flood* is an award-winning play by Stuart McDowell, chairman and artistic director of the department. In 1997, the play was performed at the Kennedy Center, where it earned numerous awards from the American College Theatre Festival. The play features recorded narration from Martin Sheen, Ossie Davis, and Ruby Dee.

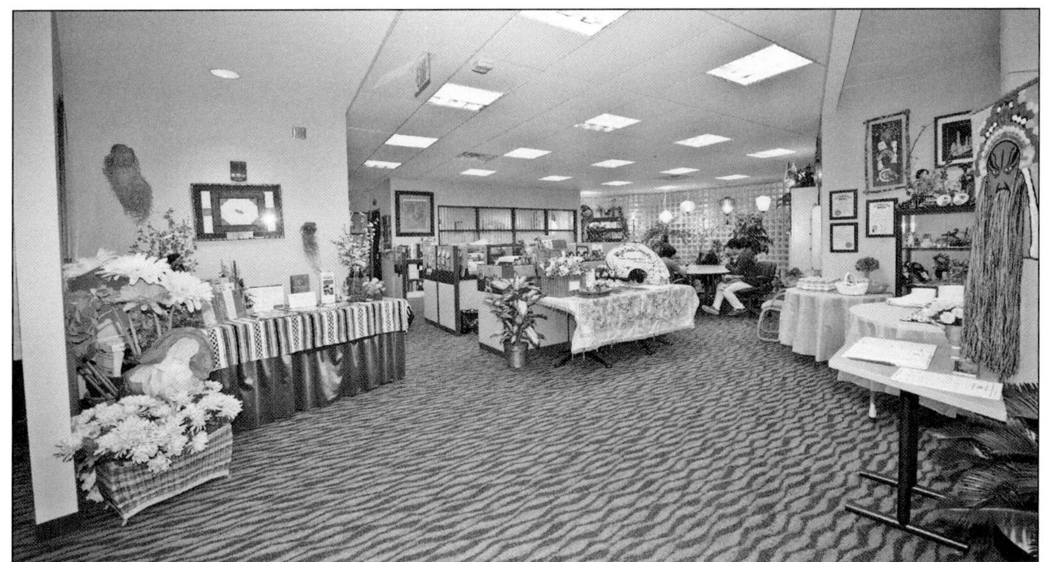

Asian/Hispanic/Native American Center. During the summer of 1997, students appeared before the University Strategic Planning Council at its open forums and met with Pres. Dr. Harley Flack to plea for the establishment of the Asian/Hispanic/Native American Center. The center addresses the needs of these students and brings forth positive images of their experiences on campus.

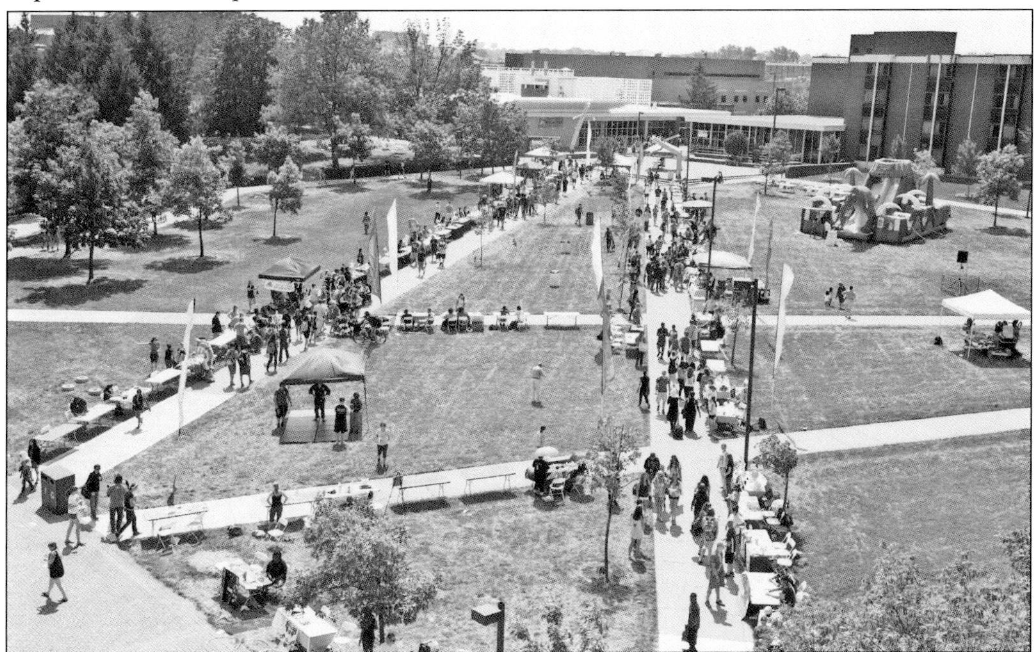

Office of Student Activities. The Office of Student Activities offers students a plethora of opportunities to get involved in various opportunities on campus. These opportunities are available through community service, fraternities, sororities, and leadership experiences. The Office of Student Activities puts on annual events such as Welcome Week, Fall Fest, Homecoming, and April Craze. Over 200 registered organizations call the office home. Throughout the year, the organizations raise money and promote diversity.

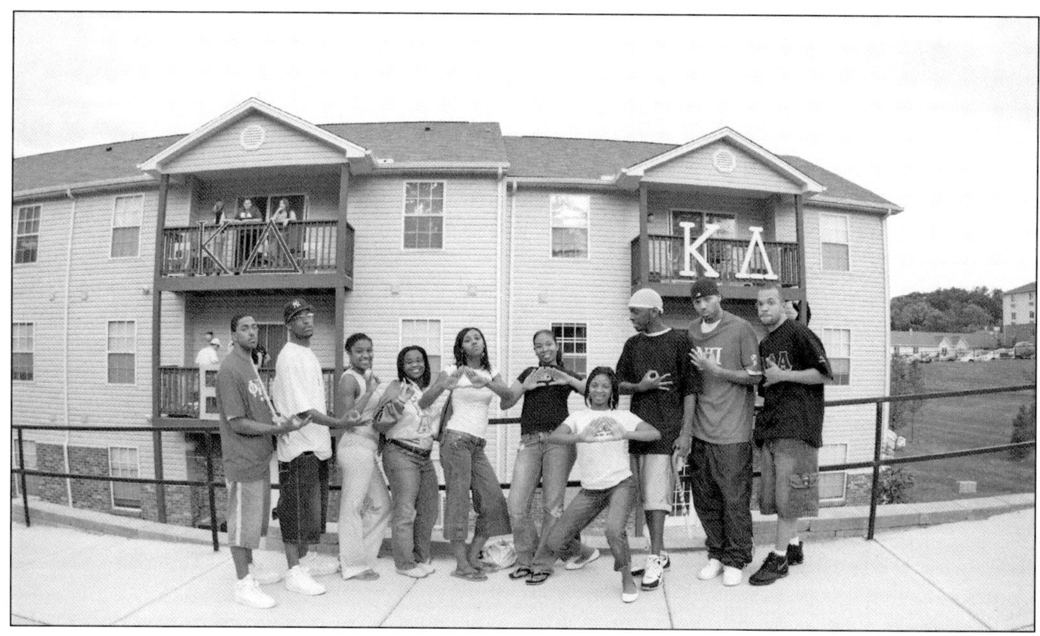

Wright State Greek Life. The Wright State Greek community is essential to campus life. Committed to public service, education, and community engagement, on-campus Greek organizations make up two separate councils, the National Pan-Hellenic Council (NPHC) and the National Panhellenic Conference (NPC). The NPHC is made up of the "Divine Nine" black fraternities and sororities. The NPC functions under the North-American Interfraternity Council of fraternities and sororities.

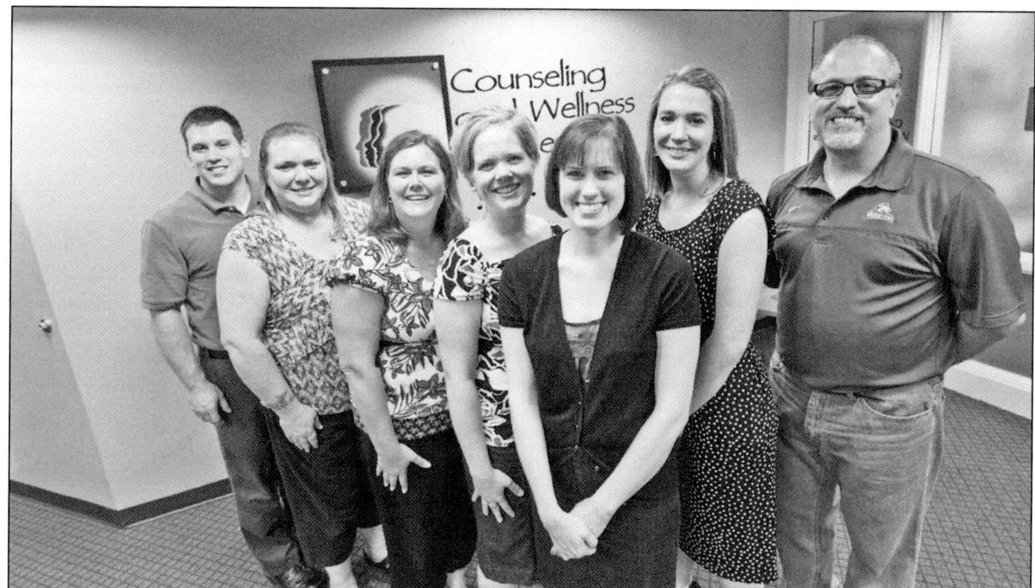

Counseling and Wellness Services. Counseling and Wellness Services (CWS) is a unit of the School of Professional Psychology. CWS promotes optimal health and wellness through the provision of quality service and training to Wright State. The diverse, multicultural community appreciates the center's welcoming environment. It offers a range of services for academic anxiety, different types of abuse, and emotional and psychological issues.

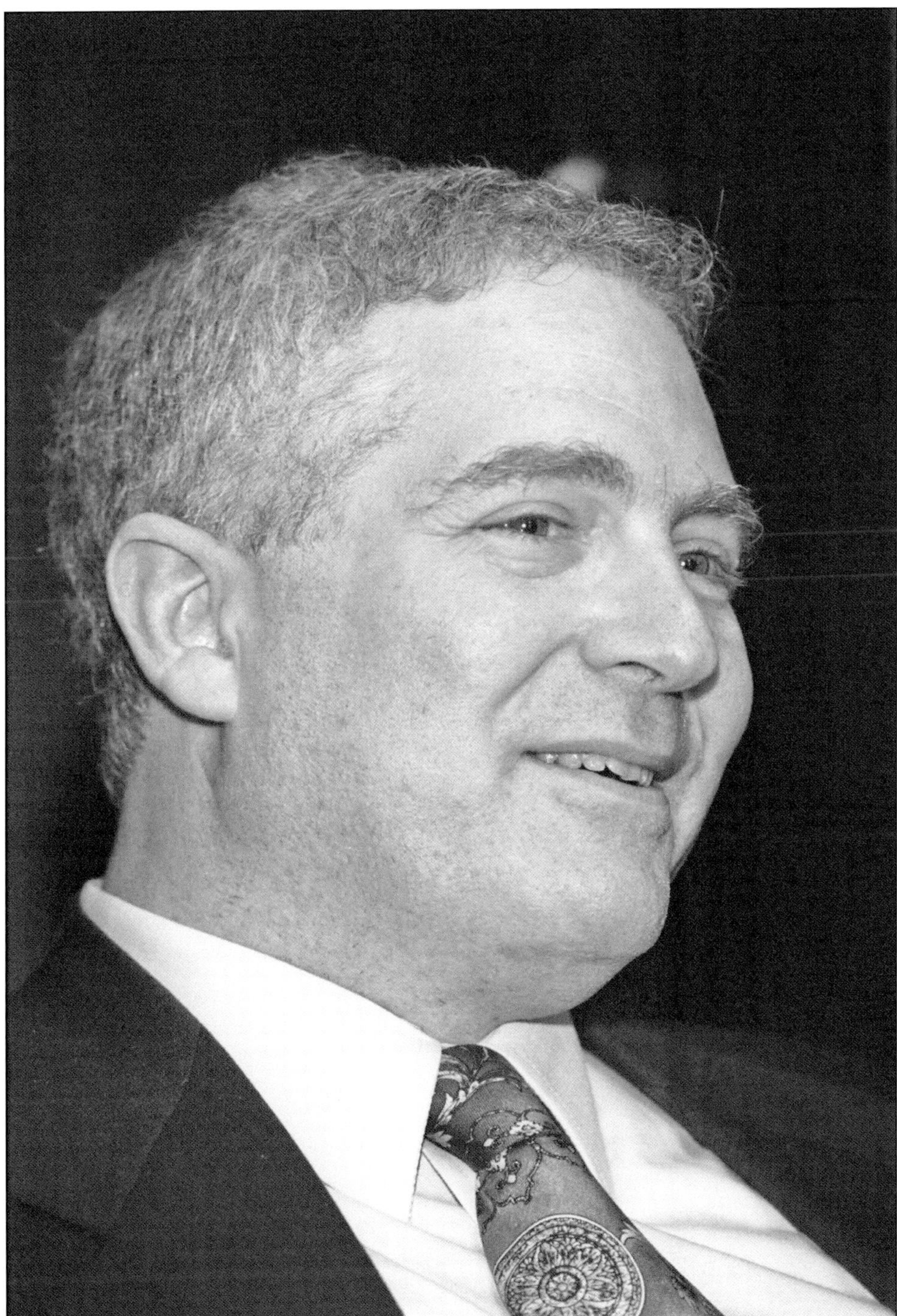

DR. KIM GOLDENBERG. Following the death of Dr. Flack, Dr. Kim Goldenberg became the university's fifth president. Prior to his appointment, Dr. Goldenberg served as a faculty member and the chief of the Department of Internal Medicine in 1983. From 1990 to 1998, he served as the dean of the medical school. Under his leadership as president, Wright State University increased its enrollment numbers and the number of research awards.

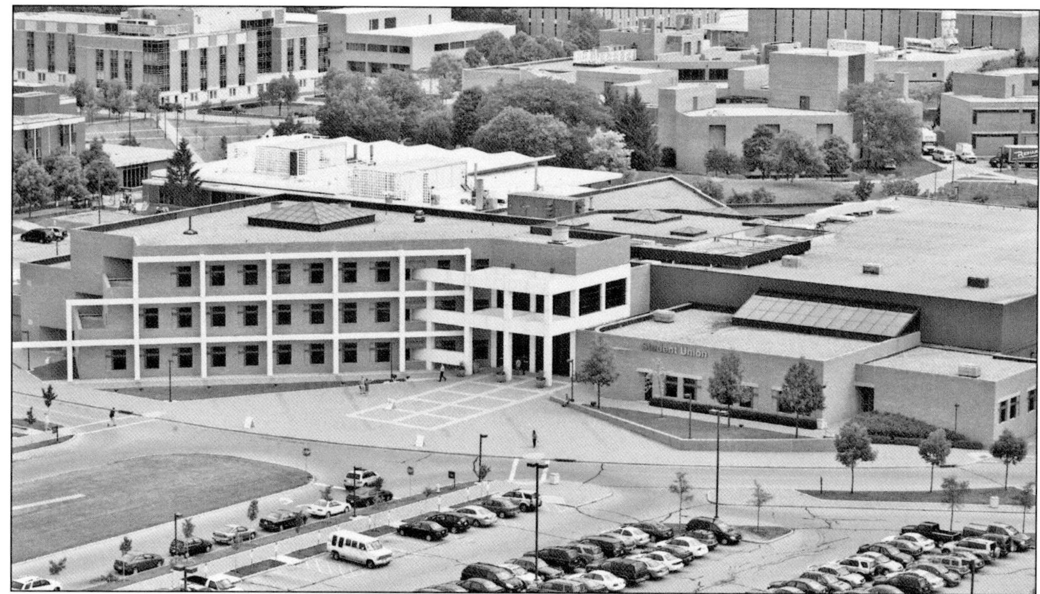

The Student Union. The Student Union is a 308,000-square-foot complex that houses a fitness center, the Union Market dining facility, the campus bookstore, conference rooms, and Raider Connect, a one-stop shop for financial aid, bursar, and registrar services. The Student Union is also home to student services such as the Office of Disability Services, the University Center for International Education, WWSU 106.9 FM, Legal Services, and the *Guardian* newspaper.

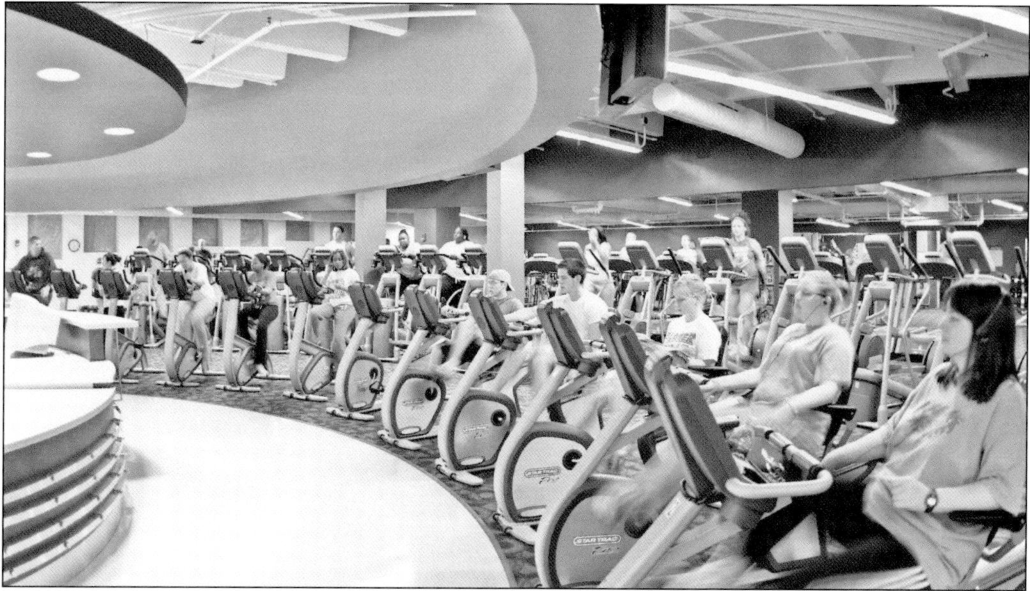

Campus Recreation Center. Located in the Student Union, Campus Recreation provides quality recreational opportunities for the campus community. It houses a state-of-the-art fitness center. For those who are outdoor enthusiasts, the Outdoor Resource Center offers hikes in the Grand Canyon, kayaking lessons, a climbing and rappelling tower, and the Low Ropes Course. The Adventure Summit, a production of Five Rivers Metro Parks and Wright State, is an event that celebrates outdoor adventure.

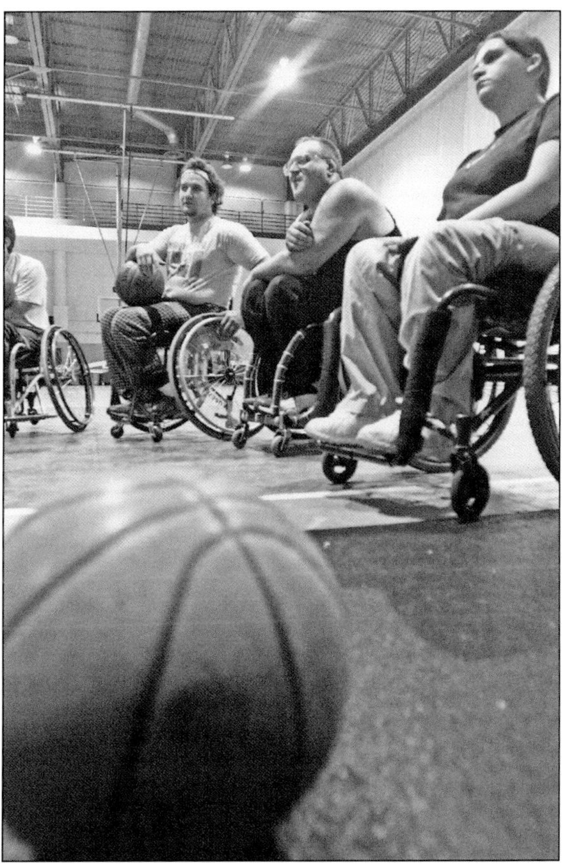

Adapted Recreation Center. Designed to offer competitive and recreational sports to students, faculty, staff, and alumni, the Adapted Recreation program caters to those with disabilities but encourages everyone to participate in aquatics, intramural sports, and outdoor recreation. The recreation center collaborates with the Office of Disability Services in order to meet the needs of those with disabilities.

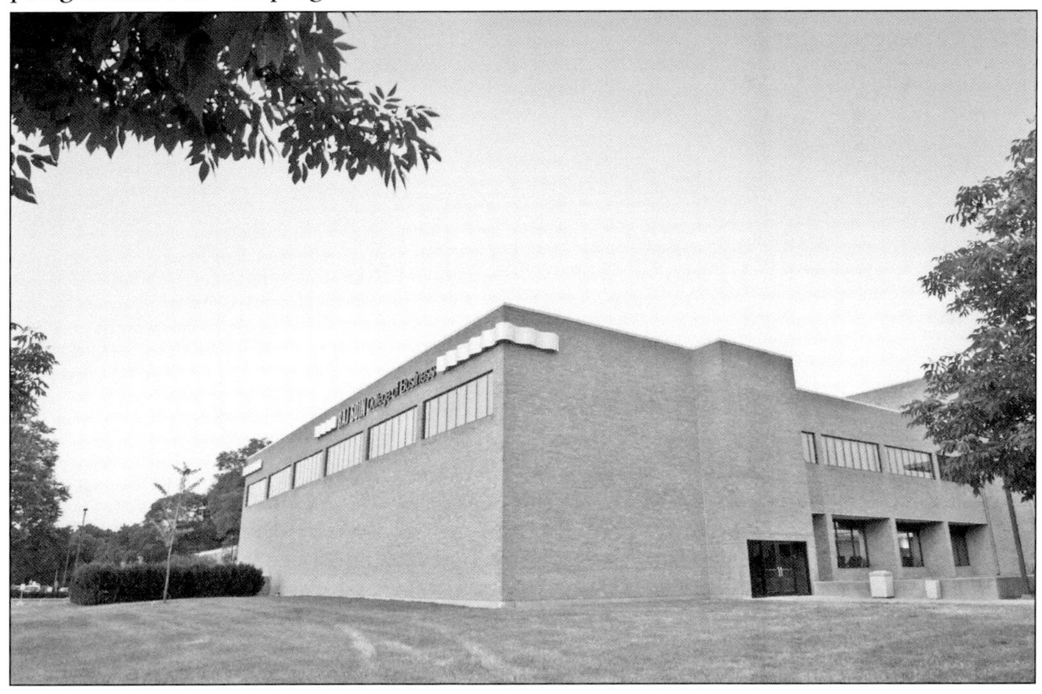

Raj Soin College of Business. The College of Business and Administration was renamed in 2000 to honor business leader Rajesh K. Soin, its benefactor. Throughout the nation, the Raj Soin College of Business has been recognized for its work in developing prominent business leaders. The College of Business was the first in the region to be accredited by the Association to Advance Collegiate Schools of Business, which is the highest accrediting body for bachelor's and postgraduate business programs.

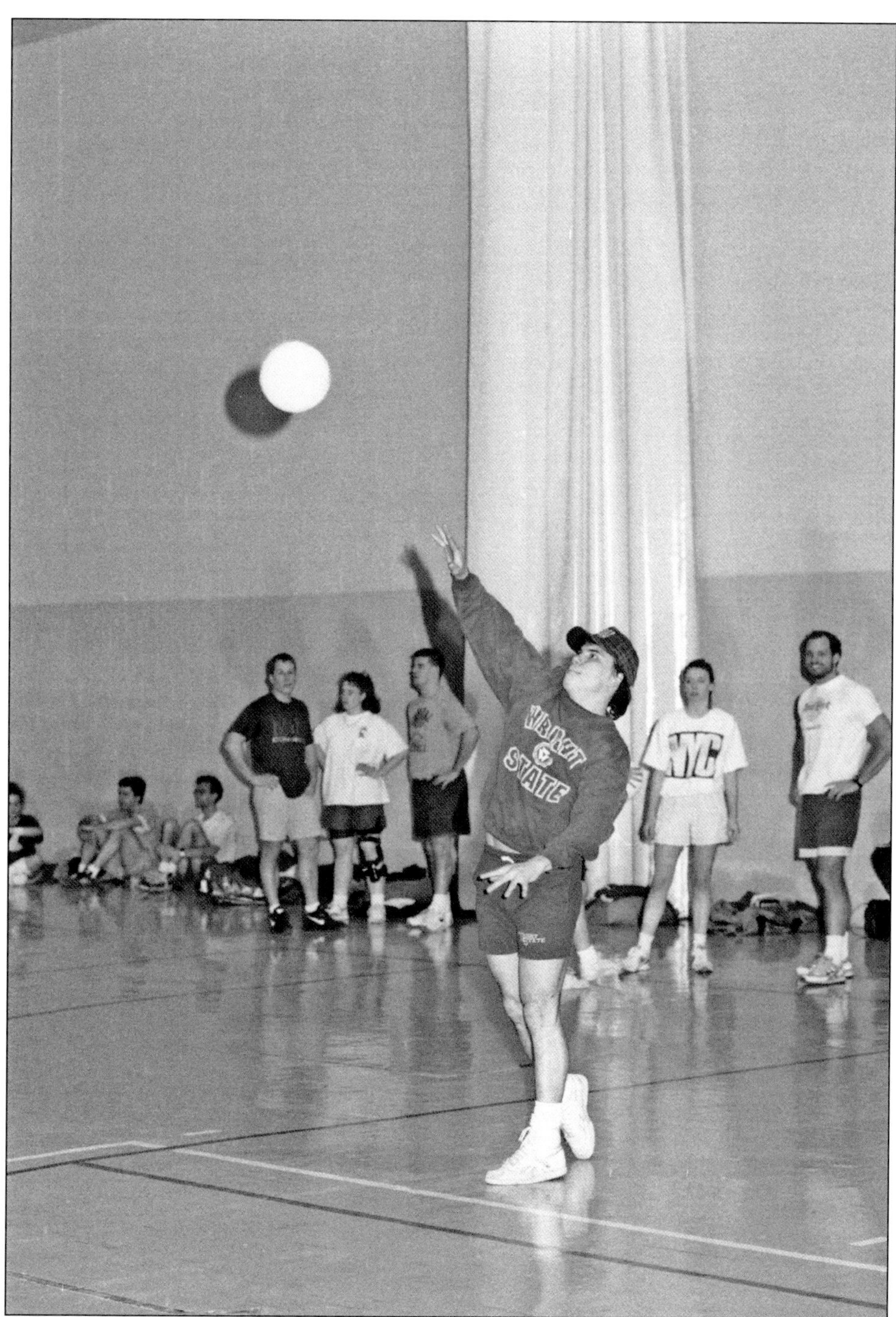

Intramural and Club Sports. Wright State offers intramural and club sports for anyone looking to relieve stress, meet new people, and stay in shape. The options include men's, women's, co-recreational, and wheelchair teams as well as individual sports and one-day special-event tournaments. The intramural sports offer Wright State students the opportunity to compete against other Wright State teams, and the club sports offer teams the opportunity to compete against teams from other colleges.

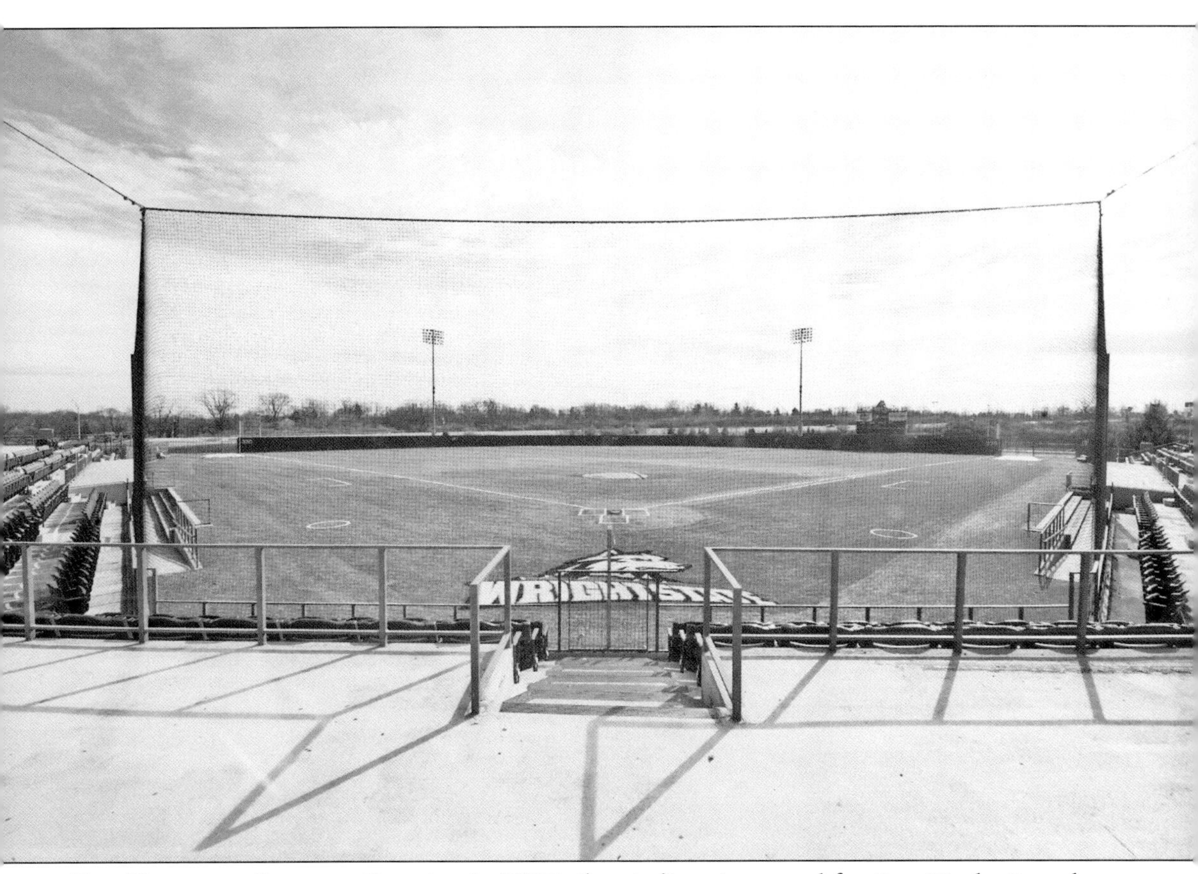

Ron Nischwitz Stadium. Opening in 2000, the stadium is named for Ron Nischwitz, who coached the Raiders baseball team for 30 years, and his son Greg, who played for Wright State for one season before losing his life in a construction accident in 1980. It has seating for 750, heated dugouts, and an athletic training facility. The stadium has hosted many games, including the 2006, 2009, and 2011 Horizon League Tournaments.

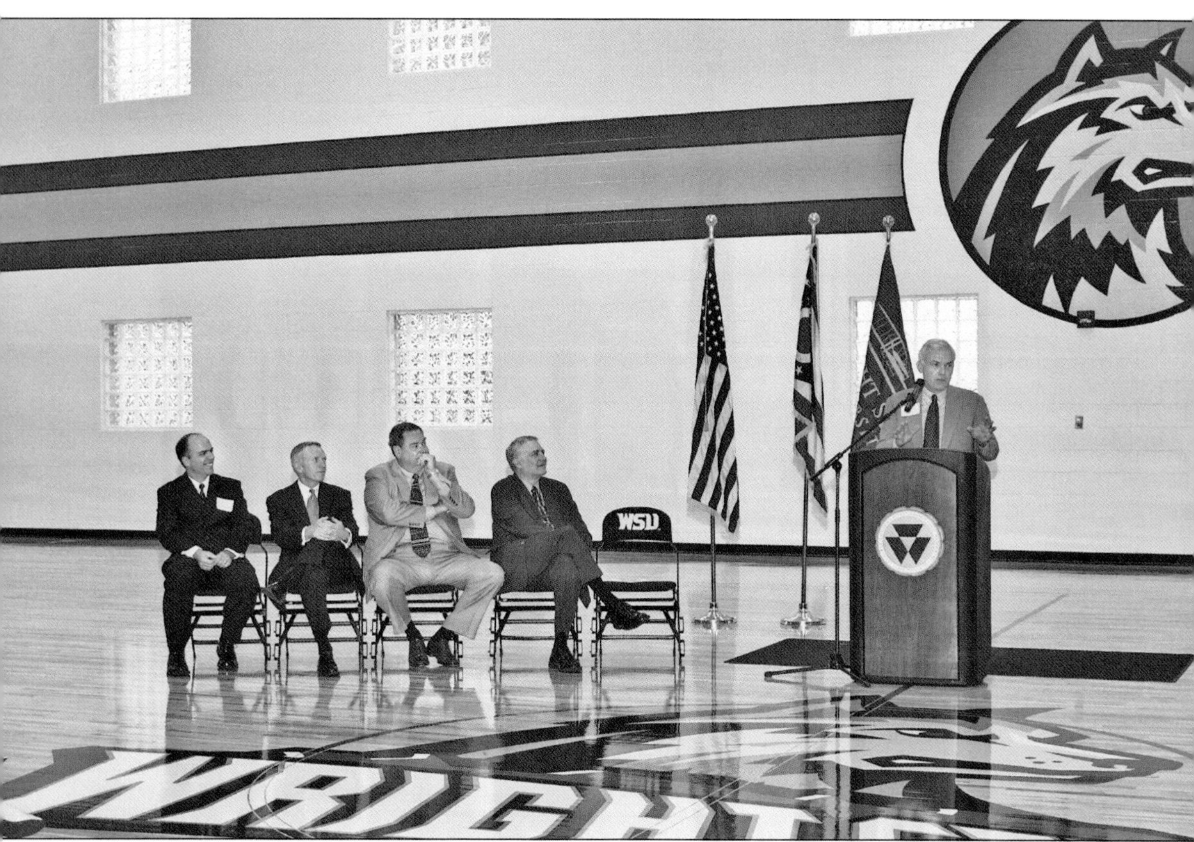

Setzer Pavilion/Mills Morgan Center. The Setzer Pavilion/Mills Morgan Center is a state-of-the-art training facility for student athletes. The privately funded facility features a full-length basketball court, weight room, locker rooms, audiovisual rooms, coaches' offices, and study lounge. The facility has been credited as a great recruiting tool for athletes and coaches. It also offers student athletes a place to study.

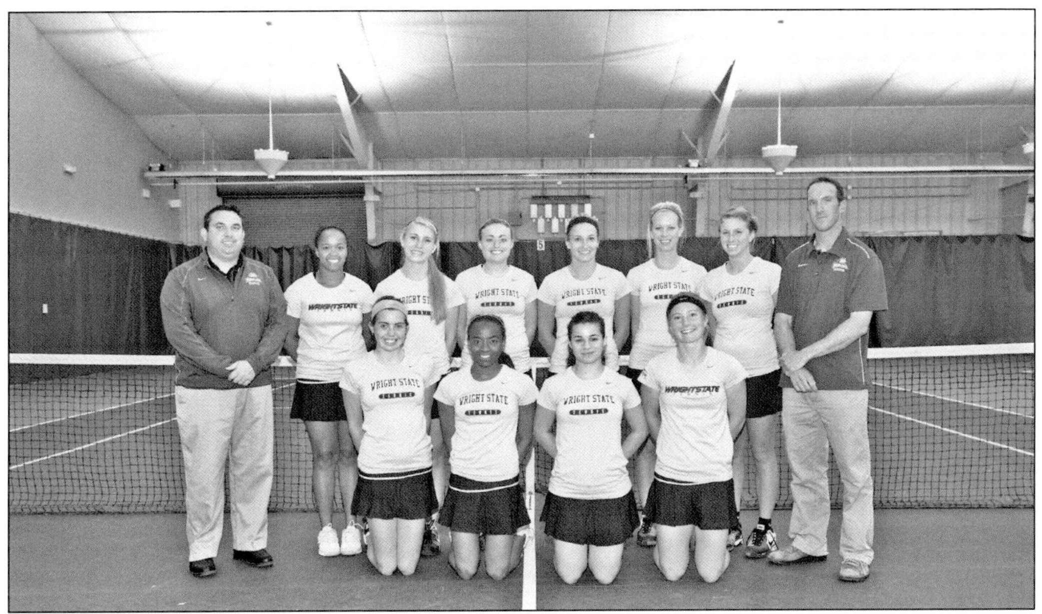
Wright State Tennis Courts. The Wright State University tennis courts are located right next to the Nischwitz Stadium. The tennis courts are home to the both the men's and women's teams. There are six courts and bleacher seating on the east side of the courts. Both the men's and women's teams have received recognition for individual and team achievements.

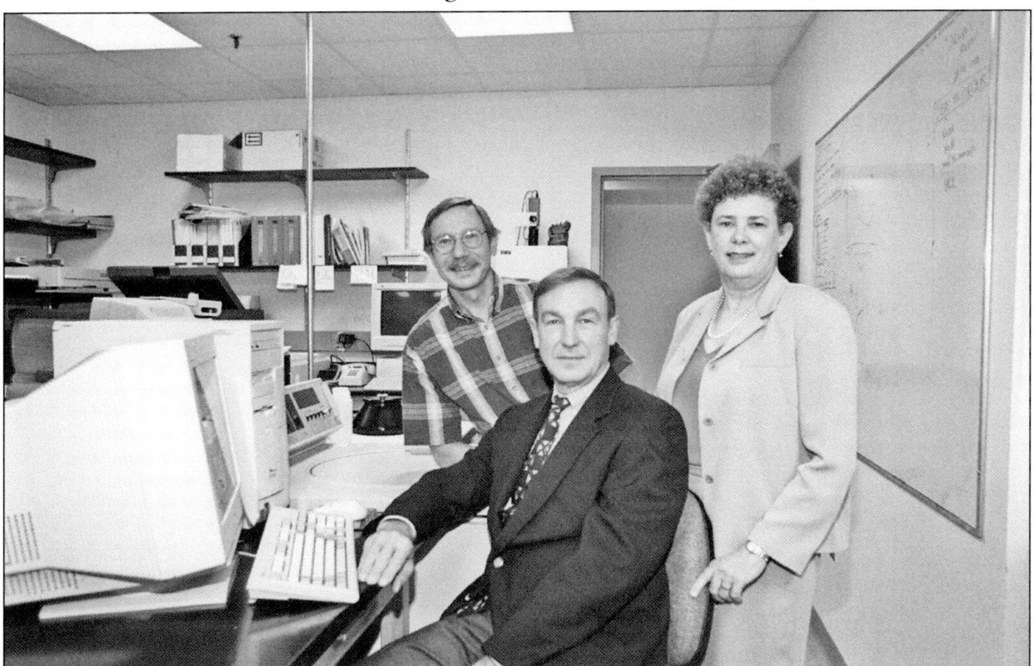
Gulf War Syndrome. As a result of the 1991 Persian Gulf War, many suffer from Gulf War syndrome. In 2000, the Boonshoft School of Medicine at Wright State University received a grant from the Department of Defense to study Gulf War syndrome in veterans. Researchers at the medical school have launched groundbreaking research that has uncovered the impacts of low-dose toxins.

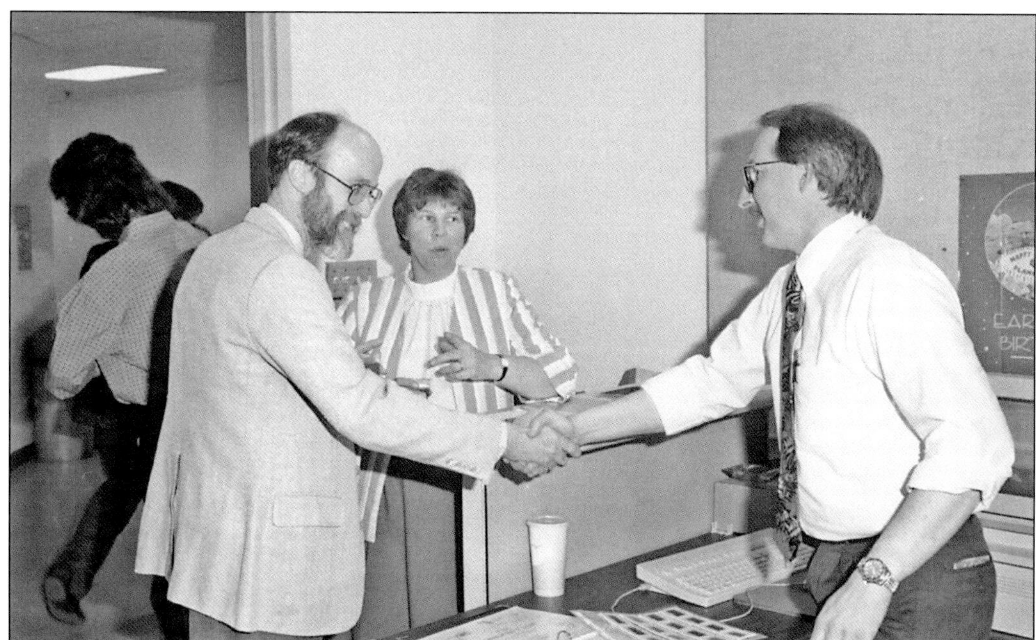

Center for Teaching and Learning. The Center for Teaching and Learning is housed in the basement of the Paul Laurence Dunbar Library. In order to enhance students' learning environments and experiences, the Center for Teaching and Learning provides various technologies and training. Through its collaboration with departments across campus, the center is able to promote teaching and learning techniques.

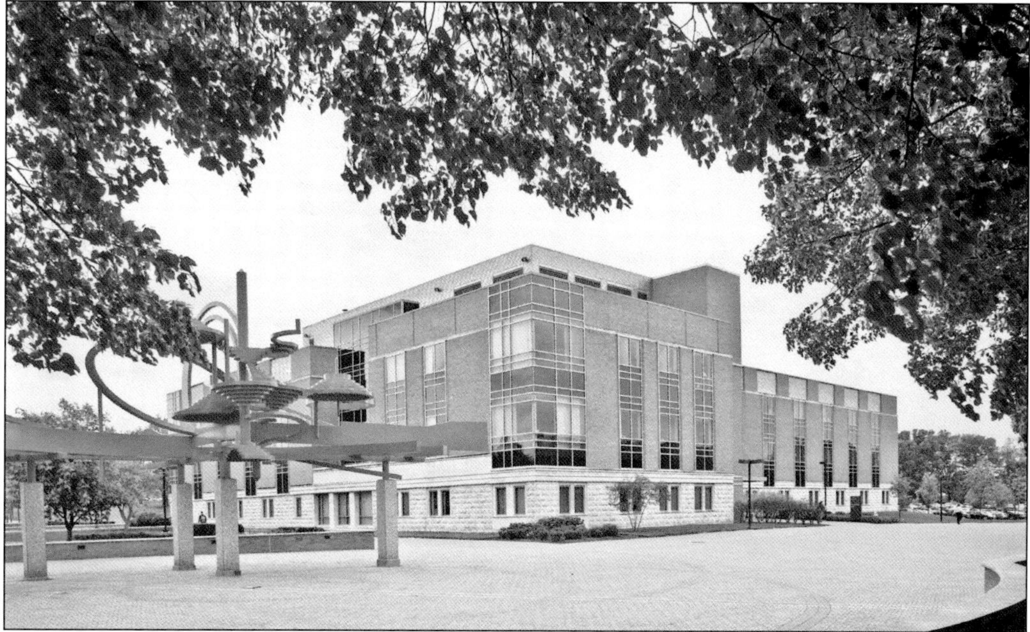

Wright State University Hall. University Hall contains many rooms, offices, and services, such as the Offices of the President and Provost, the College of Nursing and Health, Budget Planning and Research Analysis, Research and Sponsored Programs, Controller's Office, Business Services, Purchasing and Internal Audit, and Facilities Planning and Engineering.

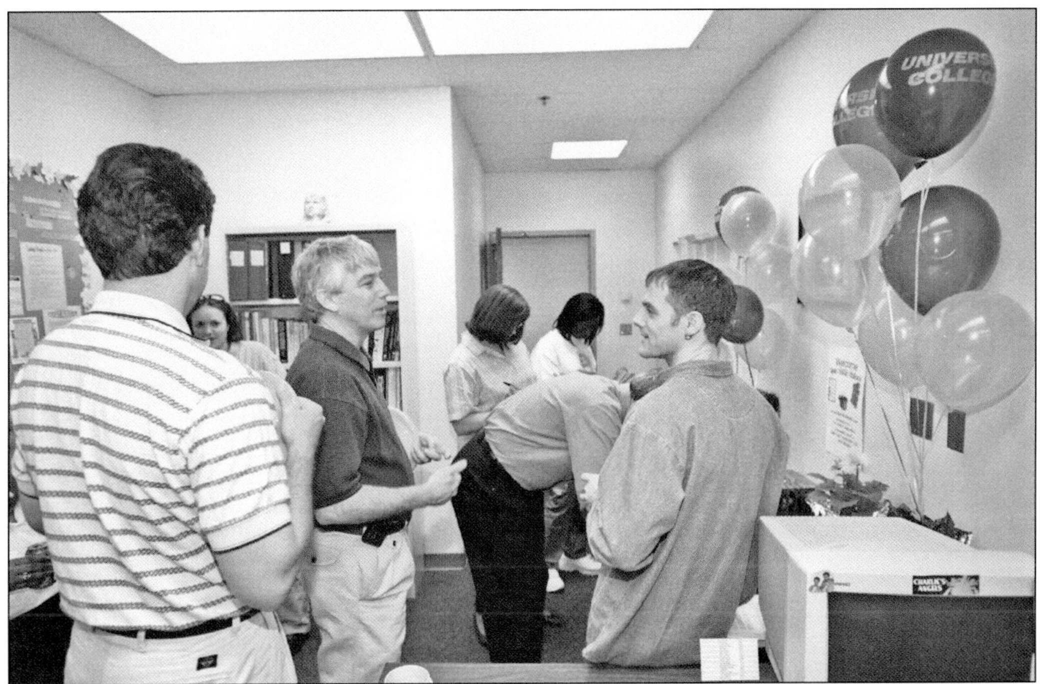

WRIGHT STATE UNIVERSITY COLLEGE. University College is the college within Wright State University that is dedicated to helping first-year students, transfer students, and adult students successfully transition into college and into their prospective majors in one of the degree-granting colleges within the university. Various services support students in meeting the necessary requirements to enter their chosen majors.

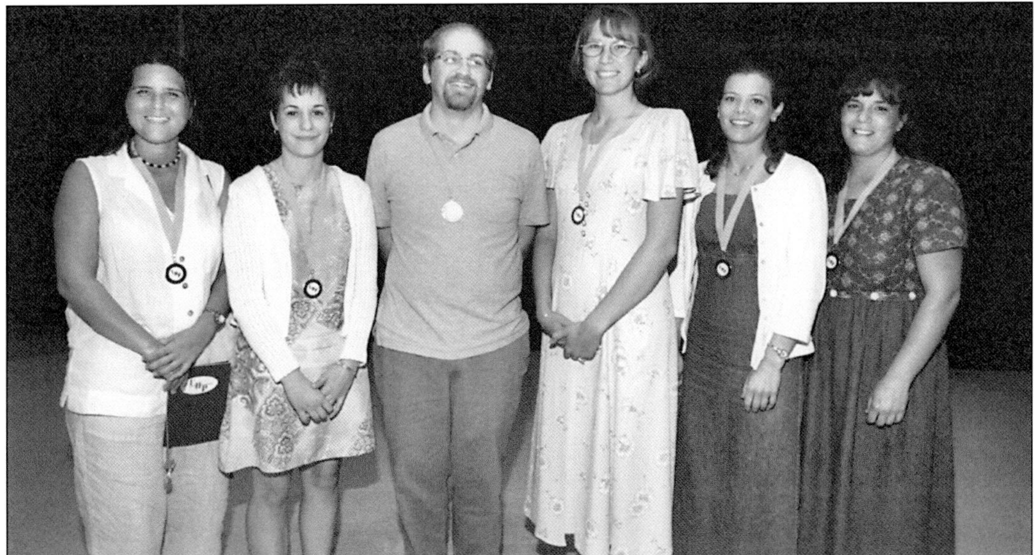

RESIDENTIAL HONORS COMMUNITY. A lot of first-year students choose to live in the Honors Community. This residence hall is a 384-bed facility arranged suite-style, with two double rooms with a shared bathroom. All of the floors are coeducational. The building features two electronic classrooms, a common kitchen, and a meeting space. It also holds a game room, a fitness center, Bridge Café, a convenience store, and a television lounge.

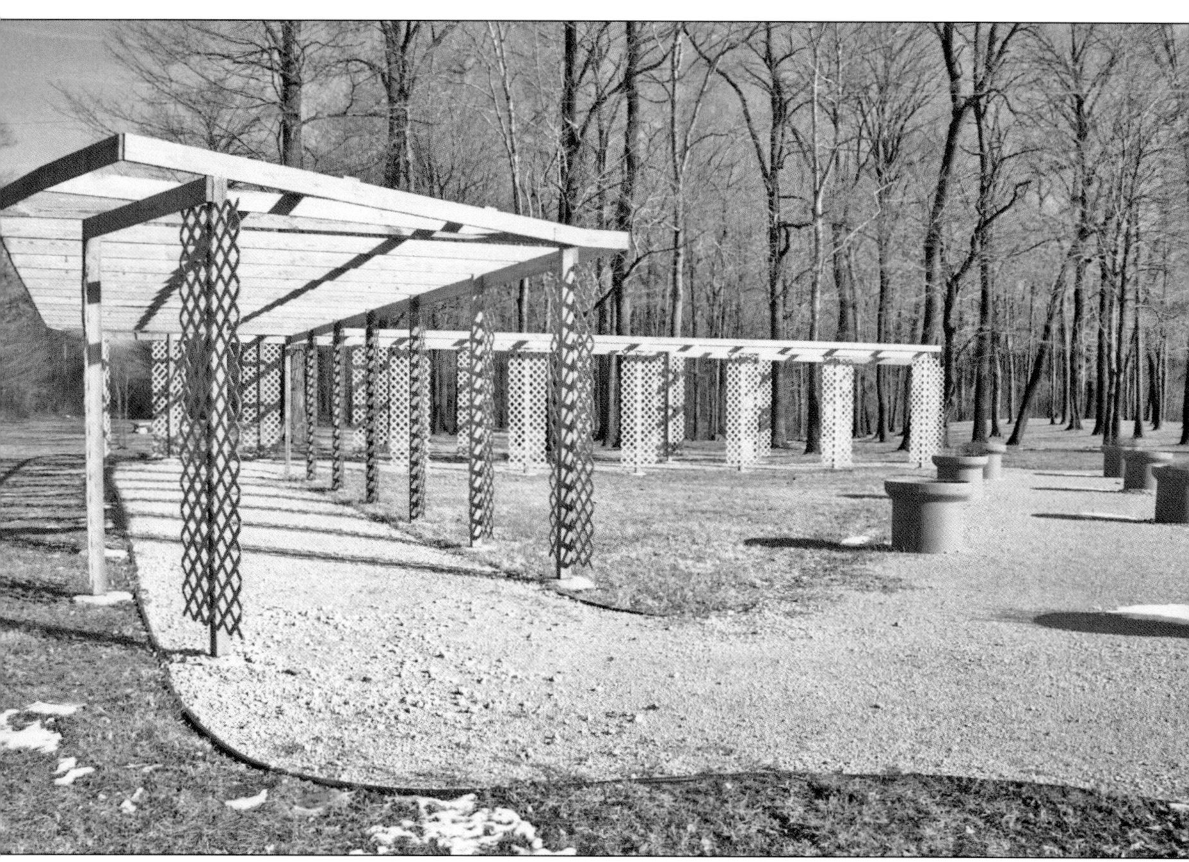

Garden for the Senses. The Clara E. Weisenborn Garden for the Senses is known to be a retreat in an environment of stress. Across from Allyn Hall, the garden has a pool that trickles around a stone mermaid sculpture. In the garden are numerous herbs and flowers, such as mint, rosemary, peonies, and dahlias. The various sights and scents lend the garden its name because the senses are stimulated.

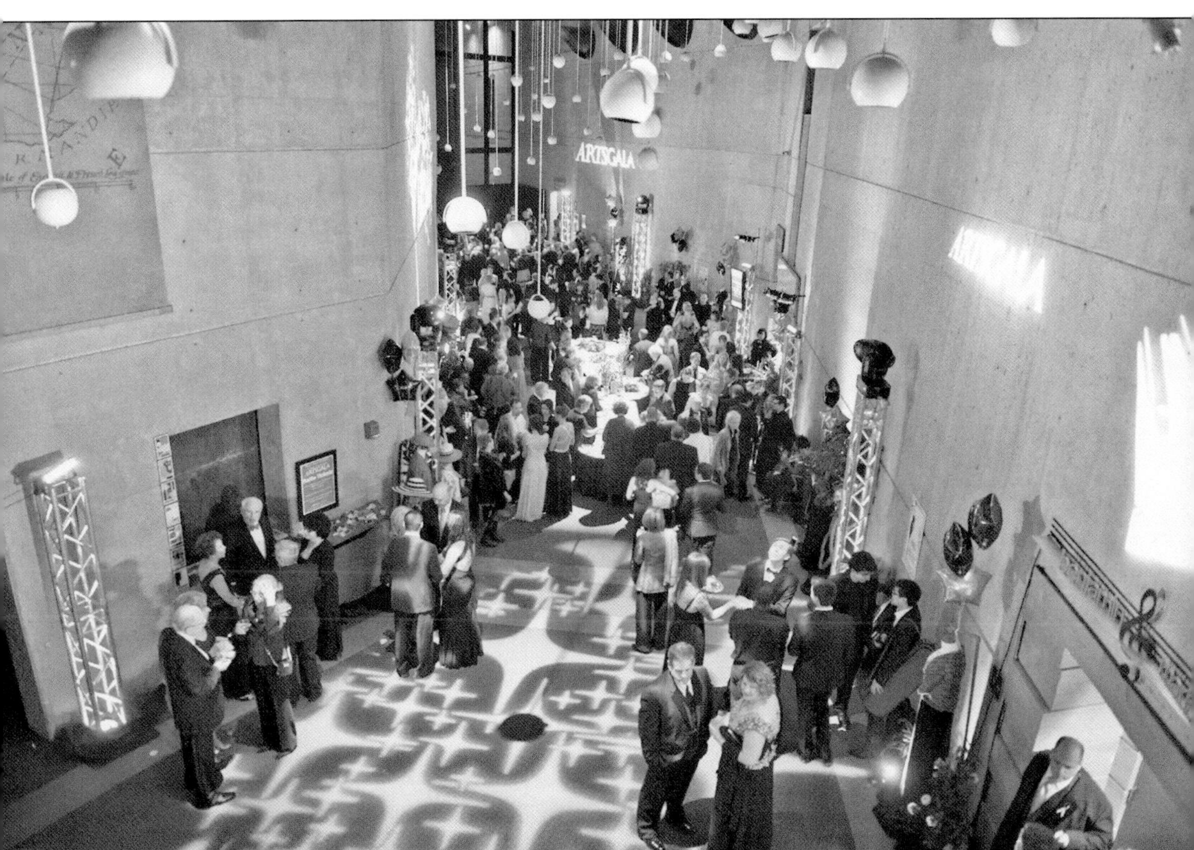

Annual ArtsGala Event. Wright State's ArtsGala is an annual event that showcases students' talents in art, music, theater, dance, and motion pictures. Known as the highlight of Wright State's arts season, ArtsGala has raised over $1.75 million in scholarship funding for arts students. This popular black-tie affair features a variety of entertainment, fine dining, and a silent auction for over 600 patrons every year.

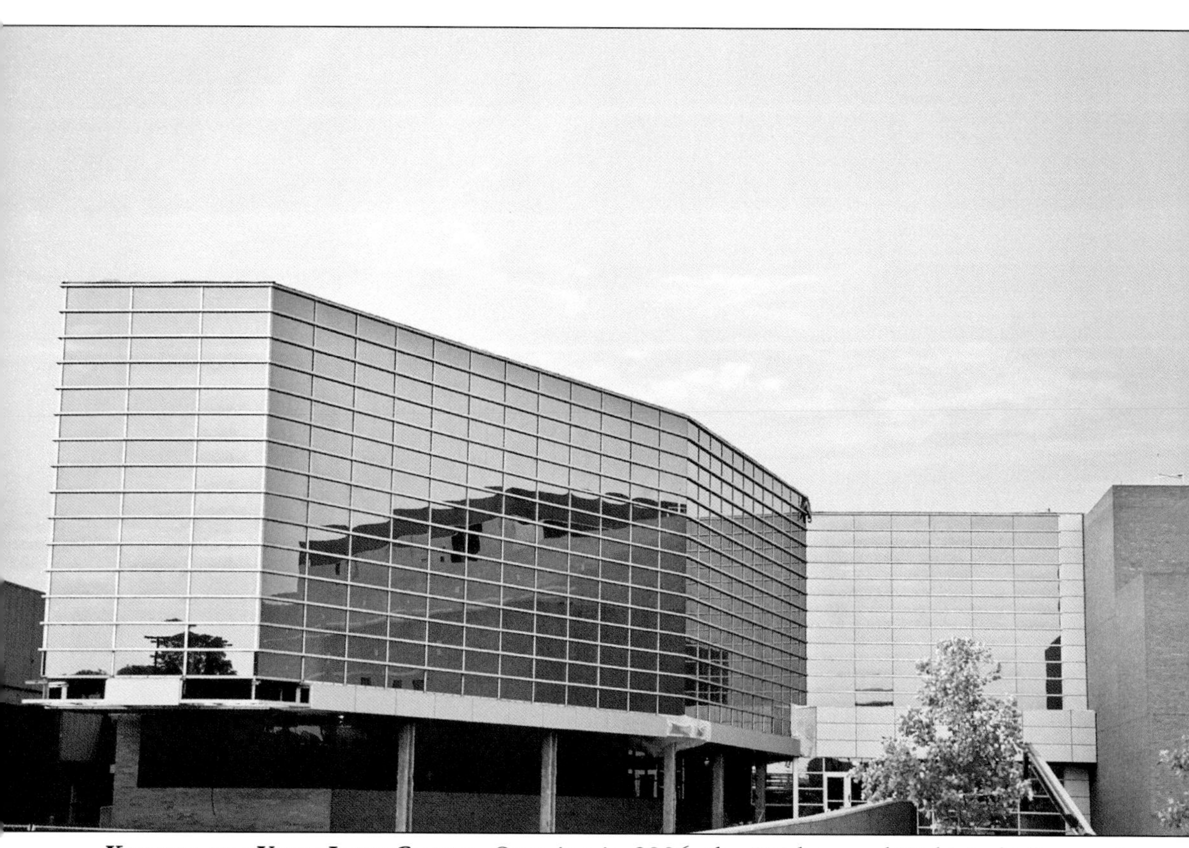

KRISHAN AND VICKY JOSHI CENTER. Opening in 2006, the Krishan and Vicki Joshi Research Center is a data technology innovation hub. The $10 million building is the headquarters for daytaOhio, as well as the Wright Center for Data, where research in bioinformatics takes place. In 2013, the center began electrical renovations that were completed in early 2014.

Six

Innovation and Excellence

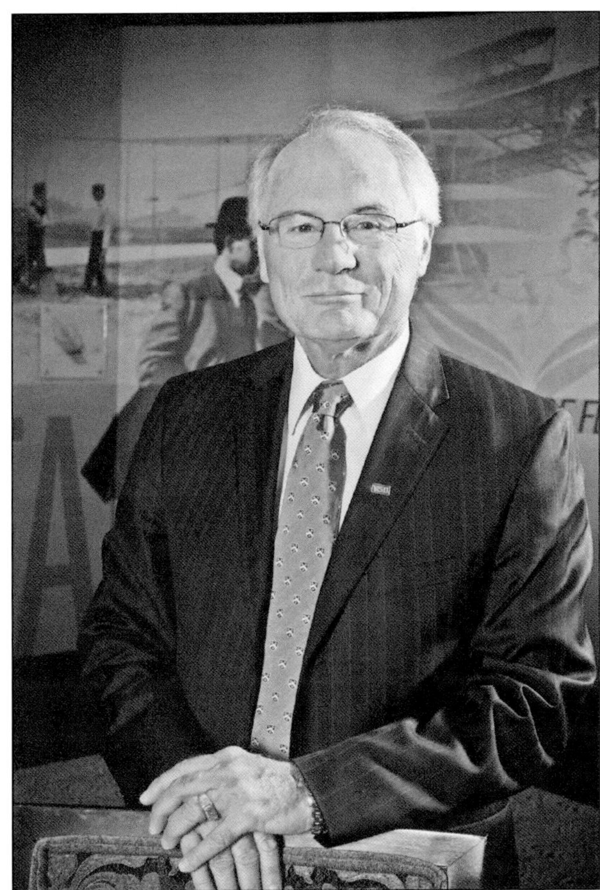

Dr. David Hopkins. In 2007, Dr. David Hopkins assumed office as the sixth president of Wright State University. Under his leadership, Wright State has emerged as an institution devoted to innovation and excellence. This is demonstrated in the university's centers of excellence. These centers collaborate with business, industry, and government, including areas of medical readiness, neuroscience, micro air vehicle research, and the visual and performing arts.

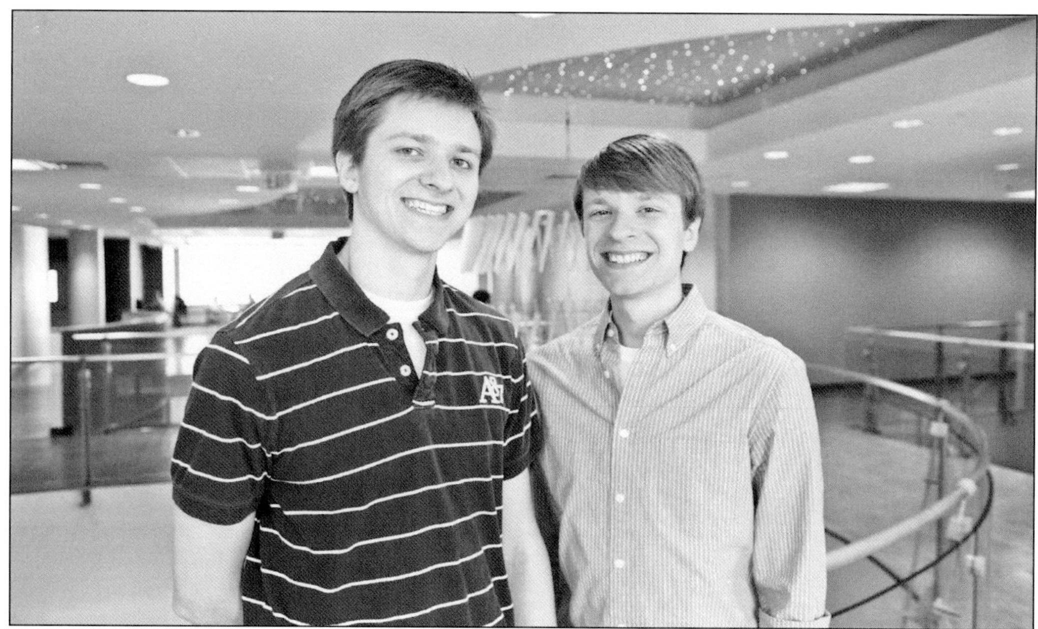

Valedictorian and Salutatorian Enrollment. Wright State has experienced an increase in enrollment numbers from high school valedictorians and salutatorians—from 301 in 2013 to 318 in 2014 and 346 in 2015. The Honors Program at Wright State University has roughly 1,200 students, a majority of whom were high school valedictorians or salutatorians.

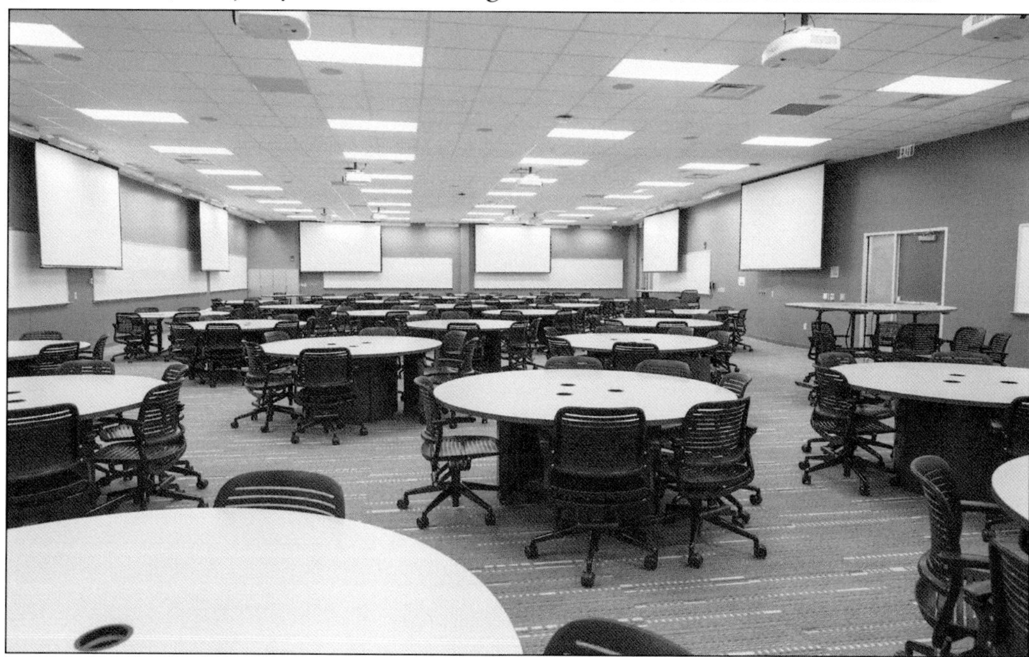

First-Generation Students. First-generation students make up approximately a third of the Wright State University undergraduate student body. As a way to help make the transition from high school to college as smooth as possible, the university offers peer mentoring programs and student success services. The Student Success Center opened in 2015. The center is equipped with classrooms, technologies, and academic support services.

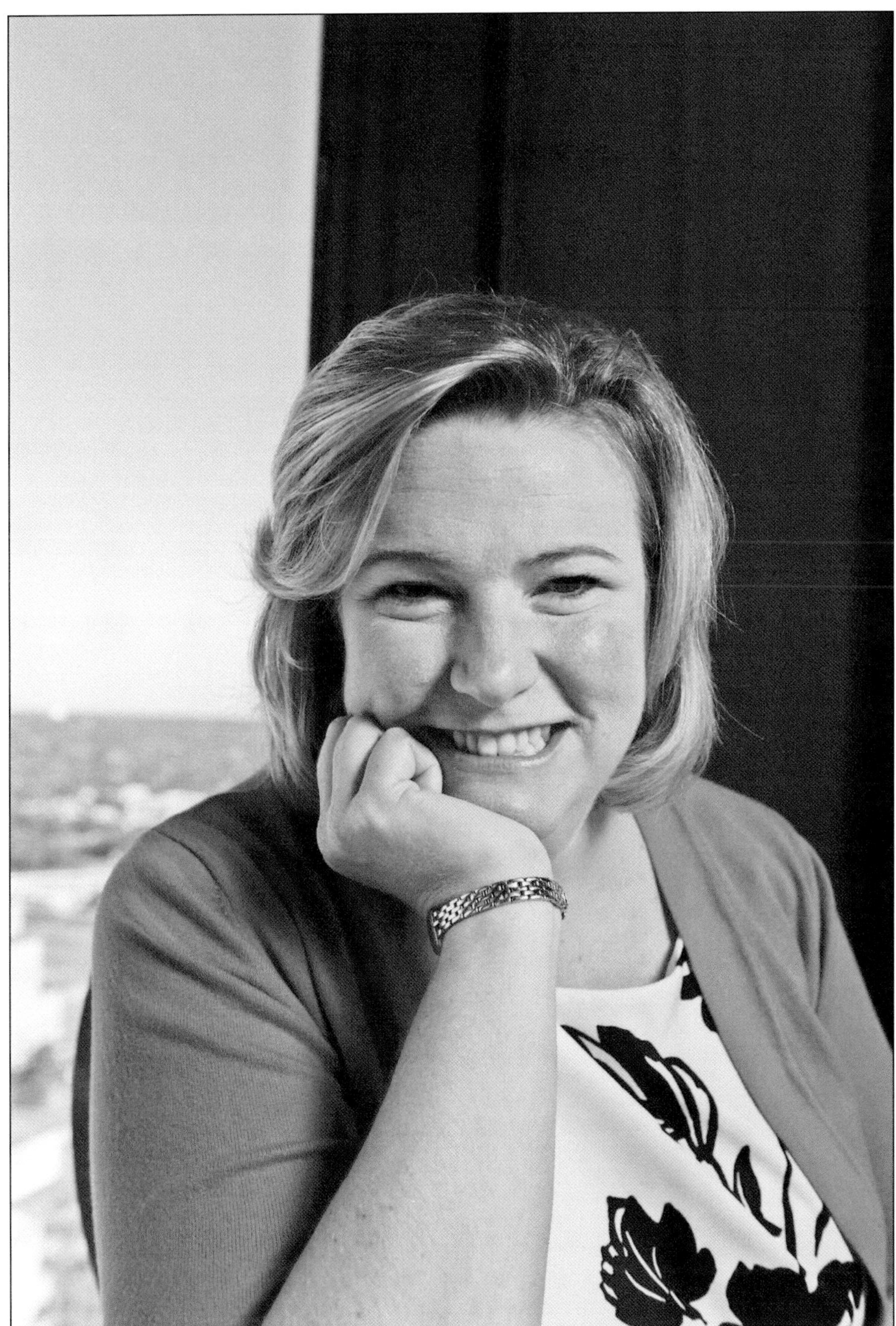

NOTABLE UNIVERSITY ALUMNI. Wright State University alumni have gone on to achieve some remarkable things in numerous fields and industries such as politics, sports, music, the military, and business. Notable university alumni include mayor of Dayton Nan Whaley (pictured), singer Nicole Scherzinger, vice president of operations at FedEx Doug Cook, NASA astronaut Michael Barratt, and retired US Navy rear admiral Deborah Loewer.

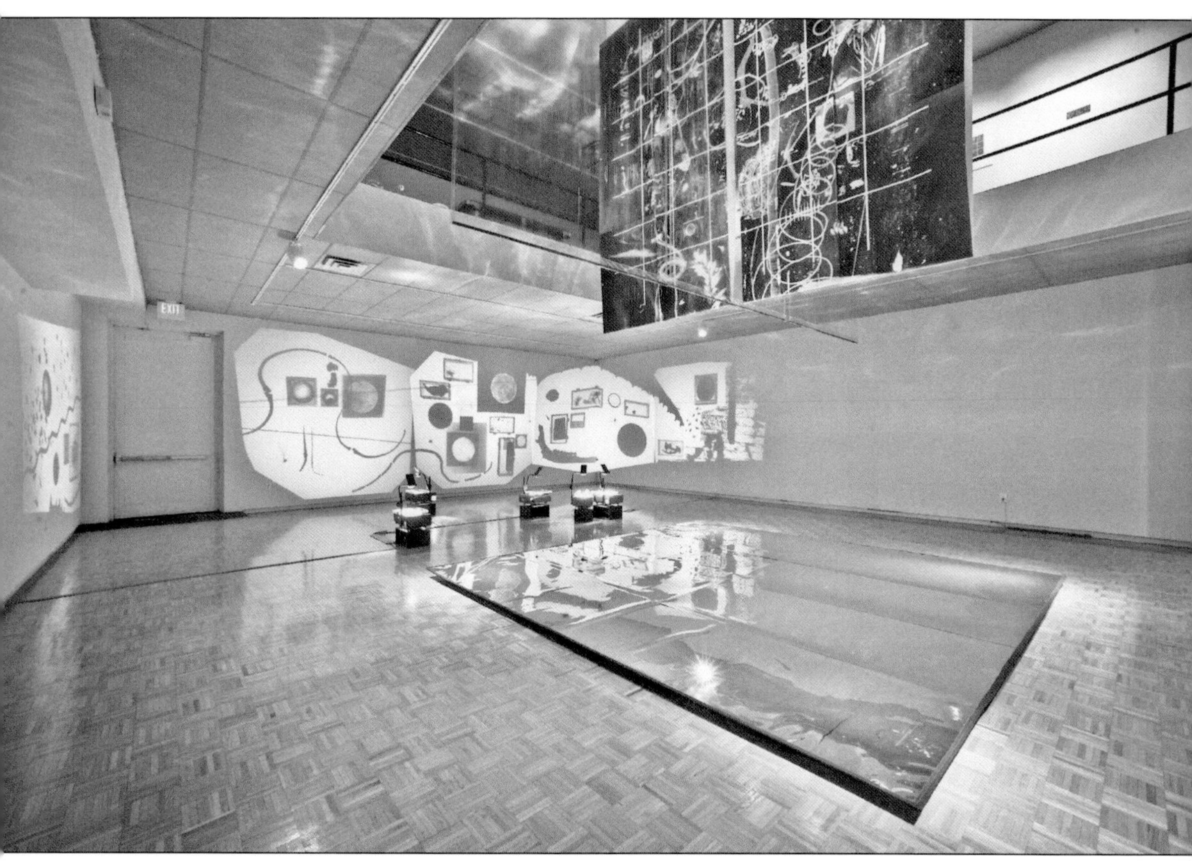

Robert and Elaine Stein Galleries. The Robert and Elaine Stein Galleries bridge the educational and cultural gap in the area by exhibiting contemporary art. The galleries' outreach programs bring awareness of the artworks as well as lectures and workshops to inform and educate the community.

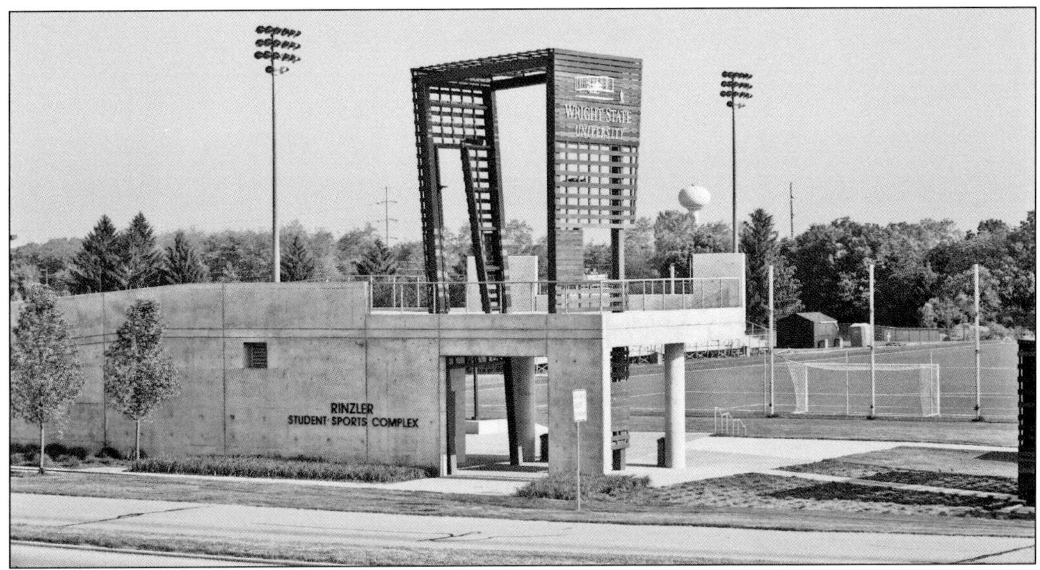

Rinzler Student Sports Complex. The Rinzler Student Sports Complex is a new facility that includes the Alumni Field. It is home to the men's and women's soccer teams. The Mulhollan Field is use for intramural sports. The complex also consists of team rooms, concession stands, and restrooms. The state-of-the-art turf and lights allow for game play during any type of weather, day or night.

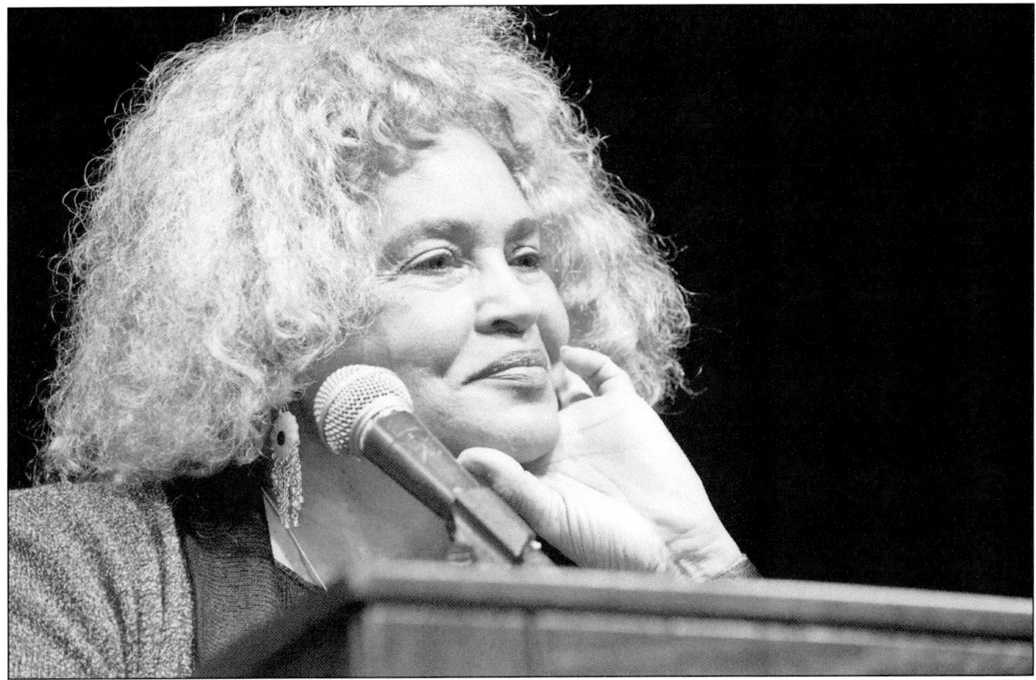

Dayton Council on World Affairs. The Dayton Council on World Affairs (DOWA) connects the greater Miami Valley with international people to dialogue on human rights, security, terrorism, and peace initiatives. Collaborating with the University Center for International Education, DOWA is made up of a diverse group of students, professors, lawyers, business leaders, and community leaders. Pictured is Charlayne Hunter-Gault.

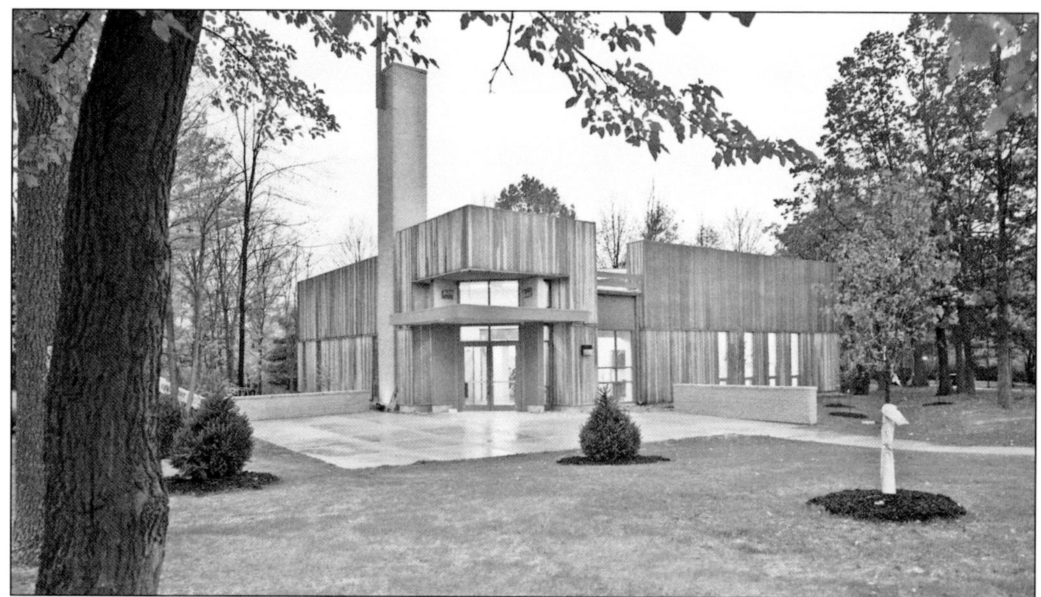

Campus Ministry Religious Center. The Wright State University community is tolerant of all religious affiliations. Owned by the Roman Catholic Church, the Campus Ministry Center center provides programming for students interested in religion and spirituality. Not only does the center offer programming for Catholic students, faculty, and staff, but other religious organizations also use the facility for activities.

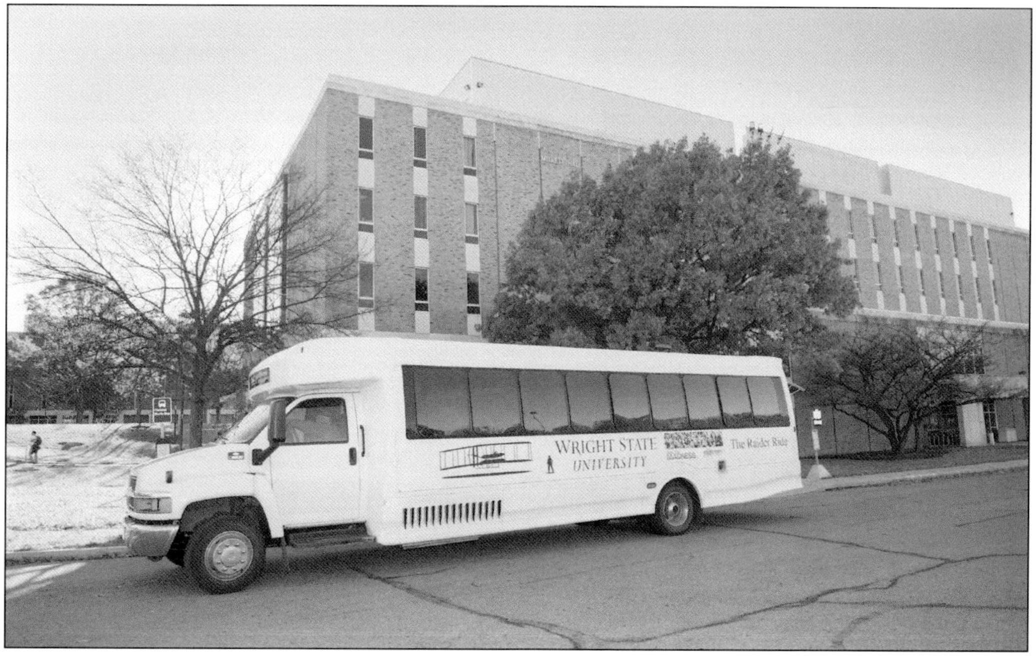

Residential and Commuter Campus Shuttle. The campus shuttle provides transportation to and from Raider Lot 20, all of the residential communities, the Nutter Center Lot 8, and the McLin Gymnasium during the school year. All of the campus shuttles are wheelchair-accessible. The shuttles run all day into the evening. When the shuttle stops running at night, students are able to call for a safety escort van provided by the Wright State Police Department.

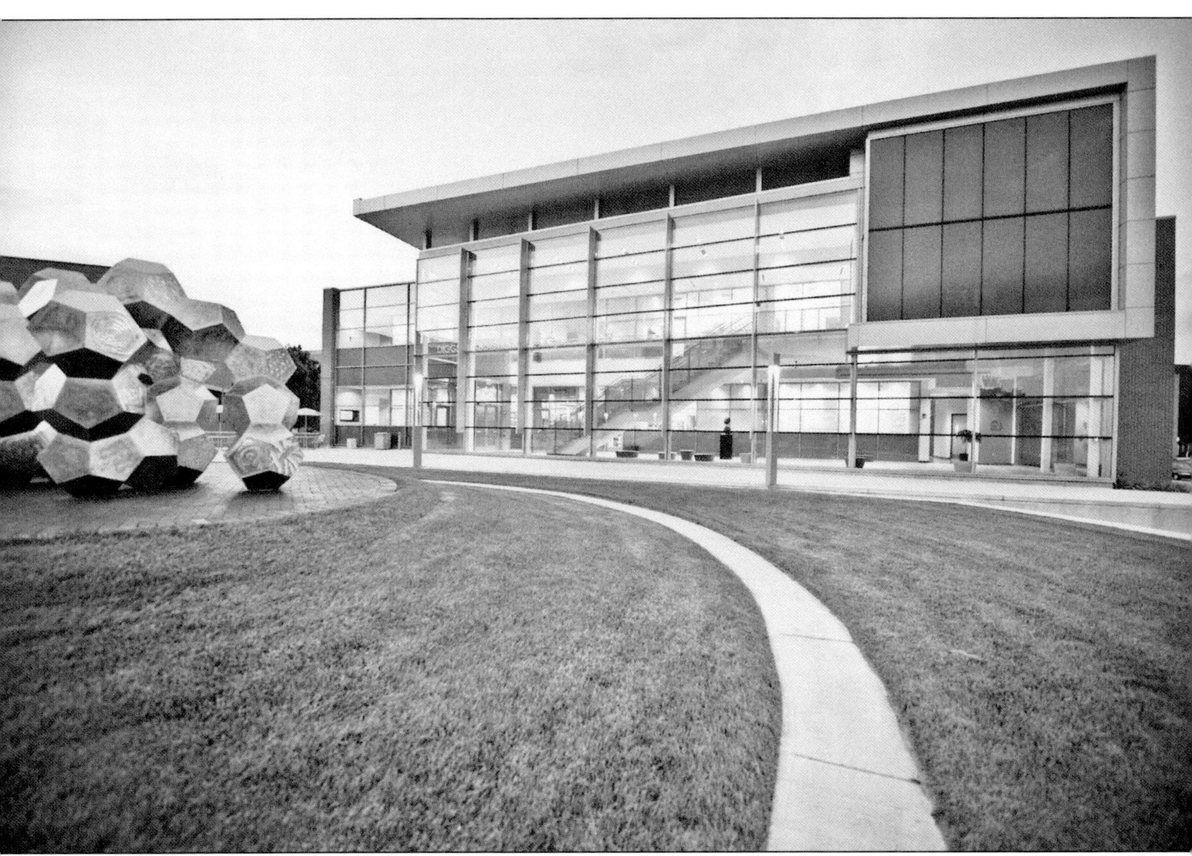

MATTHEW O. DIGGS III LABORATORY. The Matthew O. Diggs III Laboratory for Life Science Research was funded in part by a gift from former trustee Matthew Diggs Jr. and his wife, Nancy. The building is named in memory of their son. Opening in 2007, the building is one of Ohio's first green-designed research laboratories. Over 80 researchers train master's and doctoral students in molecular genetics, molecular biology, biochemistry, and cell biology.

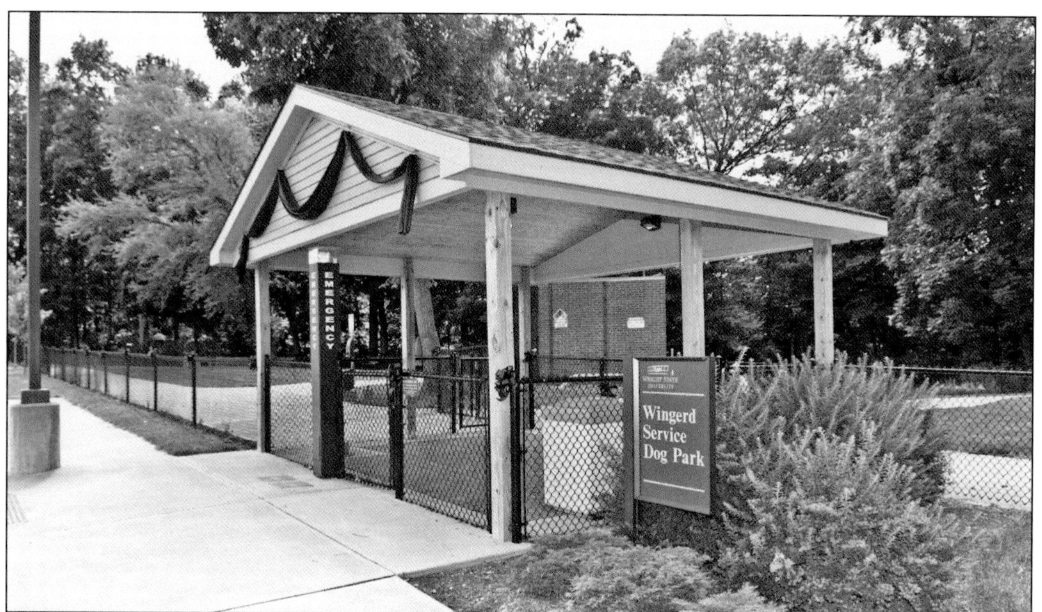

Wingerd Dog Park. Wright State University was the first university in the nation to create a dog park especially for service dogs on campus. The dog park officially opened in 2008. The park includes benches, water for dogs, shady areas for dogs and their owners, and accessible walkways for wheelchair access. Samantha Laux, who died in 2012, and the Laux family were the driving forces behind the park's creation.

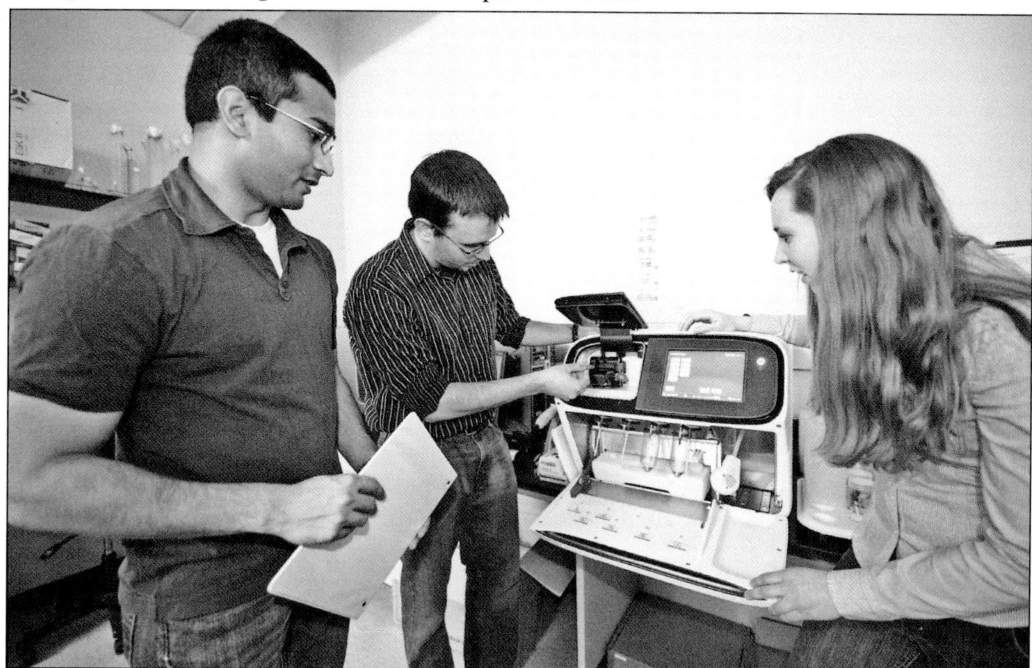

Biomedical, Industrial, and Human Factors Engineering. The Department of Biomedical, Industrial, and Human Factors Engineering focuses on improving complex human technical systems. The department is working to make it to the national stage, where it will be known for its cutting-edge research in improving systems in various areas of engineering.

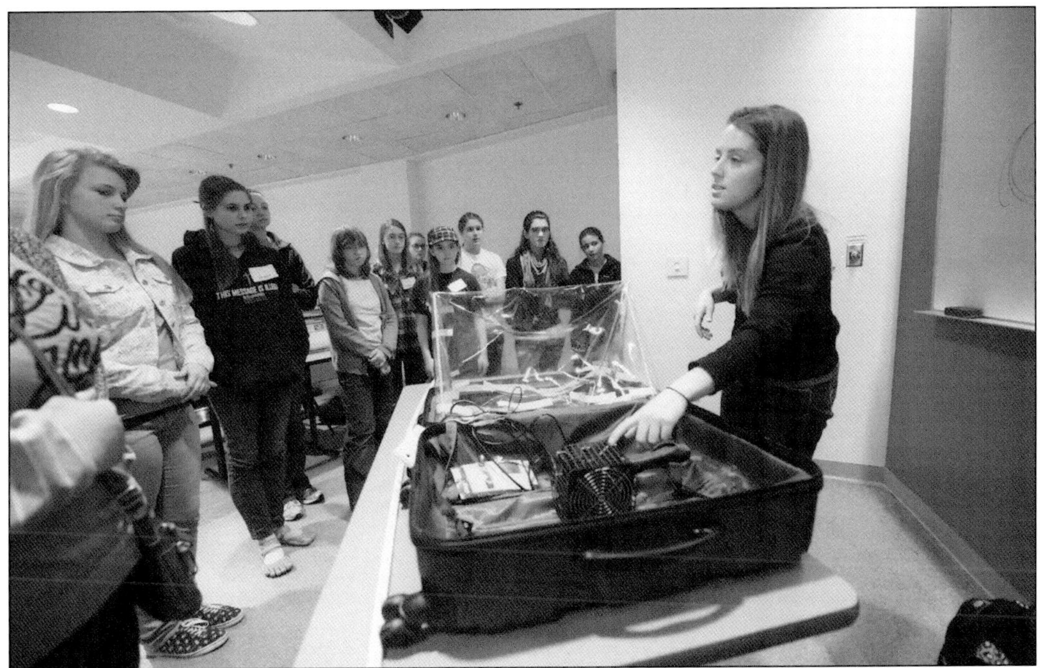

New Engineering Model. The Wright State Model for Engineering Mathematics Education is working to improve the numbers of those entering and graduating from engineering disciplines in Dayton, Ohio, and beyond the region. This model is currently being adopted nationwide, resulting in achieving its goal of improving student success in the field of engineering.

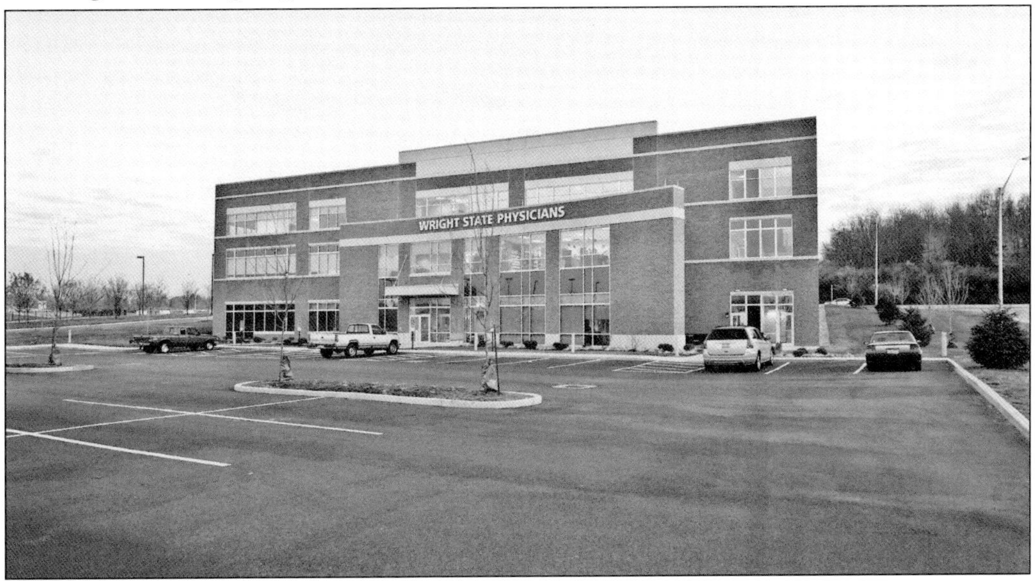

Wright State Physicians. Wright State Physicians is the region's largest multispecialty group. It is home to physicians in the practices of dermatology, family medicine, geriatric medicine, orthopedic surgery, sports medicine and rehabilitation, and women's health. To better serve patients, it includes Wright Health Pharmacy and an MRI facility operated by Miami Valley Hospital. The facility offers a central site for medical students to gain clinical expertise and for faculty to conduct translational research.

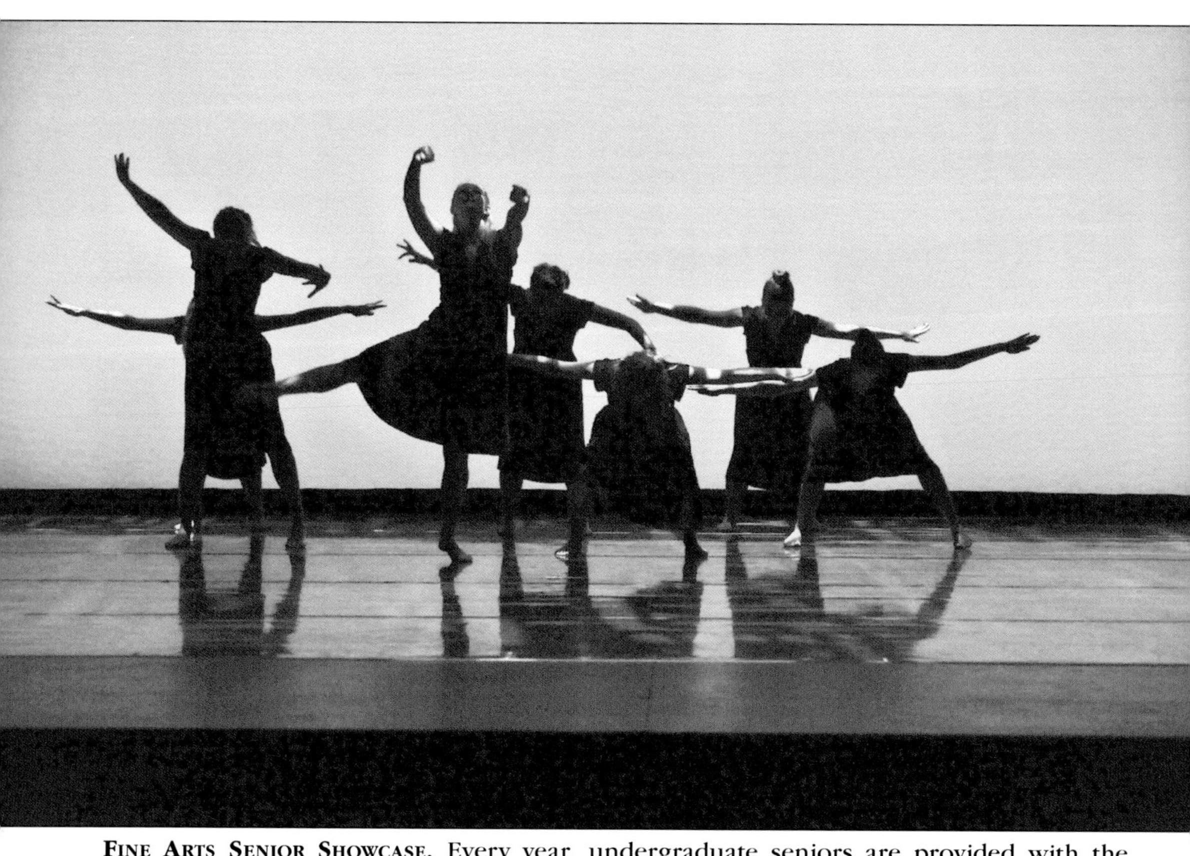

Fine Arts Senior Showcase. Every year, undergraduate seniors are provided with the opportunity to showcase their many talents in highly anticipated events such as the Big Lens Film Festival, the Senior Dance Concert, the Senior Art Show, and the musical theater Senior Showcase in New York City, which includes intensive career workshops with renowned casting agents and creative talent.

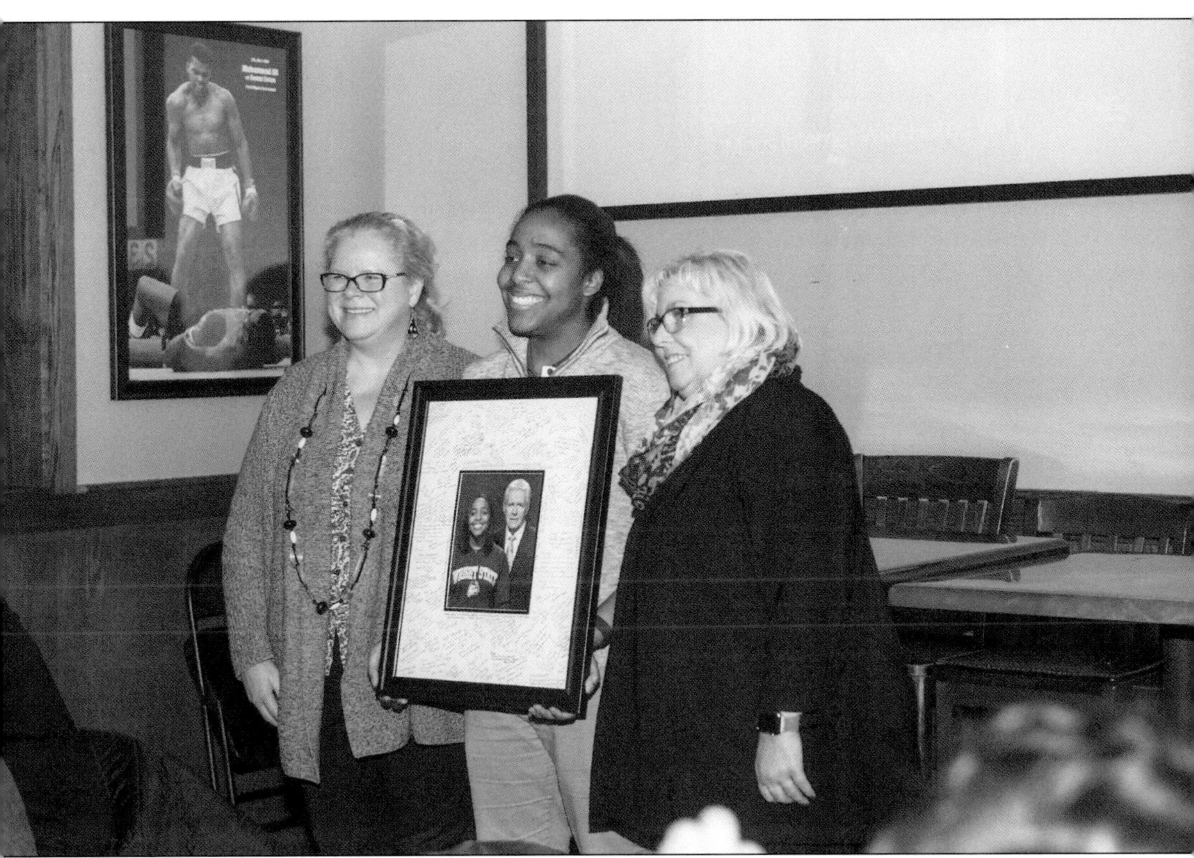

Raiders on the Big Stage. Wright State University students and alumni are no strangers to the spotlight. Emily Bingham (center) won a game of *Jeopardy!* and advanced to the semifinals in the College Tournament in 2016. She is pictured with the dean of the College of Liberal Arts, Kristin Sobolik (left), and an unidentified woman. Alumna Alexis Gomez appeared on *American Idol* in 2015 and made it to the top 24.

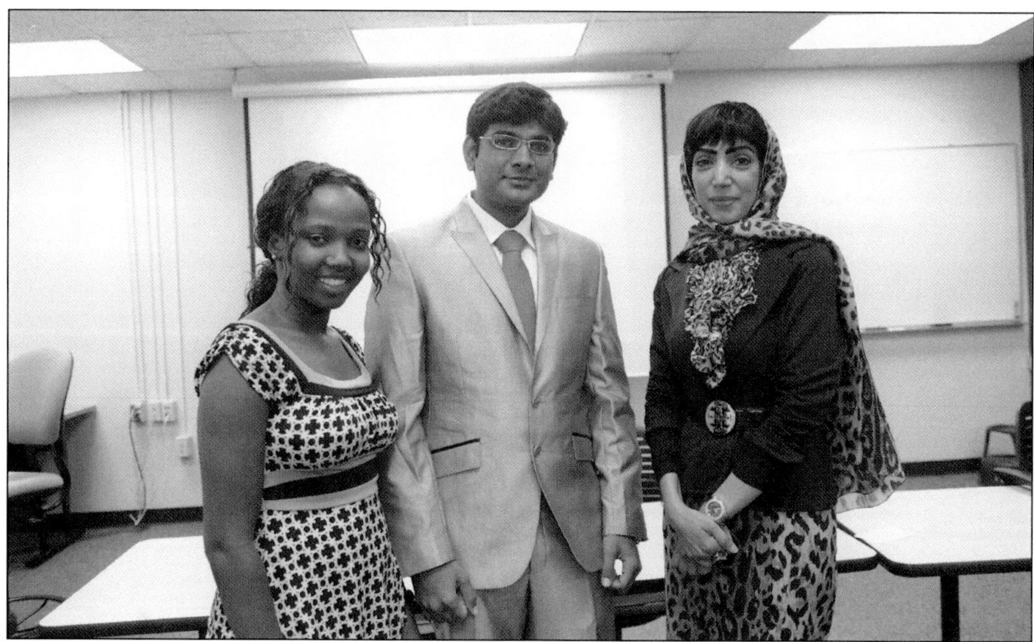

International Student Enrollment. In recent years, Wright State has seen a surge in international student enrollment, which represents nearly 10 percent of the student population. During 2015's fall semester, 1,879 students from 66 different countries chose Wright State as degree-seeking or exchange students, while the University Center for International Education organized 16 trips, with more than 250 students, to China, Costa Rica, Germany, Japan, Taiwan, Tanzania, France, Spain, and other countries.

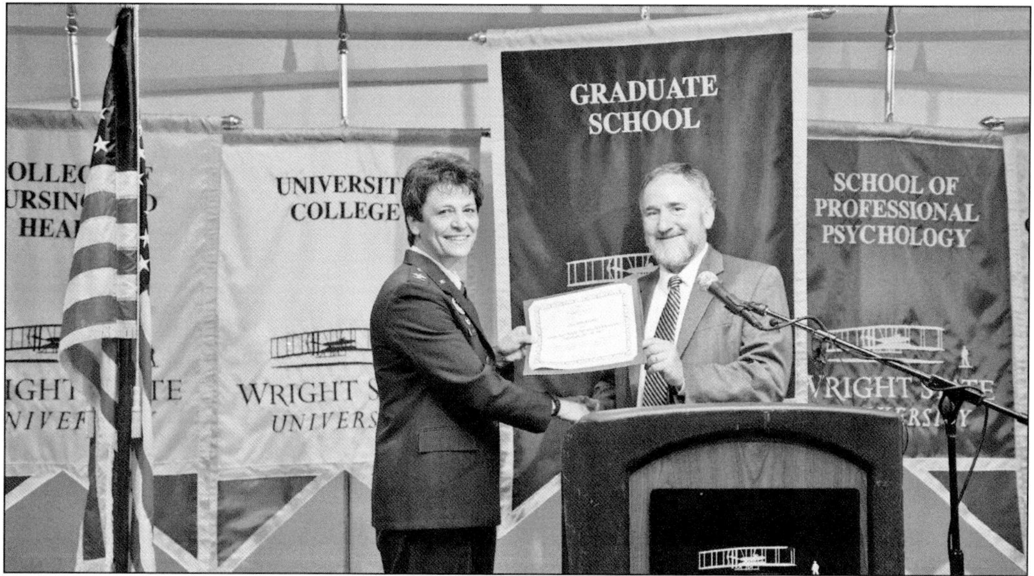

Military-Friendly Campus. Wright State University has been recognized as a military-friendly school six years in a row (2011–2016) by *G.I Jobs* and *Military Advanced Education.* It is a number one choice for veterans and active-duty military personnel. The university created and opened the Veteran and Military Center in 2014. The center offers academic and financial support for veterans and active-duty personnel.

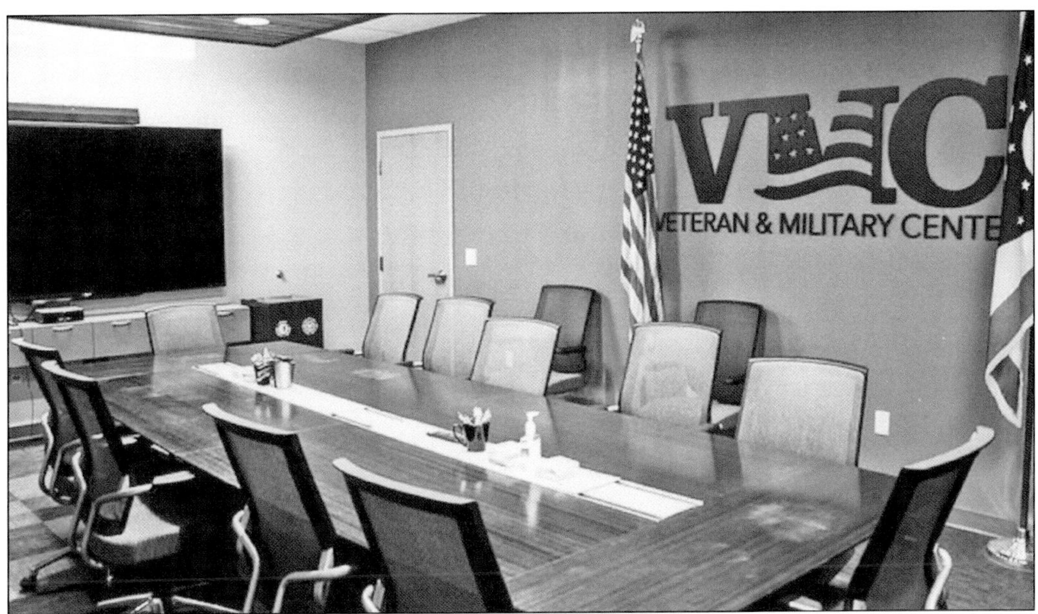

Veteran and Military Center. The Veteran and Military Center opened its doors in 2013 to offer support to students as they make the transition from the military to college. This support is provided through academic and financial help but also in courses that are only available to veterans and active-duty personnel.

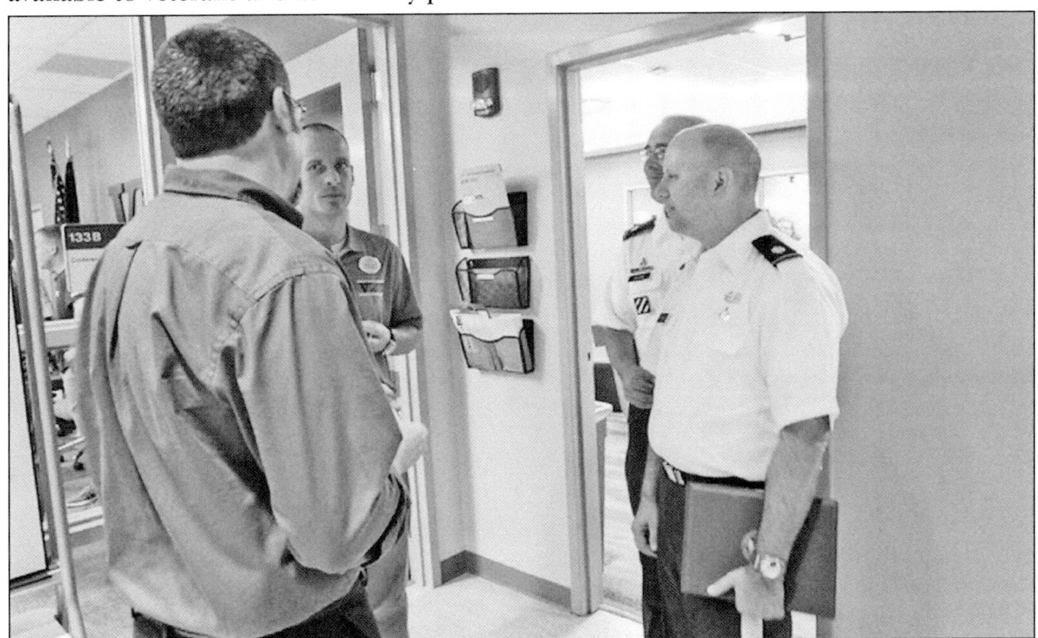

Military-Only Classes. As veterans and active-duty civilians transition into college, Wright State University offers military-only classes, which provide such individuals with safe spaces to adjust from combat situations in a new environment. These classes are made possible through the collaboration of the Veteran and Military-Connected Student Committee and faculty members such as Larry James, a retired army colonel now in the School of Professional Psychology.

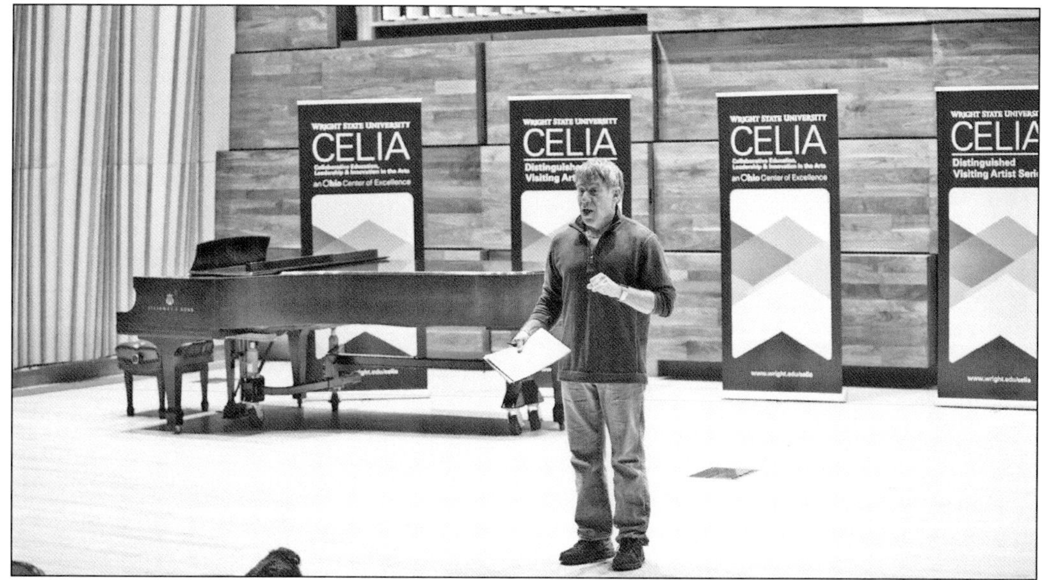

Collaboration, Education, Leadership, Innovation in the Arts. The Collaboration, Education, Leadership, and Innovation in the Arts (CELIA) initiative was created through the efforts of various campus departments to help enrich the arts community in the greater Dayton region. To bring awareness to the program and promote civic engagement, the Distinguished Visiting Artist Series was created to host world-renowned artists through performances, lectures, and exhibits.

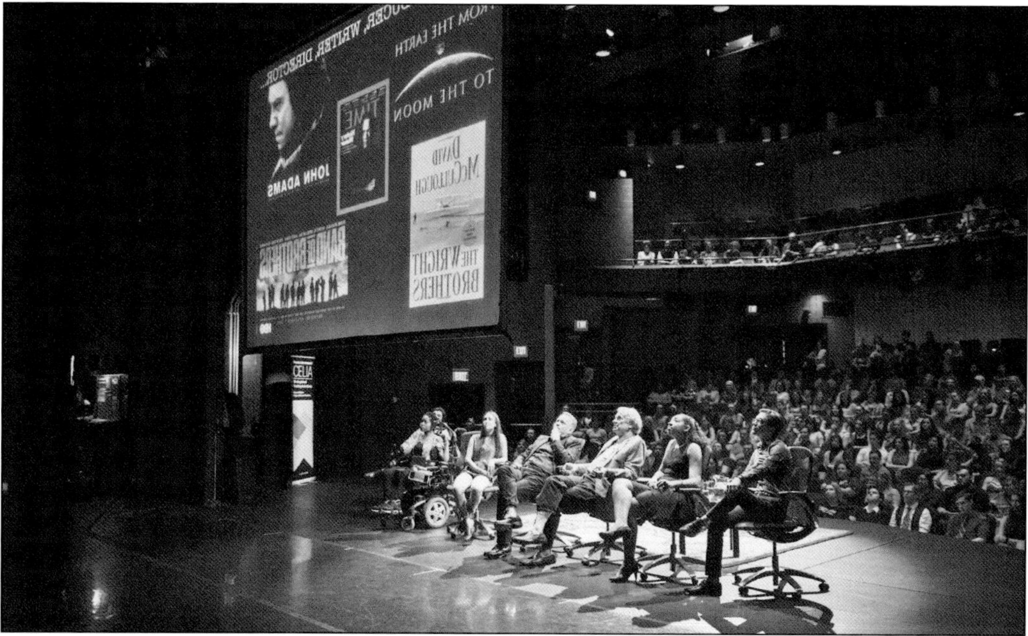

Excelling in Performing Arts. Wright State University students, faculty, and alumni are engaging in the performing arts worldwide, working in Hollywood and on Broadway. Actor Tom Hanks has a solid relationship with the Wright State University community, and in 2016, he dedicated the Tom Hanks Center for Motion Pictures. Also, he has a scholarship in his name for performing arts students.

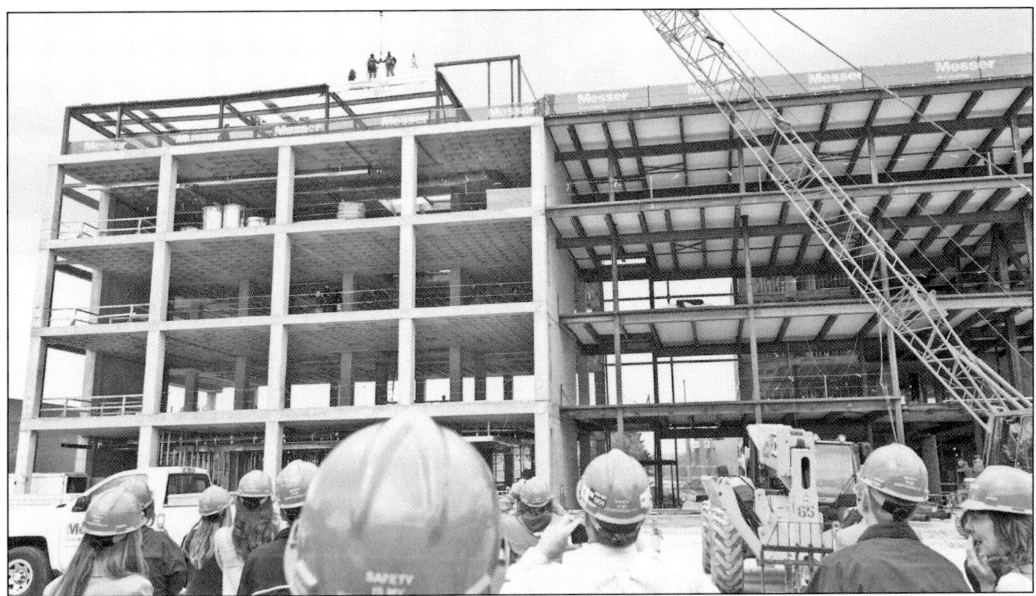

Neuroscience Engineering Collaboration Building. The Neuroscience Engineering Collaboration Building opened on April 16, 2015. The building is a result of the collaborative efforts by the university and Premier Health Neuroscience Institute to signify a partnership that promotes unity in the medical field in Dayton. Neuroscientists at the university's school of medicine and the Premier Health Neuroscience Institute are on the cutting edge of medical research.

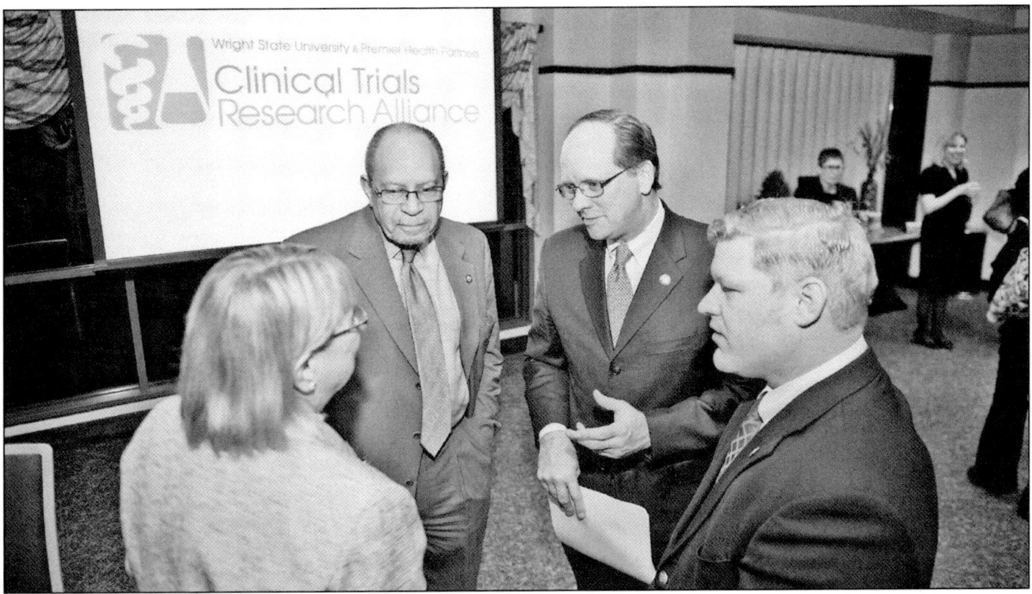

Clinical Trials Research Alliance. Wright State University and Premier Health Clinical Trials Research Alliance is a public-private initiative that combines the Boonshoft School of Medicine and Premier Health. This alliance fosters growth in the ability to offer clinical trials to patients and support research opportunities for clinicians and researchers. The Clinical Trials Research Alliance provides students with the opportunity to participate in research discoveries while helping physicians treat illnesses through clinical studies and trials.

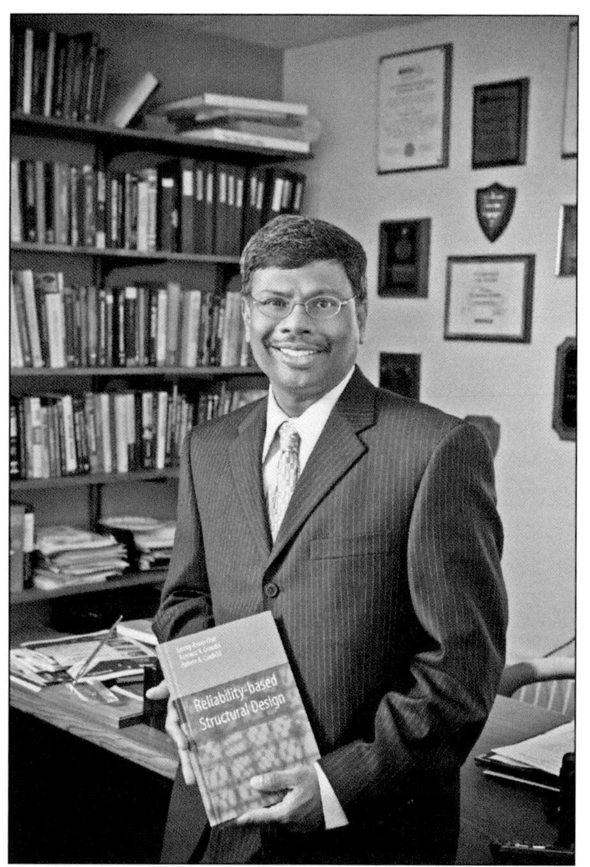

Center of Excellence for Product Reliability and Optimization. The Center of Excellence for Product Reliability and Optimization (CEPRO) is a collaborative effort between multiple departments across campus as well as a variety of companies around Dayton to produce highly efficient technologies through computation, modeling, and optimization. The results of CEPRO can be seen in projects such as laser peening, metal rolling processes, and aircraft designs.

Micro Air Vehicle Research. The Center of Excellence for Micro Air Vehicle is working to develop small, agile air vehicles with high intelligence capable of staying in the air for up to 20 minutes. Researchers state that these air vehicles may be of use in a nuclear crisis by specifically targeting spikes in radiation.

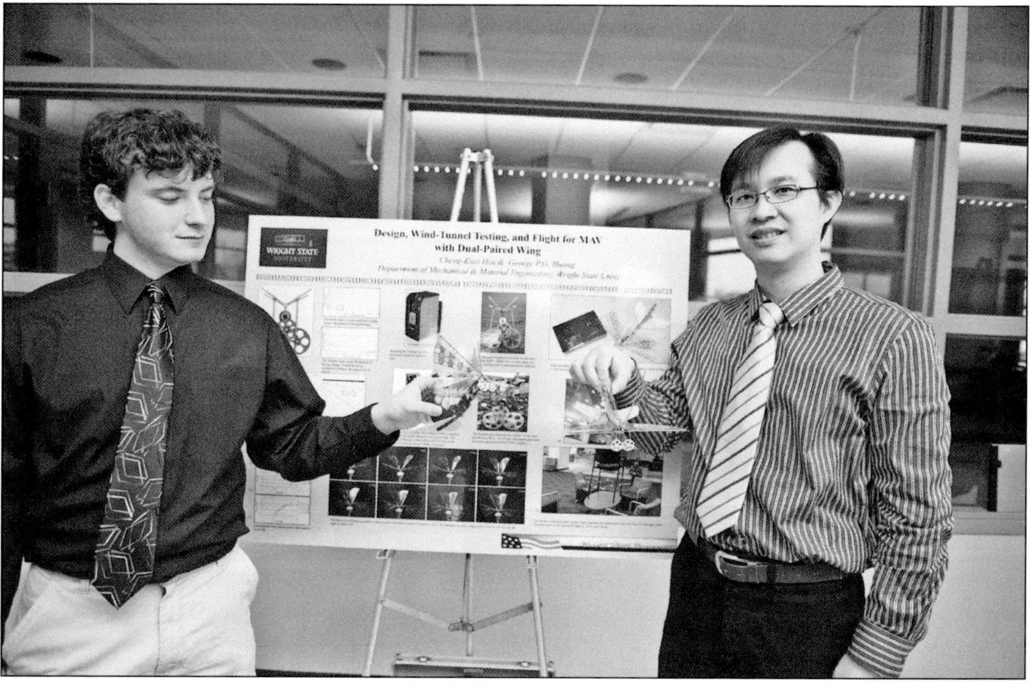

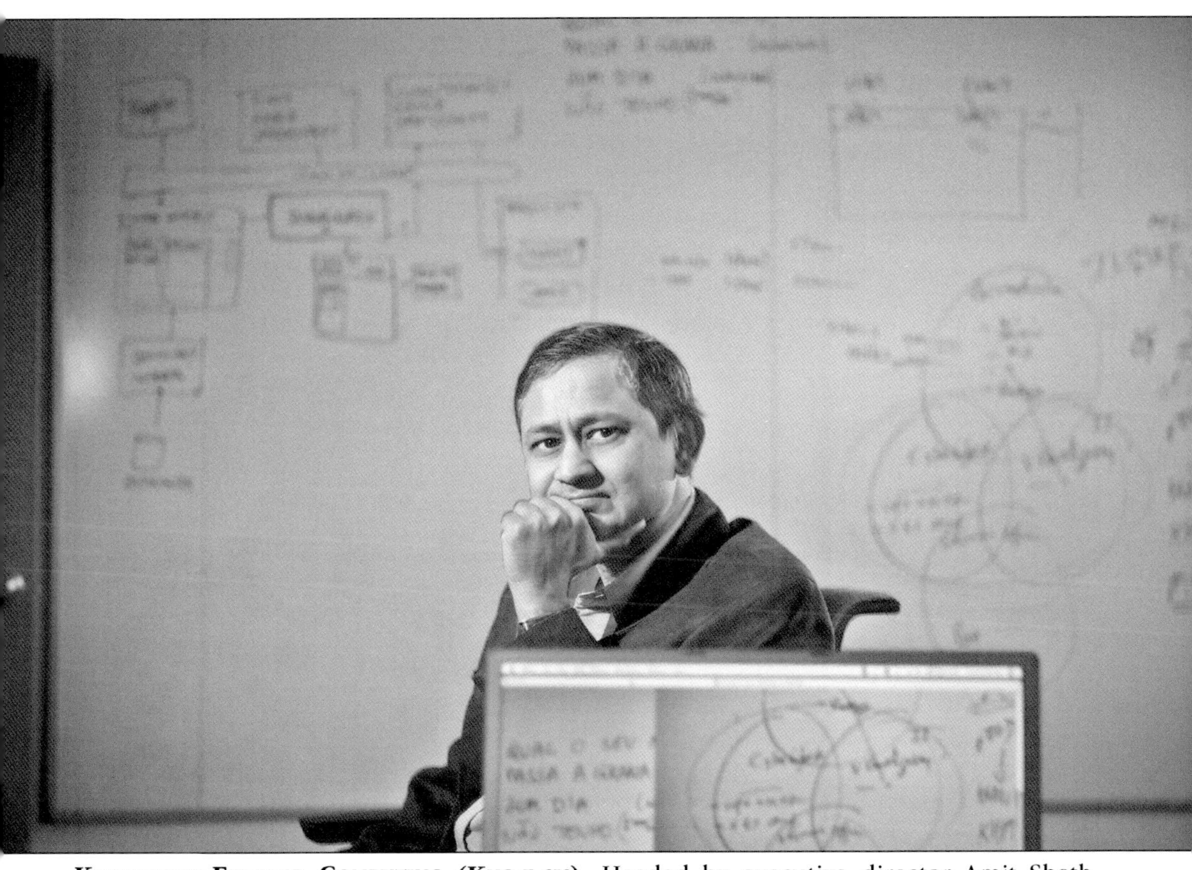

Knowledge-Enabled Computing (Kno.e.sis). Headed by executive director Amit Sheth, the Ohio Center of Excellence in Knowledge-enabled Computing (Kno.e.sis) consists of 13 labs with about 100 researchers who are faculty and doctoral students from multiple disciplines working to compute the human experience. Research conducted by faculty members involved with Kno.e.sis has been recognized and awarded by IBM, Google, and Hewlett-Packard.

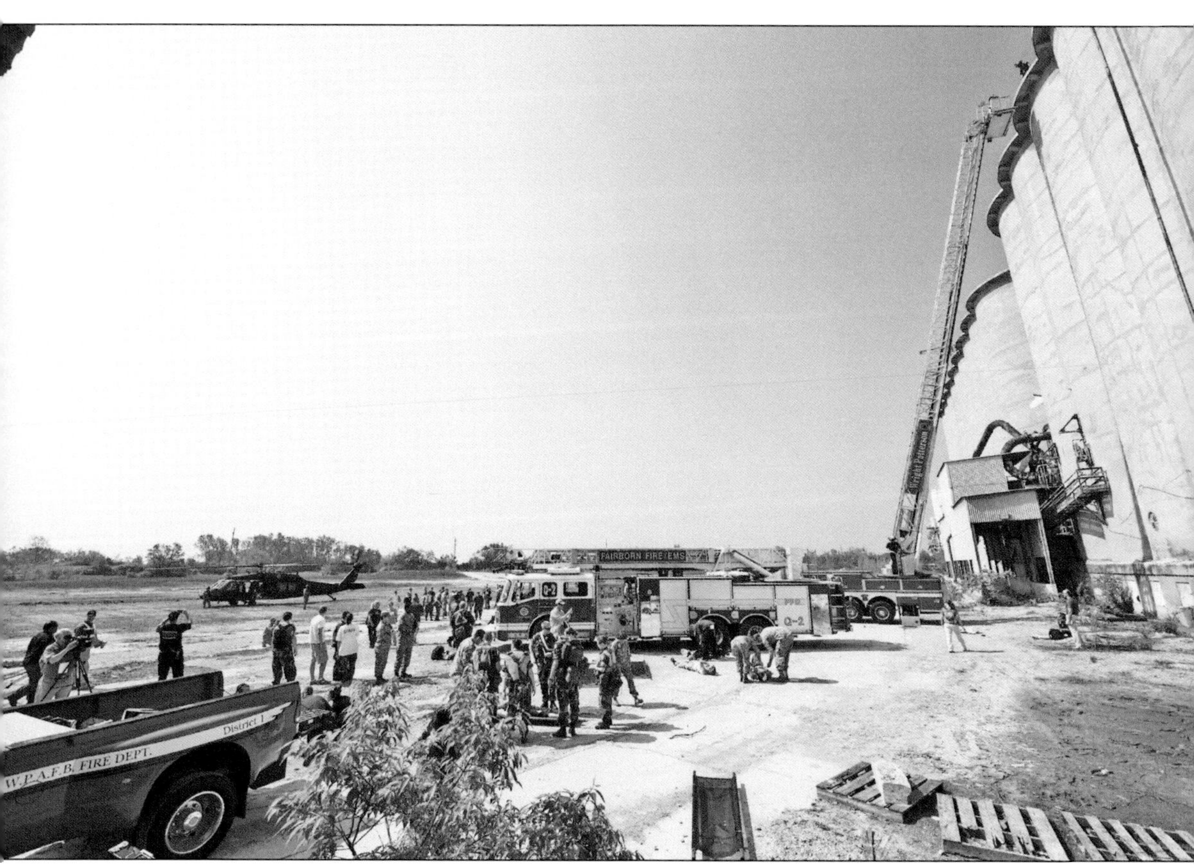

National Center for Medical Readiness. Located on 52 acres in Fairborn, Ohio, the collaborative training and research facility of Calamityville prepares civilian and military medical communities to participate and react effectively and efficiently with disaster responders. Calamityville is the first program in the nation to fully integrate civilian and military relationships as well as medical and nonmedical responses that occur in a disaster or other complex rescue situation.

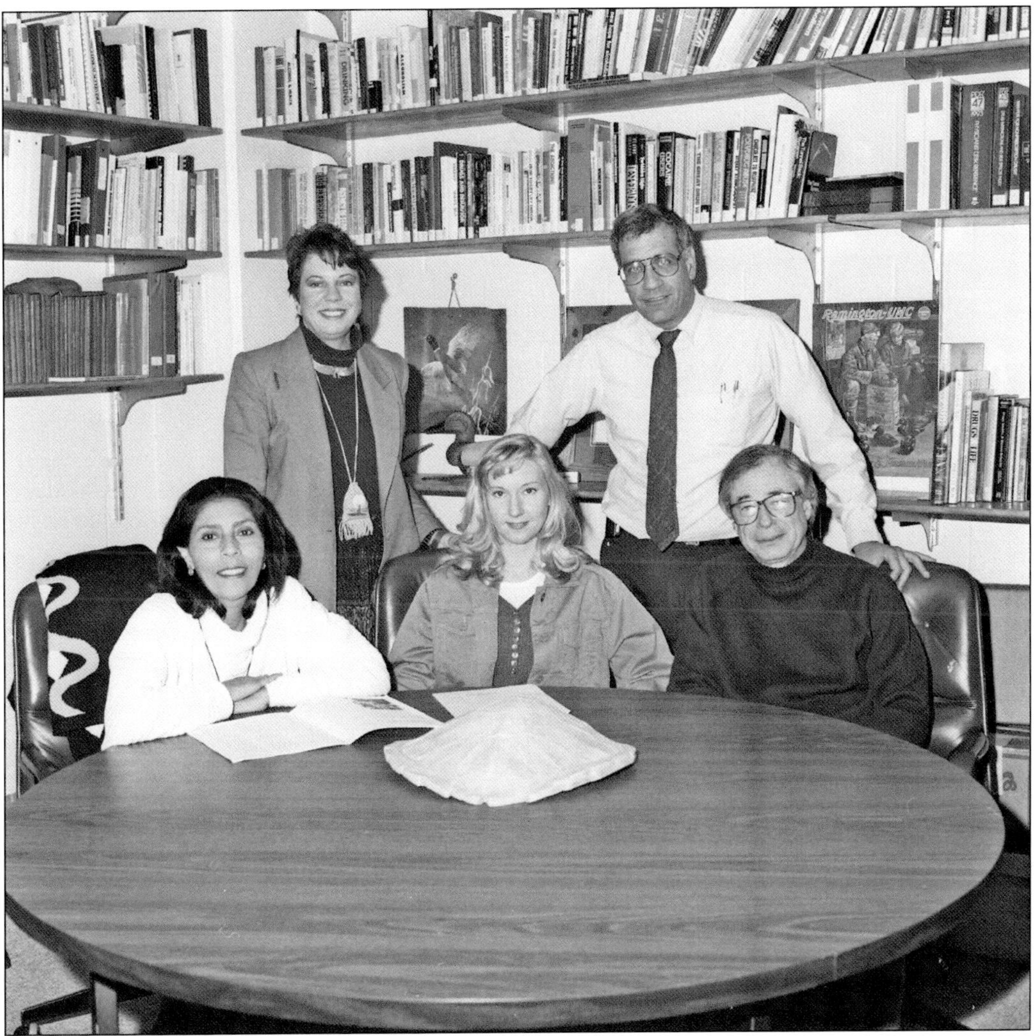

CENTER FOR INTERVENTIONS, TREATMENT, AND ADDICTIONS RESEARCH. Situated within the university's Boonshoft School of Medicine, the Center for Interventions, Treatment, and Addictions Research (CITAR) seeks to promote and disseminate information on the consequences, treatment, and prevention of substance abuse. The center studies substance abuse, intervention, and management in rural communities and the suburbs.

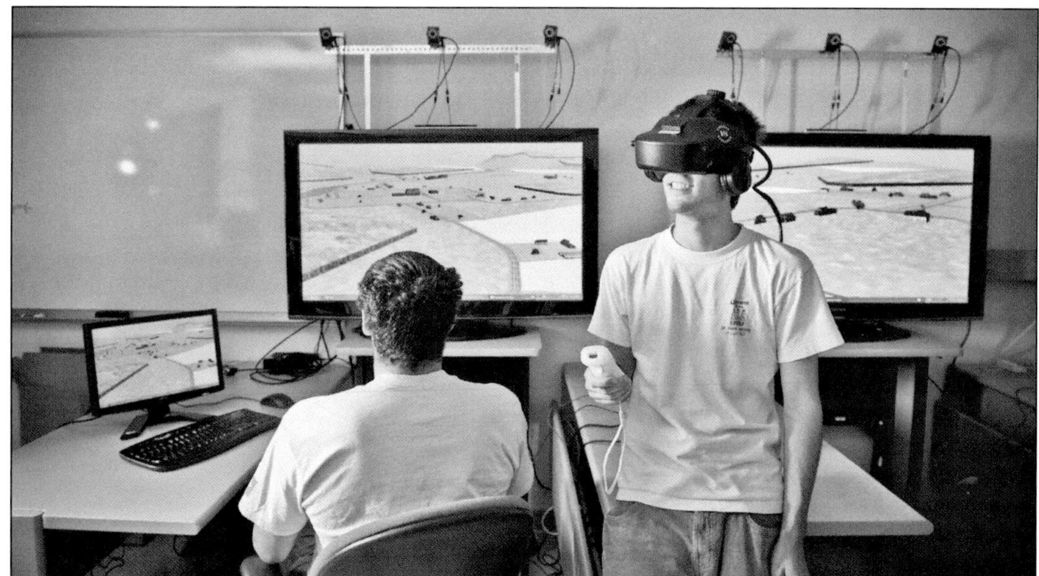

Human-Centered Innovation. The Center of Excellence for Human-Centered Innovation plays a critical role in human performance research for the Defense Department. Faculty members in the areas of engineering, computer science, biology, psychology, mathematics, and health science use the center to support humans by creating systems, technologies, processes, and organizational change to enhance daily lives.

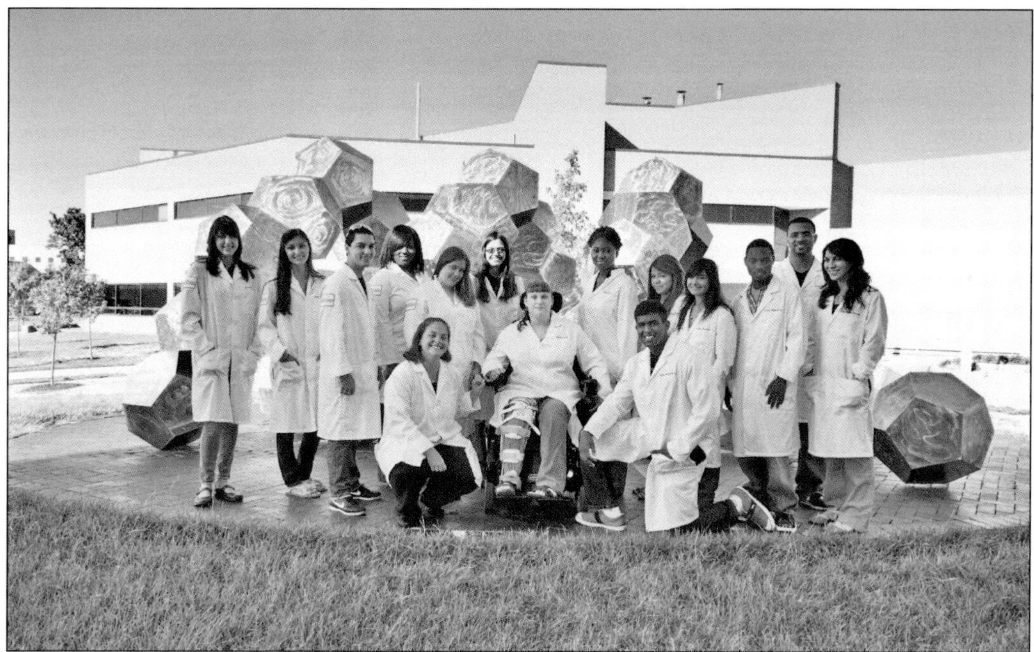

BioSTAR Program. Reaching out to junior and senior undergraduate students who are members of underrepresented minorities, disabled, or economically disadvantaged, the Initiative for Maximizing Student Diversity Biomedical Scholars Training and Research program highlights career development in the biosciences. The goal is to ultimately increase the number of these students in doctoral programs in biomedical fields.

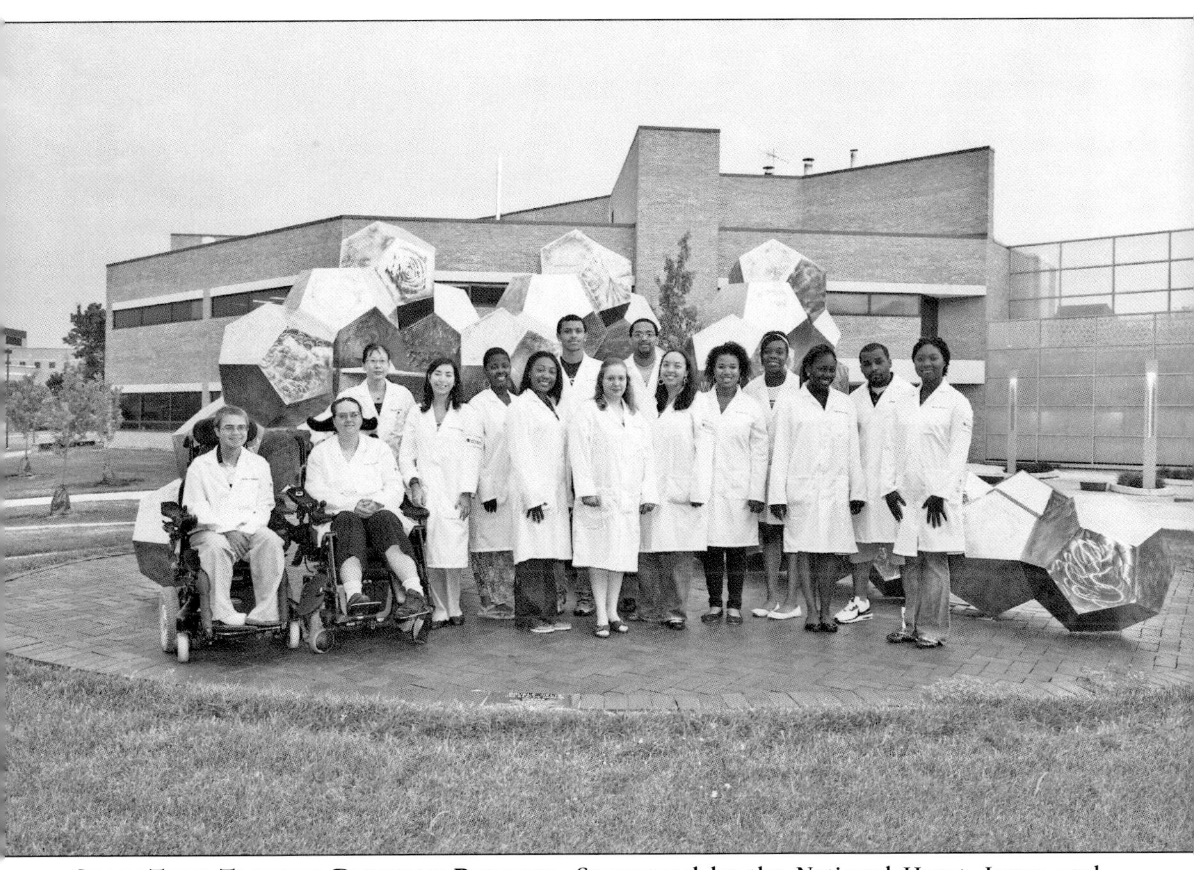

Short-Term Training Diversity Program. Sponsored by the National Heart, Lung, and Blood Institute of the National Institutes of Health, the Short-Term Training Program to Increase Diversity in Health-Related Research program, also referred to as STREAMS, is a cardiovascular-related research program for underrepresented groups as well as students with disabilities. The program highlights the importance of their involvement in biomedical research.

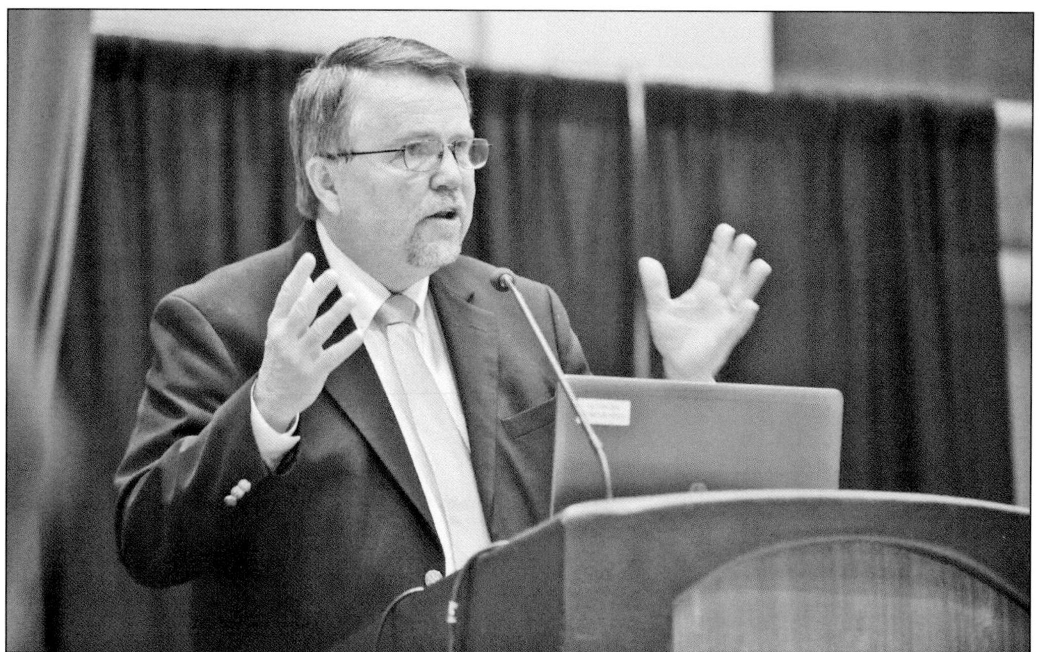

Weekends at the Alumni College. Each August, the weekends are dedicated to socialization and educational experiences for Wright State University alumni. The Alumni College provides in-class learning experiences for current courses and research from the school's most distinguished faculty members. In 2015, Robert Sweeney, executive vice president for planning and Secretary to Board of Trustees Professor, delivered the keynote address.

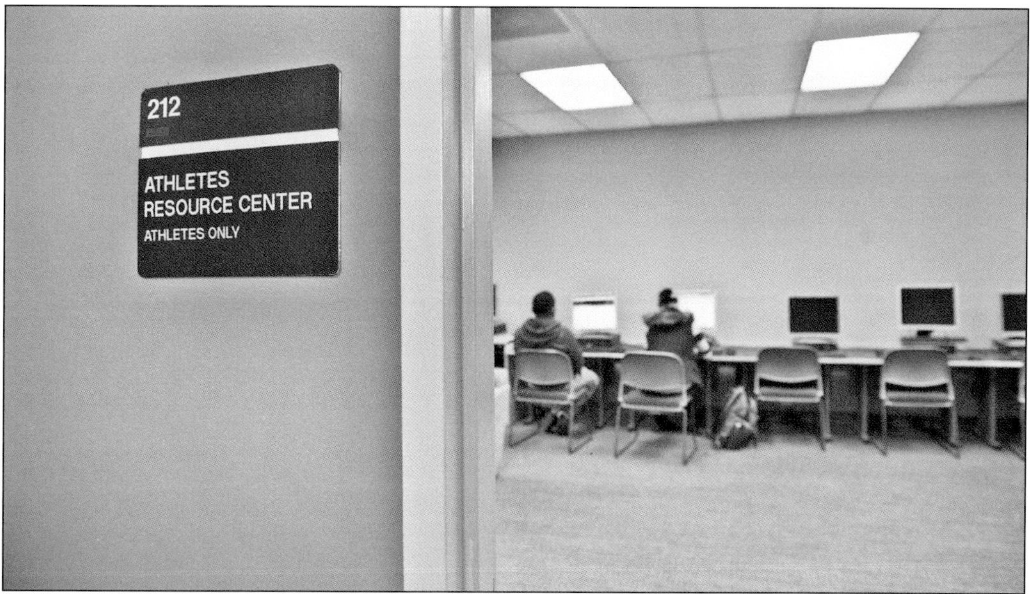

Athlete Academic Resource Center. The Athlete Academic Resource Center is dedicated to the academic success of all student athletes at Wright State. Every freshman athlete is required to spend at least six hours a week at the center, and other student athletes attend per agreement with their coaches. There are computers and quiet spaces so that students have a safe place to study and maintain decent grade point averages.

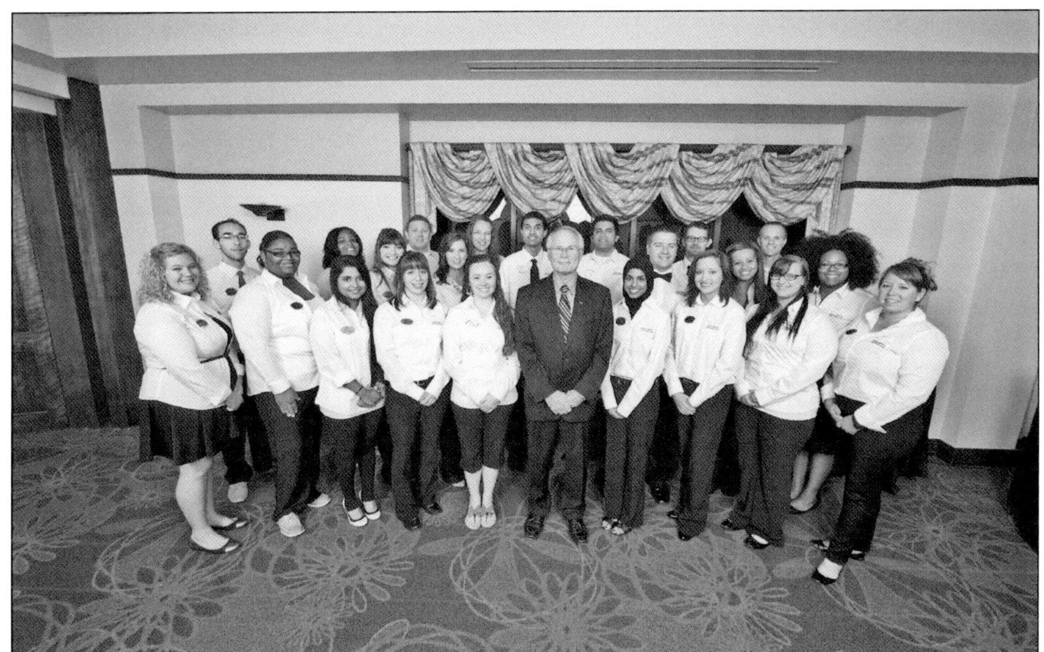

President's University Ambassadors. As the President's Ambassadors, university students represent the Office of the President and the university as a whole during special events such as presidential dinners and meetings. These student ambassadors serve a tour guides and welcome community leaders, alumni, and donors, making their role important in the university's reputation domestically and abroad.

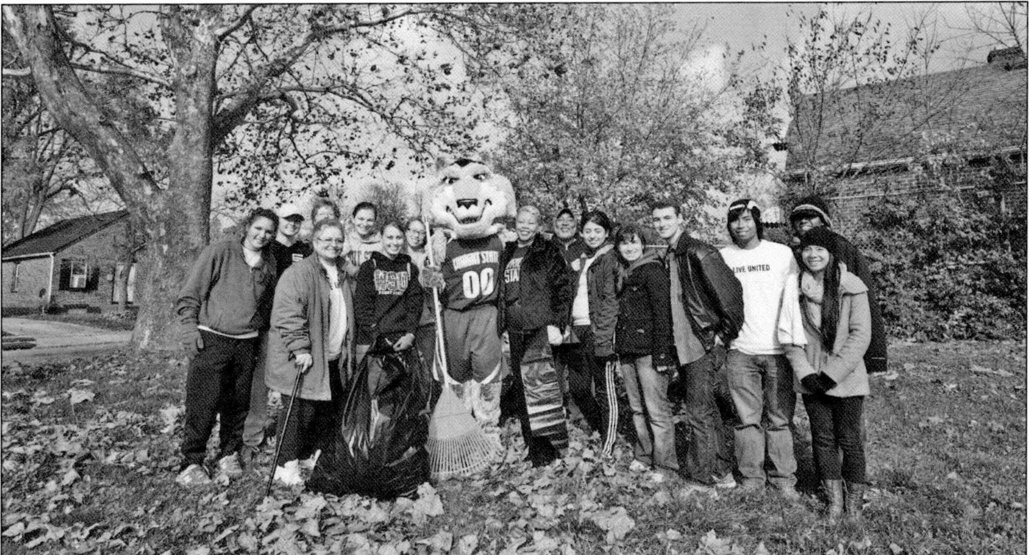

President's Higher Education Community Service. The university's commitment to public service, service learning, and civic engagement since its humble beginnings is now reflected in its being honored on the President's Higher Education Community Service Honor Roll for four years in a row (2013–2016). With the campus community logging over 400,000 community service hours, this federal recognition is cherished by the university community as well as the greater Dayton community.

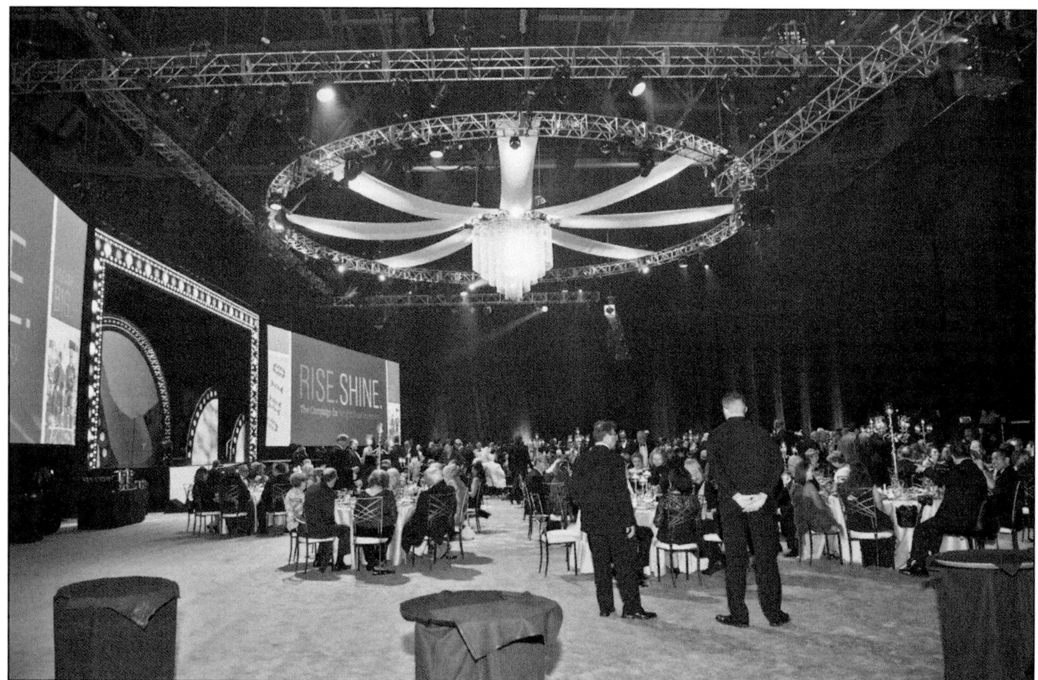

Historic Fundraising Success. In 2016, Wright State University achieved its greatest fundraising goal. With the support of Tom Hanks and the Wright brothers' niece, Amanda Wright-Lane, the university raised a whopping $152 million that will go towards scholarships, faculty salaries, and technology-focused learning spaces around campus. The campaign "Rise. Shine, The Campaign for Wright State University" is credited for the fundraising success.

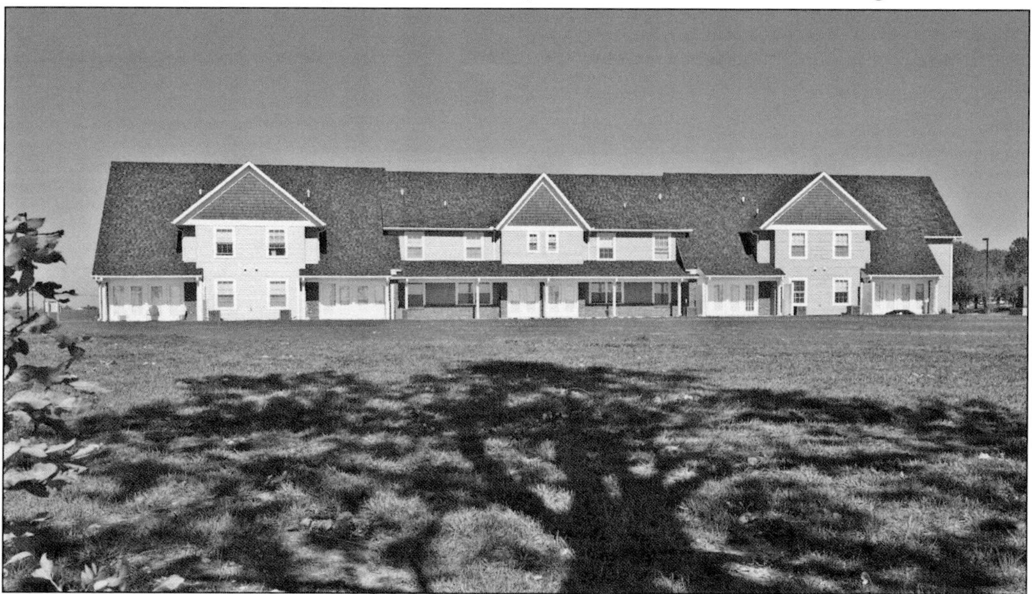

Knapke Villa Campus. Completed in the fall of 2011, Knapke Villa is on-campus housing for students at Wright State University's Lake Campus. Located just west of the campus, these fully furnished apartments offer residents a view of Grand Lake St. Marys. Knapke Villa is the first on-campus housing option for Lake Campus students.

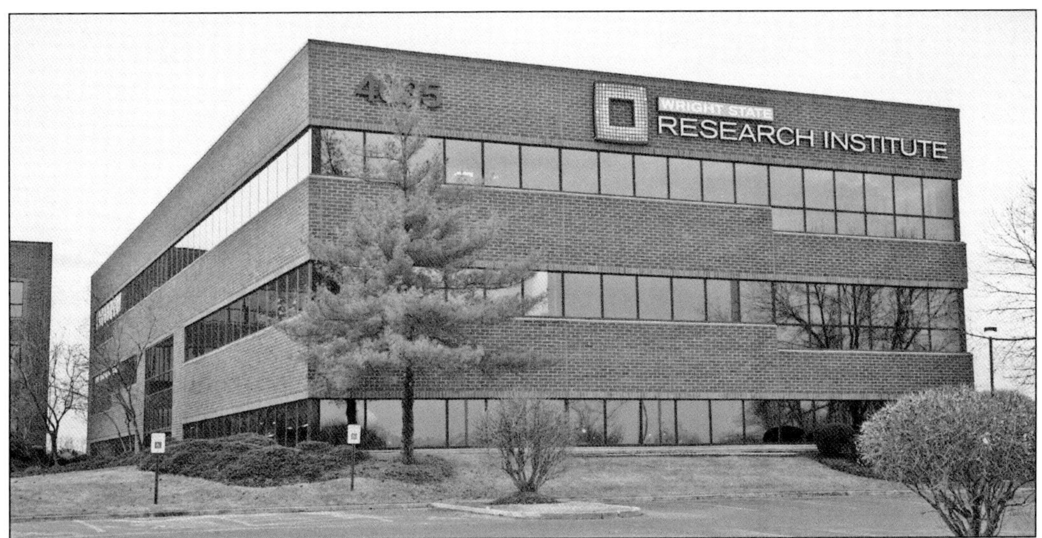

Wright State Research Institute. The Wright State Research Institute provides a common gateway to university capabilities, researchers, scientists, and staff. Focusing on applied research and services, the institute applies emerging technologies to difficult problems facing industry and government partners. The institute tests and develops unmanned aerial vehicles and also applies top-notch practices to the nation's supply chains. Additionally, it ensures the security of computing systems.

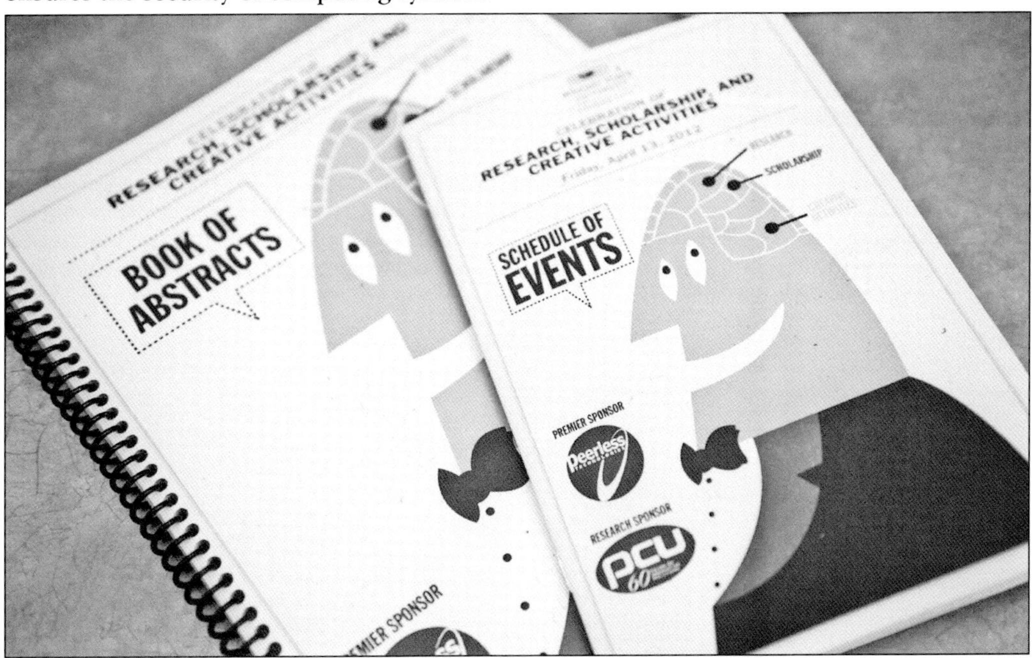

Multicultural Affairs and Community Engagement. The Division of Multicultural Affairs and Community Engagement works to transform both the lives of students on campus and the surrounding communities through social responsibility, equity, and service while preventing discrimination. The organization's vision is to institutionalize inclusion so that when students leave the university they are able to participate in society as well-informed, compassionate, and engaged citizens.

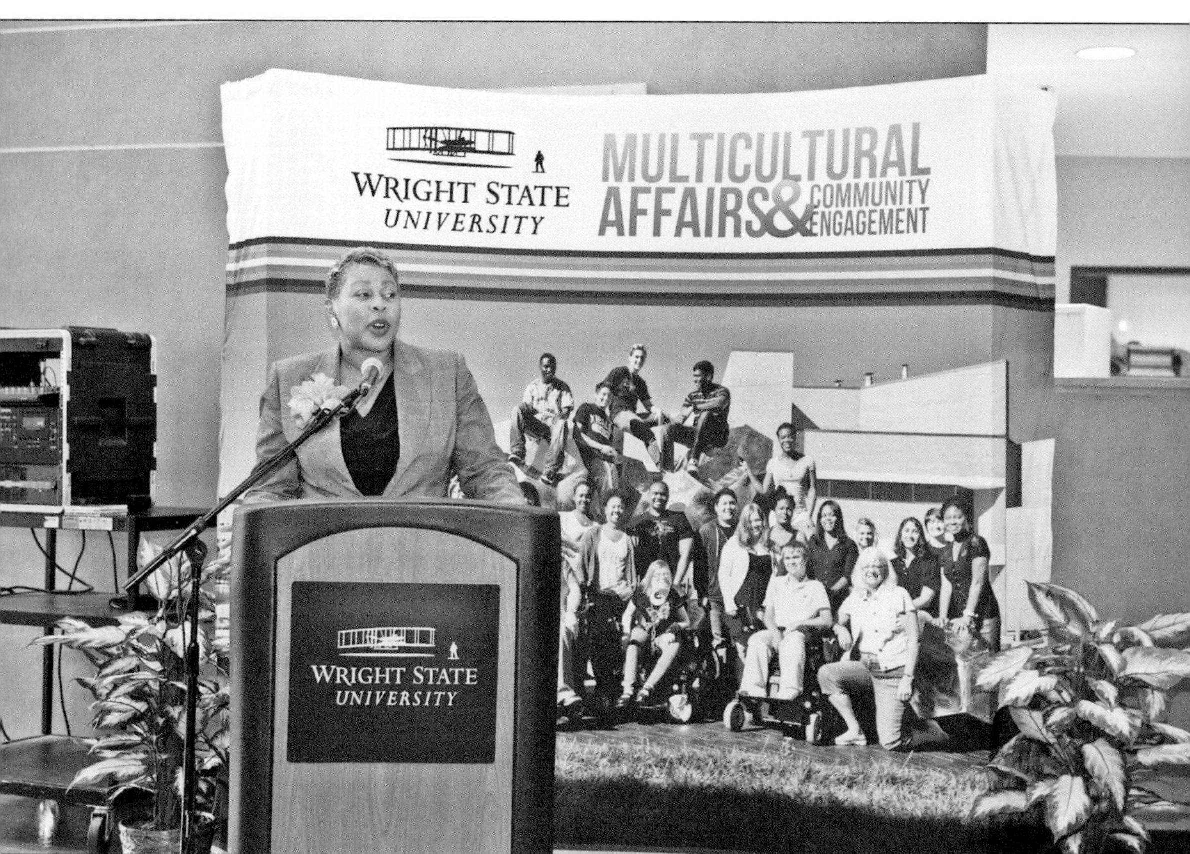

Vice President of Multicultural Affairs. In August 2012, Dr. Kimberly Barrett joined the university as the new vice president of multicultural affairs and community engagement. Barrett's current vision is to increase and strengthen diversity at Wright State. She plans to implement mini-grants as incentives to encourage faculty and to establish and build relationships with outside minority scholars and organizations to bring them to the university.

Diversity Quest Conference. Wright State University's Diversity in the Multicultural Millennium Conference is designed to bring together faculty, staff, and students from across Ohio for a day of meaningful workshops, discussions, media presentations, and activities. The goal is to foster an understanding of and a commitment to issues of diversity. The theme for 2013 was "Affirmative Action: 52 Years of Debate." The keynote speakers were Dr. Michael Eric Dyson and Marilynn Schuyler.

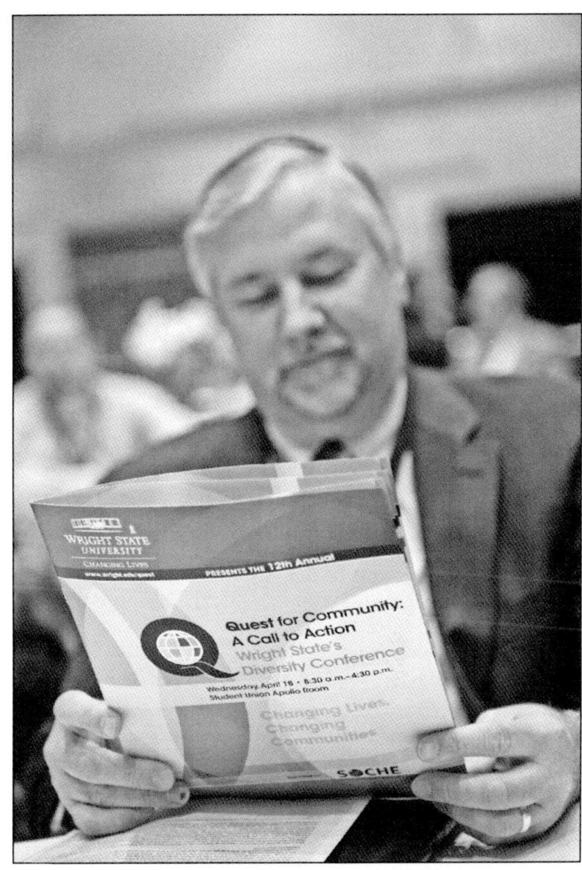

Celebration of Research and Scholarship. The Celebration of Research, Scholarship, and Creative Activities offers undergraduate, graduate, and professional students across all disciplines the opportunity to showcase their academic endeavors. Since 2009, students have exhibited and presented their discoveries, advances, and scholarly explorations. The event has been supported by businesses throughout the Dayton metropolitan region.

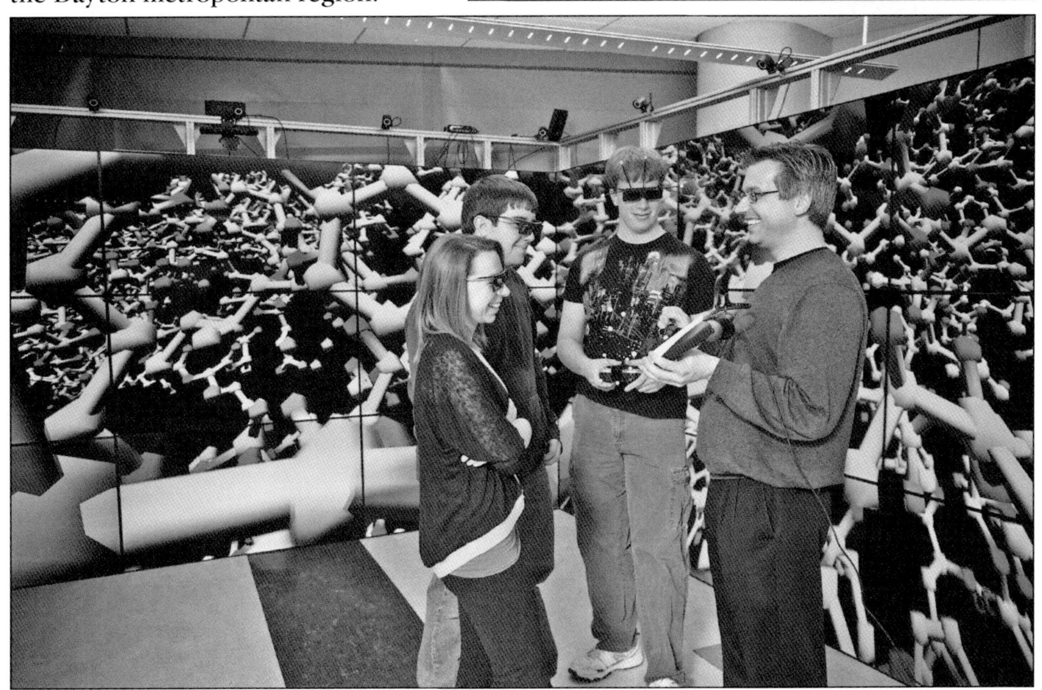

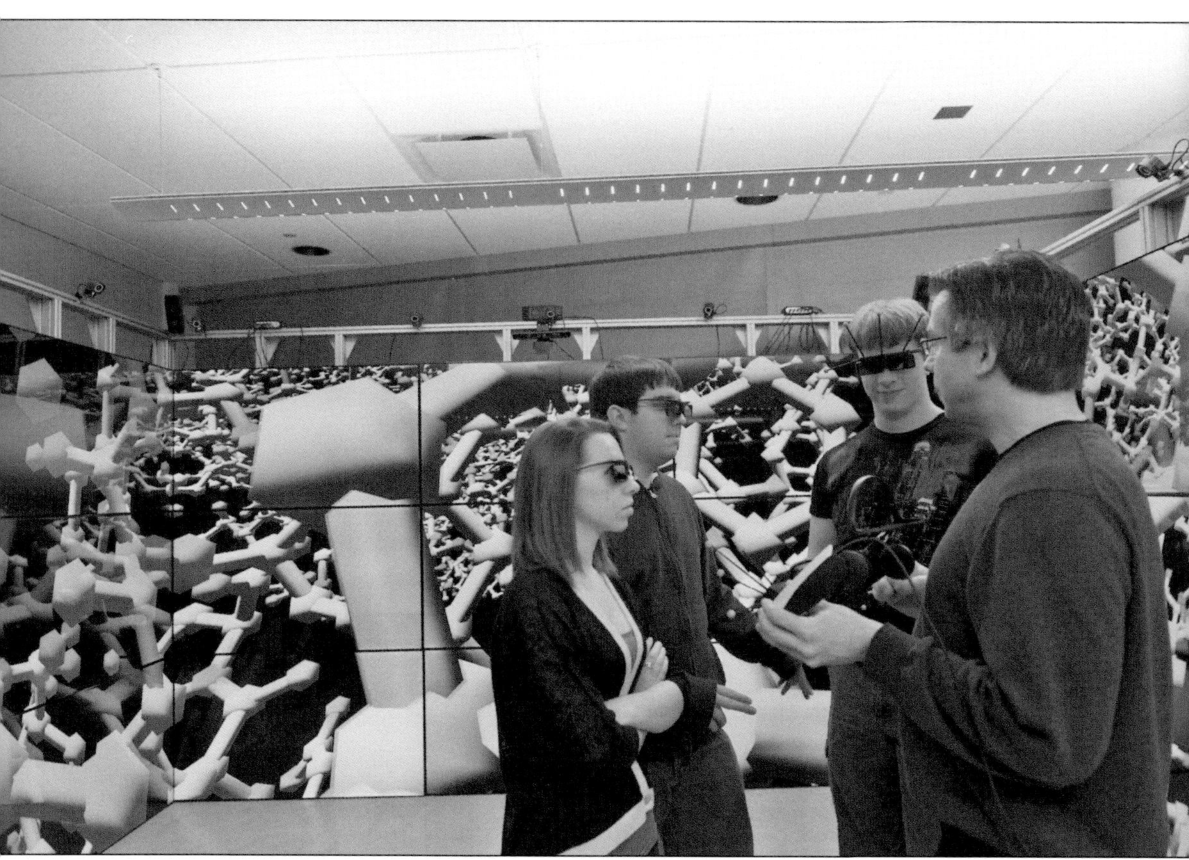

APPENZELLER VISUALIZATION LABORATORY. The Appenzeller Visualization Laboratory, located in the Joshi Research Center, was a gift from Robert and Joan Appenzeller. The laboratory, known as the centerpiece of the research facility, offers visitors an impressive virtual-reality tour underneath the Earth's surface, past factory assembly lines, and through the human bloodstream. This advanced laboratory, which features a fully immersive 3D environment, allows researchers to visualize and manipulate their research.

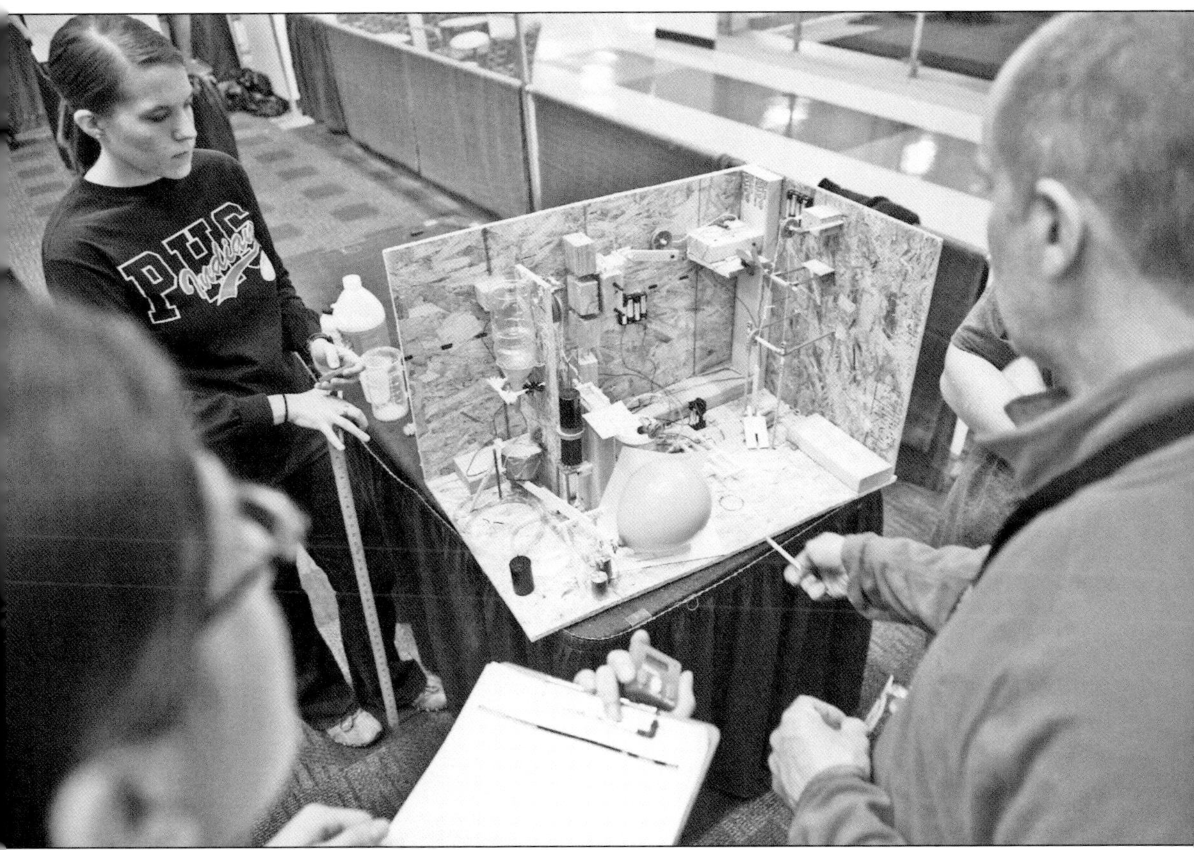

Annual Science Olympiad. In January 2014, Wright State University sponsored and hosted the Science Olympiad Invitational Tournament. The tournament is the peak of achievement for over 100 of the country's best Science Olympiad teams. The event is produced by an international nonprofit organization dedicated to improving the quality of science education, increasing student involvement in science, and acknowledging excellence in science education by students and educators through classroom activities, training workshops, and tournaments.

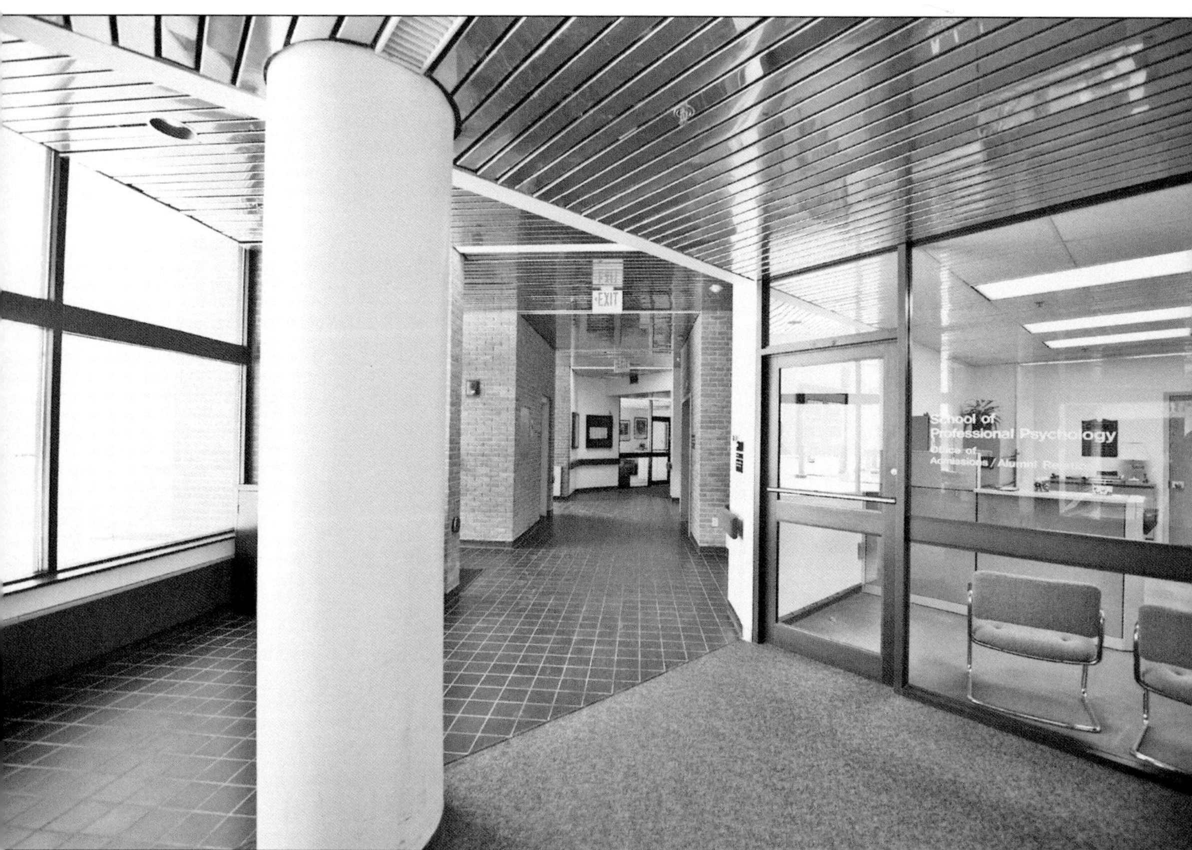

Pioneer in Accessibility. Due to its dedication to accessibility with student support services like the Office of Disability Services, ramps, elevators, a dog park, and a unique tunnel system, Wright State University has been recommended as a top-five disability-friendly campus for students with disabilities by *College Success for Students with Physical Disabilities.*

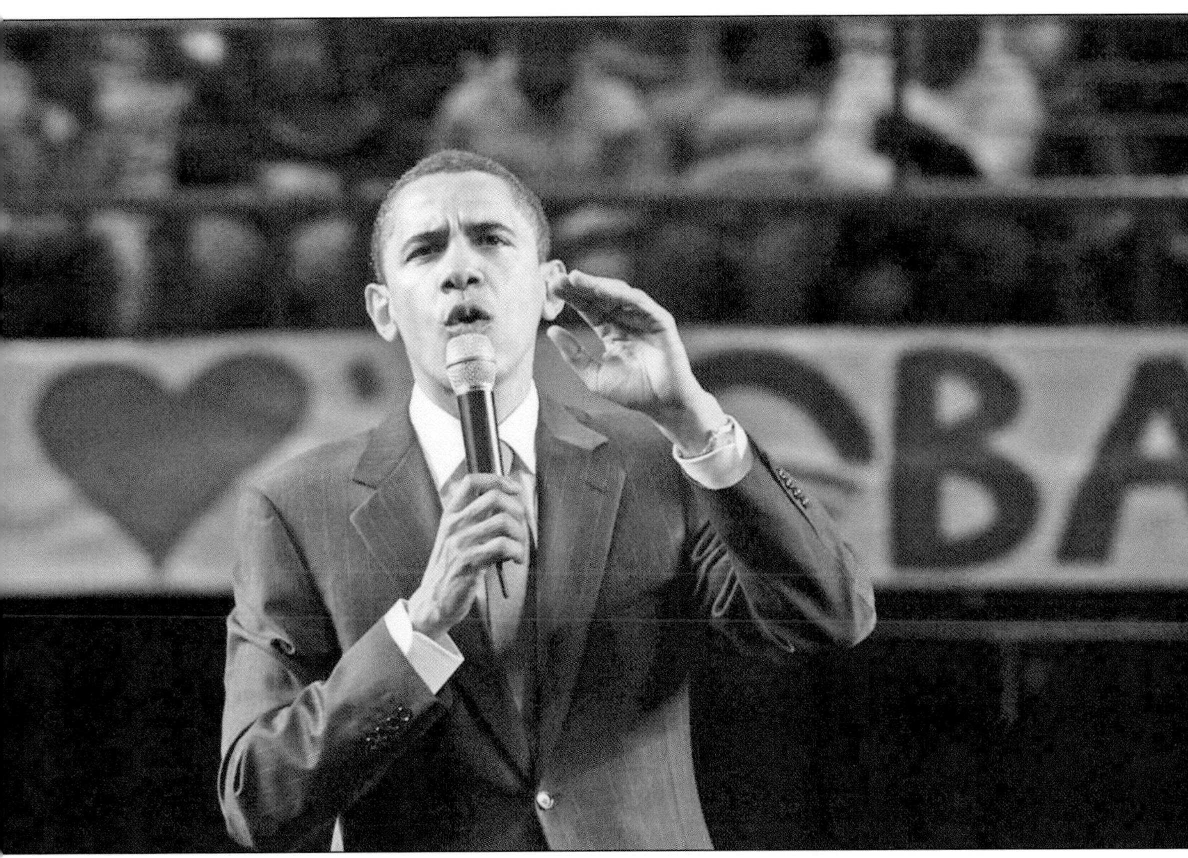

A Site for Politics. Wright State University has been a site for politics since the 1990s. Prominent politicians such as Barack Obama and George W. Bush have campaigned here. Presidential candidate Obama is pictured here at a February 25, 2008, campaign rally in the Nutter Center. In September 2016, the university was once again going to host a political event, this time a presidential debate. University president Hopkins expressed concerns over ever-rising costs as well as security, and as a result, the school decided to not host the debate.